V-Bombers

AVIATION **SERIES**

V-BOMBERS
Valiant, Vulcan and Victor

Barry Jones

The Crowood Press

First published in 2000 by
The Crowood Press Ltd
Ramsbury, Marlborough
Wiltshire SN8 2HR

© Barry Jones 2000

British Library Cataloguing-in-Publication Data
A catalogue record for this book is available from
the British Library.

ISBN 1 86126 385 6

Typefaces used: Goudy (*text*),
Cheltenham (*headings*)

Typeset by Florence Production Ltd,
Stoodleigh, Devon

Printed and bound by Bookcraft, Bath

Dedication

To V-Bomber enthusiasts everywhere – may our memories ever endure.

Acknowledgements

In writing a history like this, an author often receives snippets of information and photographs from fellow enthusiasts, plus those who have had personal contact with the subjects. All are most gratefully received and in this respect I would like to express my thanks to The Avro Heritage Centre; Gordon G. Bartley of BAE Systems; R.P. Beamont CBE, DSO*, DFC*, DL, FRAeS; Damien Burke; Ray Deacon; Bill Gunston; The Handley Page Association; Harry Holmes; Gerald Hitch; Del Holyland of Martin-Baker; Dave Jackson; Derek N. James; Philip Jarrett; Ian Mactaggart; Michael Oakey of *Aeroplane*; Gary O'Keefe; Peter G. Pavey of Rolls-Royce Heritage Trust; George Pennick; William S. Sleigh; Julian C. Temple of Brooklands Museum and my family's fortitude for sharing the past year with a trio of bombers.

Contents

Introduction

A Memorandum of Association to form the Society of British Aircraft Constructors (SBAC) was drawn up on 28 May 1916 and, while various static displays were held in Olympia, it was 27 June 1932 before the SBAC held its first flying display. This was an extension of the Hendon Air Display held the previous week, with the Society including several additions to the New Types Park for their one-day event at the same venue.

Annual shows continued until 1937, with a relocation to Hatfield being made in 1936, but the advent of war initiated the cancellation of the projected 1938 programme and it was 1946 before the seventh display took place. This two-day show was held at Radlett, in the first week of September; two years later, when the move to a permanent venue at Farnborough was made, the RAF's operational long-range bombing ability was still exemplified by the piston-engined Avro Lincoln.

In September 1951, the first prototype Vickers Valiant's appearance announced the long-awaited transformation of Bomber Command. The twin-jet-engined Canberra was in service, but the Valiant heralded the introduction to the RAF of the quadruple-turbojet, long-range, high-altitude bomber. There was also the political contribution from Belfast, the Short S.A.4, later to be named Sperrin. The following year, Avro's first Vulcan joined the second Valiant prototype and when Handley Page displayed the first of two prototype Victors in 1953, the trio of British four-turbojet-engined bombers appearing on the same stage together proclaimed the formation of the V-bomber force, which in three decades hence would see the finale of this genre in the Royal Air Force.

Those thirty years brought exhilaration and tragedy to the Service, as well as all three manufacturers. They were years when new avenues had to be traversed by all concerned; challenging times, intensified by policy fluctuations which enforced role changes that accelerated the demise of the first of the trio. This generated a knock-on effect that presented additional role requirements for the remaining pair, which would culminate in the RAF flying the longest operational missions in its entire history.

The formidable demands of this epoch, with its myriad of political and technical vicissitudes, are fascinating to recall and it is hoped that the readers of this narrative will feel that the tens of thousands of people who were involved have been afforded full justice for their magnificent endeavours and achievements.

Barry Jones
Hatton Green
Warwickshire
May 2000

V-bomber grace and beauty personified by Valiant B.1 WZ365 from No. 232 OCU, Gaydon. Author's collection

CHAPTER ONE

Birth of the Weapon

It is often interesting, though really rather futile, to speculate that if such and such had not happened, then so and so would have been different. However, the multifarious political events of the mid-1940s were such that Britain was presented with a set of circumstances that would have far-reaching consequences for its technical research facilities, its aircraft industry and the armed forces in general.

The end of hostilities against the Axis powers in 1945 could be expected to have brought about considerable change, and in many aspects it did. However, a change of leadership on both sides of the Atlantic, coupled with the realization of the Soviet Union's political aspirations, created new attitudes. Furthermore, the recent introduction of an entirely new form of aircraft propulsion that offered far greater operational capabilities and the new approaches to aerodynamics that this inevitably generated, all amalgamated to sow the seeds that would germinate into the V-bombers.

Prior to World War II, scientists in several countries were becoming aware of, and experimenting in, the field of nuclear physics relative to nuclear fission being developed into a bomb. This bomb was seen as having far greater destructive potential than could really be visualized at that time. The 500lb and 1,000lb bombs were the major operational weapons in the Royal Air Force, with a 4,000lb high-explosive ordnance on the drawing board.

In Britain, the findings of scientists Rudolf Peierls and Otto Frisch at Birmingham University concerning the chain reaction established by the separation of uranium elements 235 from 238, were enough for Churchill's wartime government to establish a committee of leading scientists. With the title the Maud Committee, its brief was to investigate all aspects of the requirements necessary to manufacture a uranium bomb, with 1943 set as a provisional target date.

In the atmosphere of suspicion and security that abounded in 1940, the choice of the name 'Maud' for the committee was viewed by some as having a certain significance, and I remember a suggestion once being aired that it was an acronym for Military Airborne Uranium Developments, which proved just as unfounded as the initial suspicion. The committee had to be called something and the Christian name of a member's nanny to his children, one Maud Ray, was as good as any and it certainly held no indication as to the work being undertaken.

By the middle of 1941, the Maud Committee had drawn the conclusion that such a weapon could be made in the suggested timescale, for a cost estimated at £5 million. The explosive power generated was estimated as being comparable to 1,800 tons of TNT, and it was believed that the adjacent area to such an explosion would be radioactive for a considerable period of time. These two factors were the only ones that approached reality, for the cost and timescale were beyond British capabilities, considering that production resources were totally committed to the war in hand and providing the conventional weaponry required to conduct it.

The committee's conclusions added a rider that co-operation with the United States would have mutual benefits. President Roosevelt's 'day of infamy' had not yet arrived and his country had not given atomic research much consideration. Sir Henry Tizard, chief adviser on weapons research to the British Government, had already given America a 'Pandora's box' of information on the current state of British research in several technical fields and the Maud Committee's suggestion was relayed to the United States. Dr Vannevan Bush, Chairman of the National Defense Research Council, expressed the opinion that the findings merited his country's attention.

President Roosevelt suggested to Prime Minister Winston Churchill in the summer of 1942 that collaboration on atomic research between the two countries would not be a bad thing, but Churchill held on to the belief that Britain could develop an atomic bomb itself, although he accepted that the original target date and costings were now not viable. However, mutual co-operation was agreed and with America now drawn into the war by Japan's attack on Pearl Harbor, it was galvanized into giving the programme its full attention.

The Manhattan Project

Established in July 1942, the Manhattan Project, named in recognition of earlier work in the field undertaken by Columbia University in Manhattan, was conducted from a research site at Los Alamos, deep in the southernmost folds of the Rocky Mountains as they enter New Mexico. The project's scientific director, Dr Robert Oppenheimer, welcomed the British scientists incorporated into various sections, and the deluge of finance and resources that the United States poured into the project soon brought home to them the gross miscalculation of the Maud Committee's original estimate for producing a nuclear bomb. The British Government was appraised of these realities and it was finally agreed that an independent research programme was unrealistic.

On the other hand, American attitudes had changed and they, for their part, felt that having got going, they were capable of proceeding without any further British input. Roosevelt was in favour of full co-operation, but the National Defense Research Council's chairman extracted an understanding from the President that British collaboration would be restricted to the requirements of World War II alone. America was already viewing the potential of nuclear energy in a commercial capacity and, bearing in mind the unreserved input that the project was receiving, it wanted ground rules established to protect future exploitation of the science.

On 19 August 1943, the Quebec Agreement was signed by Britain and America.

This confirmed full co-operation between the two countries and laid down that nuclear weapons would never be deployed against each other, or any other country, without mutual consent. Despite the feelings of Dr Bush and his Council, a year later Churchill and Roosevelt signed the Hyde Park Memorandum, which extended co-operation in atomic research between the two countries into the post-war era and was conditional upon both parties being agreed to any cancellation.

Work on the Manhattan Project culminated in the first test detonation on 16 July 1945. Mounted on a 100ft tower set on the White Sands Missile Range, east of the San Andres mountains, the atomic device was activated a second before 05.30 hours. The ensuing shock wave was felt over 200 miles, both east and west, while the intense flash was visible even further afield.

Little Boy and *Fat Man*

The White Sands device was far removed from an operational bomb, but it proved the principle. A true bomb was well on the way to being perfected, so it was a mere three weeks later, on 6 August, that the world was introduced to an aircraft-delivered nuclear bomb and the devastation that it generated. It had been appreciated that an atomic bomb would have to be a substantial piece of hardware and that the only aircraft on the United States Army Air Force (USAAF) inventory capable of delivering such a weapon was the Boeing Model 345 B-29 Superfortress.

In the summer of 1944, the newly formed 393rd Bombardment Squadron (Very Heavy), as an element of the 509th Composite Bombardment Group at Wendover Field in Utah, was chosen as the unit, with fifteen B-29s, to deliver the new weapon. On 17 December, Col Paul W. Tibbets, who was no stranger to historical events, was appointed Commanding Officer. (As Maj Tibbets, he had been co-pilot of 41-2578 *Butcher Shop*, the lead B-17E of 340th Bomb Squadron, 97th Bombardment Group (Heavy) based at Polebrook in Northamptonshire, on the first 8th USAAF heavy bomber mission against the Axis-held European mainland, flown on 17 August 1942.) During an intense work-up period, inert variants of the proposed weapon were dropped to test

the ballistics, and in May 1945 the squadron transferred to Tinian, one of the Mariana group of islands in the Philippine Sea.

Stripped of all four machine-gun barbettes, but retaining the one 20mm and two .50in machine-gun tail armament, the unit's B-29s were flown on simulated nuclear weapon missions, with special orange-painted 'Pumpkin' TNT-filled 10,000lb bombs being dropped from altitudes around 30,000ft (9,140m). These 'Pumpkins' were accurate replicas of the forthcoming atomic bombs in shape, size and weight and their carrier aircraft had been modified to accommodate them, thereby making them unable to take any standard weapon.

The first two atomic bombs were ferried from the United States to Tinian and, with the southern city of Hiroshima on the Japanese mainland of Honshu designated as the target, seven B-29s were allocated for the mission. Of these, three were reconnaissance aircraft for the prevailing weather conditions in the target area, two were tasked with observation, for which special recording equipment and scientific observers were carried, and one aircraft was based at Iwo Jima as a spare.

The seventh was B-29 44-86292, piloted by Col Tibbets and named *Enola Gay* after his mother. It had been modified to carry the first operational atomic weapon, nicknamed *Little Boy*. With a length of 129in (328cm) and a 31⅛in (80cm) diameter, the bomb weighed nearly 9,000lb (4,130kg), of which 137lb (62kg) was Uranium 235. Taking off from Tinian 2¾ hours into Monday, 6 August 1945, Tibbets arrived over the target area, set as the city's Aioi Bridge over the Ota river, 6½ hours later. At 08.15 hours, *Little Boy* was released from an altitude of 31,600ft (9,630m), detonating at 1,850ft (565m) above Hiroshima with a force equivalent to approximately 20,000 tons of TNT. Casualties numbered over 70,000 and more than 4½ square miles of the city was demolished.

Three days later, on 9 August, the shipbuilding port of Nagasaki on the southern Japanese island of Kyushu was the recipient of *Fat Man*. The primary target had been Kokurs, the home of Mitsubishi, but nine-tenths cloud over Kokurs decided the secondary target's fate. Dropped from B-29 *Bockscar* piloted by Maj Charles W. Sweeney, *Fat Man* was a 10,000lb plutonium bomb which delivered a force equiv-

alent to over 20,000 tons of TNT. On this sortie, Gp Capt Leonard Cheshire, VC, one of the most renowned RAF bomber leaders, was invited to be an observer in the accompanying B-29 *Full House*. The result of what he saw changed the whole course of his life. Six days later, Japan surrendered and World War II was at an end.

The McMahon Bill

While Allied forces were advancing on Germany in the first months of 1945, teams of technical specialists from both America and the Soviet Union were following close behind their respective land forces, in order to obtain anything in the way of knowledge relative to Germany's scientific achievements. The close wartime liaison between Britain and the United States in terms of sharing research materials was already fracturing, and when the British Allied Technical Intelligence Mission eventually went to the European mainland, some months later, it received more co-operation and assistance from German representatives than was forthcoming from US sources.

This American nationalistic disposition prevailed over co-operation in the field of atomic research and it was furthered by political events on both sides of the Atlantic. In America, Franklin D. Roosevelt died on 12 April 1945, the presidency passing to Harry S. Truman. Two months later, Britain held a general election and Winston Churchill was ejected, placing the onus of leading the United Kingdom upon the newly elected Socialist government headed by Clement Attlee. For Britain, the die for an independent nuclear arms policy was cast.

Although Attlee had not been *au fait* with the secret atomic bomb arrangements that had existed between the two wartime allies, he was quick to appreciate the vast potential of nuclear science and in October 1945 he made public the setting up of a nuclear experimental establishment. With many wartime airfields becoming available, an examination of the requirements, such as on-site space for the burial of radioactive waste and a proximity to established university laboratories, produced a shortlist of sites.

The former pre-war Expansion Period airfield at Harwell, in Oxfordshire, was selected. Built between 1935 and 1937, Harwell's initial unit was No.226

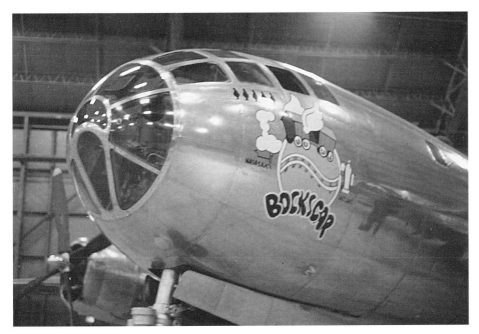

44-27297 B-29 Bockscar **today is displayed in the USAF Museum at Dayton, Ohio.**
Ian Mactaggart

Squadron, equipped with the Hawker Audax. It had hosted Anson, Battle and Wellington squadrons prior to becoming, on 8 April 1940, the home of No.15 Operational Training Unit (OTU), which it stayed as until March 1944. The following month, Harwell became an element of the airborne forces of No.38 Group, flying Albemarles and Stirling tugs for a fleet of Horsa gliders, during which time it played an important part in the feverish activities of Operation *Market*, the supplying of airborne forces confined at Arnhem. On 12 October 1944, No.13 OTU took up occupation, flying North American B-25 Mitchells until the end of the European activities of World War II. The final RAF units moved from the base to Brize Norton, further west in the county, and on 1 January 1946 the Atomic Energy Research Establishment (AERE) moved in.

The expediency of setting up the AERE was soon vindicated. The fact that Britain now had a Socialist government was viewed with a certain amount of scepticism on the other side of the Atlantic and Truman's declared attitude of 'the buck stops here' precluded any close association which did not meet full Congressional approval. America's outlay on the Manhattan Project in terms of finance and resources was enormous and, while Britain's input was appreciated during the

combined efforts to beat the Axis powers – particularly Japan, which was more personal so far as the United States was concerned – it quickly dissipated after August 1945. Despite Attlee's fervent appeals to continue the sharing of nuclear research findings, America refuted both the Quebec Agreement and the Hyde Park Memorandum, this isolationism culminating in a new Bill, the Atomic Energy Act, proposed by Senator McMahon in August 1946.

On hearing of the McMahon Bill being passed by Congress, Prime Minister Attlee wrote as follows to President Truman:

Our continuing co-operation over raw materials shall be balanced by an exchange of information which will give us, with all proper precautions with regard to security, that full information to which we believe we are entitled, both by documents and by the history of our common efforts in the past.

Truman did not even grant Attlee the courtesy of an acknowledgement; nor was Britain's case aided by the disclosure in February that the British nuclear physicist, Alan Nunn May, had transmitted American nuclear information to the Soviet Union. Relations between the two wartime allies were at an unprecedented low, and Britain immediately withdrew its lawful portion of raw uranium from the

Joint Anglo-American stocks that had been created during the war.

The British Bomb

Under the leadership of Professor Jock Cockcroft, the physicist who had been a founder member of the Maud Committee, the AERE investigated the output of uranium from the various uranium mines existing within Commonwealth countries, in order to maintain a satisfactory supply of the base element obtained from pitchblende. It was now obvious that Britain was determined to develop an indigenous nuclear weapons industry, which in itself rather surprised some members of the US government. It did produce a softening of the US attitude by 1947, to the extent that there was a slight improvement in relations (which can, maybe rather cynically, be allied to the fact that the United States was facing a shortage of uranium, while British stocks were quite healthy!). A loose agreement was drawn up early in 1948, whereby Britain would receive technical information, in exchange for the transfer of materials from its uranium stocks to the USA. However, the word 'Socialist' was becoming anathema to some American politicians and, within a year, far from this false dawn heralding lasting daylight, the American Congress had again brought down the shutters. One reason cited by Truman was Britain's closer proximity to the European mainland, which made nuclear weapons more vulnerable to 'capture', although he did not go so far as to mention just who would do the 'capturing'.

Attlee became convinced that, in view of the changeable climate of American Congressional pressure in relation to nuclear matters and the lack of appreciation by Americans of the true situation outside their own shores, it was essential for Britain to be capable of developing an operational independent nuclear capability. Construction of two atomic piles at Windscale, on the Cumbrian coast, was already under way and a facility was organized at Risley, in Lancashire, for the production of plutonium which, pound for pound, was regarded as having far greater atomic weapon potential. Dr William Penney, who had been a leading member of the British contingent engaged on the Manhattan Project, became the Chief Superintendent of the Ministry of Supply's

Armament Research Department (ARD) on 1 January 1946; together with Professor Cockcroft, he urged the government to draw up a timescale of expectancies from the fledgling establishment. The Chiefs of Staff put in their first nuclear weapon request in August of the same year, and on 8 January 1947 a governmental inner cabinet was established. The new body, consisting of the Prime Minister, Ernest Bevan (Foreign Secretary), John Wilmot (Minister of Supply), A.V. Alexander (Minister of Defence), Herbert Morrison (Lord President of the Council) and Lord Addison (Secretary of State for the Dominions), gave the official go-ahead to the development of an independent British atomic bomb.

Aldermaston and the AWRE

Dr Penney's ARD team of engineers, scientists and technicians, set up at Fort Halstead in Kent, was briefed to produce a 'gadget', as it was known, based on plutonium, that could form the core of a bomb and be capable of development into such a weapon. The science of such a device and its theoretical activation was capably executed at Fort Halstead, but the environment was not suitable for the very precise engineering tolerance requirements. Consequently, in 1950 the AERE moved as an entity to Aldermaston in Berkshire, the site of the former USAAF Station 467, which had housed the 315th and 434th Troop Carrier Groups, plus a few RAF units. Also, one of the large hangars was used by Vickers Supermarine for Spitfire sub-assembly and flight testing. On 6 June 1944, a vast fleet of C-47s hauled Horsa and Hadrian gliders off Aldermaston's operational runway for D-Day's Operation *Overlord*; post-war, the British Overseas Airways Corporation operated its training headquarters there until November 1948. Conversion to the requirements of the nuclear scientific team took only two years, and upon moving the AERE was retitled the Atomic Weapons Research Establishment (AWRE).

The programme before Penney and his team was far reaching, for not only were they concerned with the elements necessary to produce various nuclear weapons, but they were also to investigate their individual effects against different target constituents. The team's leader had joined the Manhattan Project in 1944 and, being

a later arrival, was able to assimilate the project as an entity more than the other British scientists engaged on their individual aspects. He had paid particular attention to the effects of the blast and shock waves anticipated from the detonation at White Sands and these researches were incorporated into the Aldermaston team's calculations. The schematic of their nuclear device centred around two separate subcritical plutonium components. A detonator for each component was to be simultaneously activated by firing mechanisms, which propelled supercharged explosions into the plutonium. The resultant explosions would compress the components into a supercritical mass, which would generate a blast effect of enormous velocity.

Operation *Hurricane*

The Aldermaston team forecast a device ready for test-firing by October 1952 and the codename Operation *Hurricane* was applied to the whole project. While the physics aspect of the project was a mammoth undertaking, it progressed comparatively untroubled; however, the problems associated with encasing it into an operational ballistic casing were not nearly so straightforward. There had been no British participation in this side of the work at Los Alamos and they had to start with a blank piece of paper. RAE Farnborough was charged with producing the casing and the Percival Aircraft Company at Luton in Bedfordshire developed the method of suspending the completed device within the finished product.

For some time, a location for the first British atomic test had been examined. Dr Penney wanted the test to take place in a comparatively shallow-water area and a Canadian site in Hudson Bay, off the coast of Manitoba, was initially the front runner. However, by the spring of 1952, the Monte Bello Islands group, lying about fifty miles off the north-west coast of Australia's largest state, Western Australia, had been confirmed and the time-expired naval frigate HMS *Plym* was prepared to carry the test elements to the Antipodes. It departed British waters in June and during its voyage, the required plutonium was delivered to Aldermaston from Windscale. The AWRE transferred the radioactive elements to Lyneham in Wiltshire, where they were loaded aboard

an RAF Transport Command Handley Page Hastings, to be flown to the Singapore airbase of Seletar. At Seletar, they were again transferred, this time into a Short Sunderland flying boat which delivered its cargo to the test site at Monte Bello, where they were installed within the casing aboard the frigate.

Recording and communications facilities were established within the island group, with blast-measuring apparatus sited on Trimoulle and remote-controlled photographic equipment installed on Alpha Island. Assembly of the bomb aboard HMS *Plym* was completed by the end of September and at 09.30 hours on 3 October 1952, Britain's first nuclear test detonation was successfully accomplished. A Conservative government had been elected in Britain at the 1951 General Election, and Winston Churchill, once more Prime Minister, sent a personal telegram to congratulate all concerned. An official announcement was made in the House of Commons and Dr William Penney was appointed Knight Commander of the Order of the British Empire.

Given the financial position of Britain after World War II, to have brought a successful culmination to eight years of intensive research and scientific work for an outlay of approximately £150 million spread over that time, was indeed a commendable achievement. It represented 1.5 per cent of the defence budget for the eight years and such an insignificant outlay was concealed within the Civil Contingencies Fund as the upkeep of public buildings, for security reasons. It was gratifying to the AWRE that they were able to reach their goal without the vast outlays known to be being spent in both the United States and the Soviet Union.

With the core tried and tested, the next stage of incorporating it into an operational weapon had already been initiated on 9 August 1946, when the Air Staff issued Operational Requirement (OR) 1001 for 'a bomb employing the principle of nuclear fission'. Parameters of a total weight not exceeding 10,000lb, maximum length 25ft and 5ft diameter, were laid down, with the operational release altitude bracket set between 20,000 and 50,000ft.

The codename *Blue Danube* was selected for the project and the British aircraft industry now had to produce the best aeroplane to deliver Johann Strauss II's Viennese waltz to the target.

CHAPTER TWO

Conception of the Bombers

On the day that the Monte Bello Islands were witnessing the atomic device test, RAF Bomber Command had twenty-seven operational squadrons, of which twenty-one were equipped with piston-engined aircraft and six had entered the turbojet era with the English Electric Canberra B.2. While the twin-engined Canberra was an excellent aeroplane, which greatly improved the service's operational speed and altitude capabilities, it was only a medium-range aircraft. The long-range strike requirements were still met by four throbbing piston-engined bombers, first exemplified, in the years of expansion, by the Short Stirling, which entered service with No.7 (Bomber) Squadron at the Yorkshire base of Leeming on 1 August 1940. (It has not been forgotten that the Handley Page H.P.15

V/1500 was actually the RAF's first four-engined bomber, seeing service with three squadrons between 1918 and 1920.)

The process of getting an aeroplane built into prototype form and then produced for RAF or RN service is quite convoluted, with the origins of the system dating back to April 1917. Post-World War II, amendments were implemented, but it still involved many tortuous routes through the corridors of officialdom. In 1950, further changes were brought into practice, but these only became applicable later in V-bomber development. With the destruction of the Axis powers, it was firmly believed that circumstances would follow the pattern after the 1914–18 war, when in August 1919 the British Prime Minister of the day, David Lloyd George, declared that there was no possibility of

another large conflict starting within the next five years and a good chance that such an occurrence would not happen for at least ten years. This became known as the Ten Year Rule, which in effect gave the government good grounds to cut back on all the armed forces plus their equipment. As this prophesy had been vindicated by events, there was, in 1945, every reason to hold a similar opinion.

Operational Requirement 229

In February 1942, Air Publication (AP) 970 was drawn up, in which the necessary procedures for getting a new aeroplane onto the drawing board were laid down. From this, the Operational Requirements Committee notified the Air Ministry

Alongside its bomber role, the Lincoln was also employed by RAF Signals Command. RE359 was a Lincoln B.2 based at Watton in 1961, when it paid a visit to Little Rissington, where this photograph was taken.
Ray Deacon

Bomber Command, 3 October 1952

Avro 694 Lincoln B.2

Resulting from an Air Ministry request to A.V. Roe for the range of the Lancaster to be greatly extended, the Type 694 was originally classified as the Lancaster Mark IV and Specification B.14/43 was written around the new design, which retained about 80 per cent of the original design structure. An order for three prototypes and eighty production aircraft, placed in 1943, had to be held back, due to the pressing need to produce additional Lancaster I and III aircraft. This urgency was twofold, due to the increasing losses during night raids in the winter of 1943/44 and the decision to phase out the Halifax, the loss rate of which was running at nearly 6 per cent. Renamed the Lincoln, Avro's new bomber first entered RAF service with No.57 Squadron at East Kirkby in Lincolnshire, in August 1945.

On 3 October 1952, the Lincoln B.2 was serving with the following squadrons: Nos 7, 148 and 214, based at Upwood in Huntingtonshire; Nos 61 and 100 at Waddington in Lincolnshire; Nos 83 and 97 at Hemswell, also in Lincolnshire; Nos 116, 199 and 527 at Watton in Norfolk.

Powerplants:	Four 1,750hp Packard Merlin 68, 68A or 300 inline engines.
Weights:	Empty 44,148lb (20,026kg); loaded 82,000lb (37,195kg).
Dimensions:	Span 120ft 0in (36.57m); length 79ft 3½in (24.15m); wing area 1,421sq ft (132sq m).
Performance:	Maximum speed 295mph (474.7km/h)
	Cruising speed 238mph (383km/h)
	Service ceiling 22,000ft (6,706m)
	Maximum range 3,750 miles (6,030km)
	Maximum bomb load 14,000lb (6,350kg) for 2,640 miles (4,248km).

Boeing Model 345 B-29 Washington B.1

Although the political climate between London and Washington was still hovering around zero degrees centigrade, Britain took on loan seventy refurbished B-29s under the post-war Military Aid Programme, as a stopgap to increase Bomber Command's potential. Being pressurized, the B-29 had an operational altitude advantage of 11,000ft over the Lincoln. The Soviet Air Force had been receiving turbojet fighters at an alarming rate since 1948 – thanks to the British government's misguided generosity in supplying Rolls-Royce Nene engines as an attempt to rekindle the wartime goodwill – and the Lincoln was of a bygone era when pitted against the MiG-15. So, on 22 March 1950, the first RAF B-29 touched down at Marham in Norfolk with a new name, the Washington. By May of the following year, the following squadrons were operating the Boeing aircraft: Nos 15, 44, 57 and 149 based at Coningsby in Lincolnshire; Nos 35 (the Washington Conversion Unit), 90 and 115 at Marham and No.192 at Watton.

With the serials WF434 to WF448, WF490 to WF514 and WF545 to WF574,

the Washington served with the RAF for four years before being returned to the United States as Bomber Command's last piston-engined type.

Powerplants:	Four 2,200hp Wright Cyclone R-3350-23 radial engines.
Weights:	Empty 74,500lb (33,793kg); loaded 120,000lb (54,432kg).
Dimensions:	Span 141ft 3in (43m); length 99ft 0in (30.18m); wing area 1,736sq ft (161.27sq m).
Performance:	Maximum speed 357 mph (574.5km/h)
	Cruising speed 342mph (550.3km/h)
	Service ceiling 33,600ft (10,241m)
	Maximum range 3,250 miles (5,230km)
	Maximum bomb load 20,000lb (9,072kg) for 1,000 miles (1,609km).

English Electric A.1 Canberra B.2

The first aircraft having been delivered to No.101 Squadron at Binbrook in Lincolnshire on 25 May 1951, by 3 October 1952 the Command's first turbojet-powered bomber was serving with Nos 9, 12, 50, 101 and 617 Squadrons, all at Binbrook, while No.109 Squadron was in the process of replacing its Mosquito B.35s at Hemswell. Canberra crews, who converted from piston-engined aircraft via the Gloster Meteor, would later form the nuclei of nearly all V-bomber flying personnel.

Powerplants:	Two Rolls-Royce RA.3 (series 101) turbojets each producing 6,500lb (2,948kg) thrust.
Weights:	Empty 22,200lb (10,070kg); loaded 46,000lb (20,870kg).
Dimensions:	Span 64ft 0in (19.5m); length 65ft 6in (19.96m); wing area 960sq ft (89.18sq m).
Performance:	Maximum speed 570mph (917km/h) at high altitude, 518mph (833.5km/h) at sea level
	Service ceiling 48,000ft (14,630m)
	Maximum range 2,660 miles (4,281km)
	Maximum bomb load 6,000lb (2,722kg) for 1,105 miles (1,778km).

Canberra B.2 WD950 on test prior to joining Bomber Command. Author's collection

Directorate of Technical Development (DTD) of their considered need for a replacement for the Lincoln. This took the form of Operational Requirement (OR) 229, which the Air Staff issued on 17 December 1946 and, in view of the considered lack of urgency so far as international tension was concerned, it embodied principles that required extensive research in almost every aspect.

During World War II, the de Havilland Mosquito had proved the theory that a bomber could get to its target and back, so long as it flew high enough and fast enough to avoid interception. In so doing, the requirement of a defensive armament was negated and the design could be tailored to the shape needed to carry the crew, bomb load and fuel at the stipulated performance. It was appreciated that the long-range bomber could not just be an enlarged Mosquito, but the principle of relying on speed and altitude without any defensive armament was considered the path to follow, despite the fact that contemporary US designs still catered for tail armaments. In January 1947, the Defensive Research Policy Committee (DRPC) was established, with Sir Henry Tizard, the Scientific Adviser to the Air Staff during World War II, at the helm. Although consideration had at one time been given to a rocket, possibly based on the German V-2, being the prime delivery vehicle for a nuclear weapon, just about everything examined, especially the range and payload, proved that such a concept was impractical and in 1948 this whole idea was rejected. It was therefore cast in stone that the atomic weapon would be a bomb, transported to the target by aircraft. The DRPC considered that a British stockpile of approximately 1,000 atomic bombs would constitute a genuine deterrent. When more thought was given to this assessment, it was appreciated that the West was in fact an integral unit and not just Britain on its own. An independent atomic bomb arsenal was essential but 200 units were later agreed to be a sufficient number.

Originally OR239 was issued, in which a range of 4,000 miles (6,436km) and an all-up weight of 200,000lb (90,720kg) was stipulated. The MoS had doubts about the industry being capable of meeting these requirements and, following a period when the OR was held in abeyance, it was eventually cancelled. Therefore, OR229 was couched in terms that specified a four-

Impression of an early H.P.80 design, to meet Specification B.35/46, based on wind tunnel models. Author's artwork

turbojet power source, a still-air range in the order of 3,500 miles (5,632km), a maximum operational altitude of 45,000ft (13,700m) which very early on in the programme was increased to 50,000ft (15,240m) and a capability of delivering a 20,000lb conventional bomb load at 575mph (925km /h), which translated into approximately Mach 0.87. An all-up weight of 100,000lb (45,360kg) was suggested, in view of the length of existing bases, but once the design teams had got their slide rules out and had been notified by engine manufacturers of anticipated thrust output figures, the all-up weight was increased to 115,000lb (52,160kg). There was also a stipulation for the aircraft to be capable of carrying a 'special' weapon. Although the Monte Bello Islands test was some years away, it had been established that a bomb would have a maximum diameter of 5ft (1.5m) and its length would not exceed 25ft (7.6m). These parameters determined the size of the bomb-bay to be incorporated in a design.

Specification B.35/46

The Air Ministry Research Directorate examined the basic requirements of the Air Staff and, following amendments considered necessary, the OR was passed over to the Ministry of Supply (MoS), who formally drew up Specification B.35/46 for issue to the aircraft industry. As this was a requirement in entirely new fields in so far as powerplants, operational altitude, speed and weapon load were concerned, the industry was more or less able to start with a blank piece of paper and, as was to

be expected, the approach by individual firms was very varied.

The specification was issued on 9 January 1947 to six companies, Armstrong Whitworth, Avro, English Electric, Handley Page, Short Brothers and Vickers-Armstrongs, with the proviso that their submissions were to be received by 31 May, which was a fairly tight schedule. The original OR was hardened into B.35/46 by the stipulated requirements of a five-man crew sited within one pressure cabin, an all-weather capability built around the wartime H_2S radar system and the aircraft was to be highly manoeuvrable throughout its entire speed/altitude operational envelope. The crew was to comprise two pilots, two navigators doubling up as bomb aimers, plus an electronic countermeasures operator and their pressure cabin was to be capable of ejection as a complete capsule in an emergency.

The Rejects

It has to be said that the design teams were far from being daunted by the project, despite treading down new paths in almost every aspect of aerodynamics. Several companies had already experimented in different fields and understandably leaned heavily on the results of their researches. English Electric had a proven design in the Canberra and their submission embodied all their experience with this, to the extent that it was in effect a larger version of one of the designs in the Canberra's development, but with six engines buried in a slightly swept high-wing and a T-tailplane. It was anticipated that the company would have little or no

Model of Avro's early submission to B.35/46, with the large circular engine intakes and wing-tip fins. Avro Heritage

capacity for the production of its B.35/46 design, once Canberra started to be ordered, and consequently their submission was rejected at the Tender Design Conference held in July. As events turned out with the Canberra, production having to be farmed out to Avro, Handley Page and Shorts, as well as filling the company's Preston plant, this was the correct decision, which left the project office free for its later P.1/Lightning design.

Vickers-Armstrongs at Weybridge in Surrey had made a bid for the civil market after World War II with their Viking, then Viscount, designs, both of which were proving very successful. 163 Vikings were produced, with the design forming the basis of the Valetta and Varsity for the RAF. 445 Viscounts would eventually be built, many of which were for foreign customers. The company's experience in four-engined bombers was limited to the Type 447 Windsor, which was unique in having a mainwheel undercarriage assembly underneath, and retracting into, each engine nacelle, of which the outboard pair were also designed to have twin 20mm Hispano cannon in remotely-controlled barbettes. Three Windsor prototypes had flown before the project was cancelled in March 1946.

The Weybridge project office answered B.35/46 with a rather conventional design incorporating a 26-degree-swept, high-aspect ratio wing and a very long fuselage. Again, the Conference considered this design was too conservative, embodying an approach that was too contemporary rather than envisaging an aircraft that would be in operational service ten years hence. Consequently, the Vickers-Armstrongs proposal, which does not appear to have been given a company type number, was rejected.

The Advanced Bomber Project Group

The four remaining companies' approaches were, in the opinion of the Tender Design Conference, too radical for them to be able to provide a true appraisal, so they turned the designs over to the Royal Aircraft Establishment (RAE) at Farnborough for an evaluation. However, the RAE too considered that the ultra-futuristic designs were beyond their existing aggregate of experience and they delegated the head of the Aerodynamic Flight Section, Morien Morgan, to form an Advanced Bomber Project Group (ABPG).

With an eighteen-strong team of the RAE's leading structural engineers and aerodynamicists, Morgan soon found that the specification range was going to be one of the most difficult factors. To attain it, wing areas would have to increase above those submitted, which in turn would increase the all-up weight and the length of runway required to get the aeroplane into the air. One obstacle was cleared when the RAF agreed to the lengthening of existing runways at the bases that would be designated for use by the new aircraft. The Group was also able to convince the Air Staff that if their suggested 115,000lb (52,160kg) maximum all-up weight figure was raised, wing loadings could be reduced, thereby benefiting operational altitudes.

The Winners, from Avro . . .

The other two designs, the Avro 698 and the Handley Page H.P.80, were two very different approaches to the specification. Avro's Roy Chadwick became Technical Director in 1946, with Stuart Davies taking over Chadwick's former mantle of Chief Designer, and Bob Lindley became head of the Project Office. As Avro was a member of the Hawker Siddeley Group, together with Armstrong Whitworth, they were able to incorporate the data that the Baginton company had accumulated during its tailless aircraft research programmes; however, they considered that, on balance, such a configuration gave too great a wingspan, which in turn induced an unacceptable all-up weight penalty. By progressively reducing the wingspan, while maintaining the desired wing area, the triangular delta shape evolved – and Chadwick had already produced at home, around 1946-47, a rough sketch of a delta-winged passenger aircraft design which he considered had merit.

To proceed to a bomber from this original thought was fairly straightforward,

More Pruning

Of the four B.35/46 designs before the ABPG, the Armstrong Whitworth and Short Brothers' submissions were the most advanced in conception. Armstrong Whitworth at Baginton, outside Coventry, had been engaged on tailless aircraft research since November 1942, with the emphasis on the perfection of a laminar-flow wing. The DTD had formed a Tailless Advisory Committee and a laminar-flow wing section, designed by Professor A.A. Griffiths, had been flown on Hawker Hurricane IIB Z3687 in March 1945, with Gloster Meteor III EE445 also being engaged in the research programme. The Baginton-based company first flew RG324, their AW.52G all-wing glider design, on 2 March 1945 and followed this with two prototype AW.52s built to Specification E.9/44. These were turbojet-powered flying wing aircraft, the first, TS363 powered by two Rolls-Royce Nene 2 engines, having its maiden flight on 13 November 1947. With this experience behind them, it was natural for the company's design to meet B.35/46 to be based on an all-wing concept.

Impression of the Short P.D.1 design, as it could have appeared, had it continued in its original configuration. Author's artwork

Short Brothers too had been engaged on tailless aircraft research, with their thinking being aided by Professor Geoffrey Hill, who had been responsible for the Westland Pterodactyl family of flying-wing aeroplanes in the 1930s. He had a long-standing friendship with David Keith-Lucas who was, in 1949, to become Chief Designer at Shorts and who considered that Hill's pivoting wing-tips employed on the Pterodactyls would alleviate the trailing-edge control-surface flutter associated with highly swept wings. The company's answer to Specification B.35/46 was the P.D.1 (Preliminary Design 1), which consisted of a large, deep fuselage, without a tailplane but featuring a substantial swept fin and rudder. The shoulder-mounted wing had a leading edge sweep of 42.5 degrees, with roots thick enough to take four buried turbojet engines. The trailing edge centre section commenced from the roots at zero degrees, then swept back at 30 degrees at quarter-span, decreasing to 18 degrees at the rotating outer sections. These would act in opposition as ailerons or in unison as elevators.

Both designs were evaluated by Morien Morgan's Group, who saw considerable merit in them, with particularly good all-up weight figures that conferred a better than specified cruising altitude. However, it was felt that not enough data existed to confirm the longitudinal stability question for either design and the time factor of researching this aspect, together with the costs involved with such a programme, did not encourage further development. Consequently both designs were rejected.

Armstrong Whitworth's flying wing research continued with their AW.52 design until 1950, when RAE Farnborough took over the laminar-flow programme and the aircraft's entry in the

aeronautical history books concerns the fact that on 30 May 1949, pilot J.O. 'Joe' Lancaster became the first British pilot to use an ejector seat in an emergency, when the first prototype had to be abandoned due to developing violent pitch oscillations in very rough air.

Short Brothers considered that their wing was worth developing enough for Professor Hill to join with Keith-Lucas and design first a glider, then a powered aircraft, employing what they called the 'aeroisoclinic' wing. The SB.1 glider encountered turbulence from the towing Short Sturgeon on its second lift-off, such that the glider's pilot, Tom 'Brookie' Brook-Smith had to cast off before any real height had been attained and he came down, hitting the runway nose-down at over 80mph. A powered variant, the SB.4 Sherpa, with two Turbomeca Palais turbojets, first flew on 4 October 1953. The aeroisoclinic wing was incorporated in subsequent company projects, such as the P.D.8 photo-reconnaissance aircraft design, the P.D.10, a projected version of the Supermarine Swift fitted with the wing and the P.D.13 to meet Specification M.148T/NA.39. This was won by Blackburn Aircraft and became the Buccaneer. Tom Brook-Smith found the Sherpa virtually viceless in its handling properties and considered that the P.D.13 would have been a superb aeroplane, but whether it would have been better than the Buccaneer in the roles in which the Blackburn design was eventually employed, we shall never know.

It is worth noting that the ABPG also gave some thought to an expendable bomber to meet B.35/46, but the economics of developing the necessary avionics and the limited operational life-span of such as aircraft determined that the idea should be abandoned before anyone in Whitehall thought it was a good idea!

with the aerodynamic research undertaken by Horten and Lippisch in Germany during World War II proving extremely useful. At this stage, the company type number 698 was applied to the design and a scale model was produced. Four engines and a crew compartment were buried in the wings, the engines being fed through intakes in the leading edge. This progressed to the engines still being retained within the wings, but the air intakes became two large circular ducts situated one either side of a central crew-carrying nacelle. The thickness of wing allowed the engines to be staggered in pairs, one above the other, with their respective orifices also staggered, being positioned at about three-quarter chord and at the wing trailing edge in pairs. Small wing-tip fins were fitted and two individual bomb-bays were incorporated outboard, one either side of each pair of engines, which were themselves separated by a large fuel-tank bay. The tricycle undercarriage main-wheel units were to retract forwards, with the nose wheel retracting rearwards; this element of the design was one of the few to be carried over to the finalized production aeroplane.

Wind-tunnel model of H.P.80 in 1946, with the wing-tips swept upwards to form fins. Handley Page Association

By early 1948, this H.P.80 wind-tunnel model had a conventional fin and rudder, with engines in separate nacelles. The nose has the H$_2$S scanner housing, that progressed into the Victor. Handley Page Association

. . . and from Handley Page

Handley Page's original offering benefited from the research which had been undertaken by the company's Experimental Designer Gustav Lachmann in the mid-1930s. He had been primarily instrumental in developing the slotted wing, to which Handley Page attached great importance as the means of reducing stalled flight at take-off and landing. His brief to Lachmann was to undertake research into the aerodynamic problems associated with an aeroplane bereft of the weight and drag penalties of an orthodox tail assembly. The resultant design was a small monoplane with a wingspan of 39ft 10in (12m) and length of 18ft 3in (5.5m). It had a wing-sweep angle of 45 degrees outboard of the centre section, on which were mounted two de Havilland Gipsy Majors fitted as pusher engines. A small fin/rudder assembly was positioned at the extremity of the wings with an additional dorsal fin mounted on a bulbous central nacelle that accommodated the two-man crew of pilot plus observer. The aircraft sat on a fixed tricycle undercarriage.

However, with the Hampden in production and the Halifax about to reach a similar status, Handley Page would not approve the diversion of manpower necessary to build a prototype, so in 1937 its construction was placed with a small company named Dart Aircraft Limited, based in Dunstable, Bedfordshire. The finished aircraft, unimaginatively nicknamed the 'Manx' because of its lack of conventional tail unit, was delivered to Handley Page's airfield at Radlett, Hertfordshire, shortly after the outbreak of World War II and was designated Experimental Aeroplane No.186, with the Class B registration H0222. It was 25 June 1943 before the 'Manx' first flew, an event which was greatly assisted by the fact that it hit a bump on the Radlett runway. It was given the company type number H.P.75 in June 1945 and after being fitted with larger elevons, it put in about 26 hours of flying before making its last flight on 2 April 1946. In keeping with the short-sighted attitude that prevailed in those days, it was burned as scrap in 1952.

Sir Frederick advocated incorporating data gathered from the H.P.75 in his company's submission to B.35/46. There

was also an official Tailless Aircraft Advisory Committee, set up as a joint Ministry/ Society of British Aircraft Constructors body during World War II. H.P.'s Research Engineer Godfrey Lee was a member of the Committee when it visited the new wind-tunnel establishment at Völkenrode, outside Brunswick, and the AVA at Göttingen in September 1945. On his return to the United Kingdom, further impetus was given to the swept-wing concept. As he stated, 'the swept-wing/jet engine was a historic pairing, for the jet is only efficient when going fast and the swept-wing enabled aeroplanes to fly reasonably fast without compressibility drag rise, with wings of sensible thickness/chord ratio.'

Consequently, type number H.P.80 evolved as a swept-wing design with a substantial fuselage, a small tailplane set on a stubby dorsal pylon at the rear with large fin and rudder assemblies sweeping upwards at each wing-tip. During the development of the design, the idea of

varying the angles of sweep along the span gradually emerged from discussions involving Lee, the aerodynamicists, wind-tunnel specialists, Lachmann and the Chief Designer George Volkert. No one person suddenly shouted *eureka!* and the format was laid; it just gradually materialized. A wind-tunnel model was produced in 1947, together with a General Arrangement drawing showing four engines buried within a wing centre section swept at 53 degrees at the quarter chord, with a 16 per cent thickness/chord (t/c) ratio. A slot-type air intake was set in the leading edge on either side of the fuselage. The wing-sweep angle changed at one-third span to 35 degrees and 9 per cent t/c, which in turn changed again at two-third span to a 35-degree sweep with a 6 per cent t/c at the fin/rudder intersection.

The foundations of the V-bomber force's constituents had been set, but the story had yet to undergo many changes, not least being the involvement of two more contenders.

CHAPTER THREE

Belfast's 'Insurance' Bomber

Morien Morgan and his Advanced Bomber Project Group were well aware of the fact that in short-listing the Avro and Handley Page proposals to B.35/46, they had selected entries which would pitch the companies into new aerodynamic realms. Furthermore, the answers would not be forthcoming in five minutes – five years was a much more realistic timescale. Nor was there any guarantee in 1947 that either approach would be successful in meeting the great operational demands of the specification. There was no doubt that lengthy programmes of research and testing would be necessary before the RAF would receive its new high-altitude, high-speed bomber. Today, advanced computers, sophisticated wind tunnels and research facilities, a great range of newly developed materials, together with a vast databank of accumulated high-speed turbojet-powered experience, are available for the design offices. By comparison, the winners of Specification B.35/46 were only a couple of steps above having the facilities to perfect the wheelbarrow.

'Just in Case'

In true British fashion, it was considered advisable to make provision for a compromise, which might not have all the advanced aerodynamics of the two main contenders, but would be an 'interim aircraft' that could be produced and put into RAF service in a reasonably short span of time, should any major problems materialize with the more radical aircraft. Operational Requirement 239 was re-activated in January 1947, with Specification B.14/46 being written around it, and Short Brothers were offered a contract. The basic provisions of the OR were a four jet-engined replacement for the Lincoln, with the capability of carrying a 10,000lb (4,535kg) nuclear bomb over a 3,500-mile (5,630km) range at a speed of 575mph (925km/h). The operational ceiling for dropping the weapon was to be

45,000ft (13,700m). This figure was later amended to 50,000ft (15,240m) and the range increased to 5,000 miles (8,045km).

With the contract offered to Short Brothers, history was being repeated. Back in 1936, the company had met Specification B.12/36 and produced the Stirling as the first of a new generation of four-engined bombers for the RAF. Now, ten years later, they were going to provide the Service with the first of the new four-turbojet-powered bombers. That this piece of nostalgia did not come to fruition can be firmly laid on the doorstep of Vickers-Armstrongs' Chief Designer, George (later Sir George) Edwards, whose contribution to the V-bomber history will be relayed in a later chapter.

The Design

Short Brothers allocated the designation S.A.4 to their design and, although the specification had been drawn up in 1946, it was a year later before it was officially handed to the company. The timing was rather unfortunate for Short Brothers, as long-standing plans to relocate from Rochester in Kent to the Northern Ireland capital, Belfast, were well in hand in 1947. Inevitably, this caused a certain amount of delay in the S.A.4's early detail design days, although the company's Chief Designer, David Keith-Lucas, had formulated the basic aircraft while still in Rochester.

From the outset, a limiting Mach number of 0.85 was set, which was quite a bold step, as this figure had only been exceeded in Britain up to then by VW120, the third prototype de Havilland D.H.108 tailless research aircraft, which was about as far removed from a four-engined bomber as it was possible to get. Conventionality, in terms of shape and structure, was adhered to by Keith-Lucas's design team, so that the resultant configuration had been established by the end of 1947. One sound decision was made in so far as all flying

controls were non-powered. The manual system employed a series of irreversible screw jacks, cable-driven from the cockpit, with actuated servo tabs on the wing trailing edges.

The fuselage was fundamentally the same as that proposed for the company's rejected aeroisoclinic wing design, but with a conventional tail unit. The Specification's stipulation that the aircraft was to have a 10ft 6in (3.2m) deep bomb-bay in order to accommodate the proposed *Blue Danube* weapon, meant that the S.A.4 featured a shoulder-wing layout, with the main spars passing above it. Sharply tapered to square tips, the wing, with a 17-degree angle of sweep on the leading edge, was set at a 4-degree angle of incidence and had 1 degree of dihedral along the whole span. A root t/c ratio of 12 per cent was employed, with the overall wing having an aspect ratio of slightly above 6:1. Either side of the nacelles, large fillets set at 5 degrees negative incidence extended from the wing leading edge to fair into the nacelle side panels.

Using a comparatively thin wing section meant that, contrary to contemporary British aircraft design thinking, the engines could not be buried within the centre section. Keith-Lucas departed from the conventional by proposing a configuration with one engine above the other on either side, with the jet pipes passing one above and one below the continuous wing spars. The engines were positioned ahead of the front spar and were attached to it by tubular-sectioned bearers. In designing the engine nacelles, the Rolls-Royce Avon RA.3 was the chosen power-plant. However, when construction actually got under way, these particular engines were not far enough in development to be supplied and consequently four RA.2s had to be allowed for, which involved several modifications to the starting controls, as the RA.2 required electric starters. A 12in addition had to be incorporated in each nacelle width to accept anti-icing pipes and alterations made to the jet-nozzle fairings.

The shoulder-wing configuration, coupled with the great depth of the fuselage, presented a challenge when it came to the undercarriage design. Initial thinking lay in a unit retracting into the engine nacelles, but these already had considerable depth in order to house the superimposed engines. Therefore, British Messier Ltd at Gloucester designed a tricycle undercarriage with a steerable two-wheel nose unit and a very impressive piece of engineering for the inward-retracting main wheels housed within the wing centre section. Although originally planned to have one giant single wheel on each leg, British Messier came up with a pair of very neat four-wheel bogies that spread the load more efficiently and

presented a much smaller mass to the airstream when activated. Dunlop Maxaret braking was incorporated in each wheel. The units retracted into enormous bays in the centre section, each being enclosed by a pair of large doors hinged to the wing root and the individual main-wheel leg. It is worth mentioning that this was certainly the first time that a four-wheel bogie undercarriage had been designed in Britain and it is debatable as to whether it was before Convair applied a similar unit to their B-36, which also first appeared with large single wheels. Each wing contained seven bag tanks, while a further eight were housed in the fuselage, the twenty-two tanks carrying a total of 6,170 gallons (28,050 litres). In Short Brothers, history was again repeated for the Stirling also featured a very substan-

tial undercarriage, which had a far more complicated retraction cycle than the S.A.4.

A profile of the S.A.4's fin and rudder assembly was test-flown on a modified Sunderland, to investigate the servo flying control system, which was found to be fully responsive and easy to operate. The tailplane was set at 13-degree dihedral, in order to clear the efflux from the superimposed engines and a G.Q. twin braking parachute system was stowed in the fuselage tail-cone.

One important factor of the S.A.4 was applied to all three V-bombers, that of the pressurized five-crew capsule. Saunders Roe were the first British company to develop such a compartment for a high-altitude turbojet bomber and its success can be evaluated by the fact that they

The two Short S.A.4 prototypes under construction, alongside the structural test airframe. Author's collection

The first prototype S.A.4 VX158, on the display line and flying in its 'Farnborough Special' colour scheme, at the 1951 SBAC Display. Author's collection

proceeded to produce units for Vickers-Armstrongs and Avro. Pressurized to a maximum differential of 9lb/sq in, the capsule carried two pilots seated side by side, behind which the radio operator, navigator and air bomber sat facing aft,

working at a full-width plotting table. The air bomber left this station and undertook his bomb-aiming duties in a pressurized tunnel extension with glazed panels at the end, sited forward of the crew compartment. In the S.A.4, only the first pilot sat

on an ejector seat, the rest of the crew making their emergency escapes down a tunnel at the lower rear of the compartment, leaving the aircraft via the ventral entry hatch. The whole question of the V-bomber crew's emergency evacuation procedure was a contentious issue that will be featured later in this narrative.

Construction Commences

Short Brothers' contract covered the construction of three airframes, one of which was for static testing only, while the two flying prototypes were allocated serials VX158 and VX161. From the start, in anticipation of receiving a quantity order, the company laid down production jigs and the three fuselages were built in these jigs, one alongside the other. From the jigs, the fuselages went down the shop floor for final assembly. There is no doubt that had the S.A.4 been ordered in quantity, these jigs would have saved many months and would have provided the RAF with four-turbojet bombers at an earlier date than actually occurred.

During construction, the decision was made to incorporate a system of self-contained hydraulic jacks within the bomb-bay roof, to facilitate the lifting of weapons into the bay. The nose radar bay also had to be enlarged to cater for an increase in size of the proposed scanner. When the first prototype had almost been completed, yet another change was made, this time to the design of the airbrake,

positioned on the wing trailing edge outboard of the engine nacelles. Instead of a single surface hinged downwards, a fail-safe design was installed, that split when operated to present a surface to the airflow above and below each wing.

The original Specification B.35/46 had stipulated that, while the principal weapon-delivering ability was to be radar guided, provision had to be made for visual bombing. Short Brothers' B.14/46 contained a similar demand, but this was not incorporated in the S.A.4 until much later, when VX158 was modified and fitted with a new nose-cone.

Official thinking in Britain was ahead of both the United States and the Soviet Union when drawing up the ORs and specifications for the bombers, in that there was no provision for defensive armament whatsoever. Beside speed and altitude, reliance was placed on discharging large quantities of *Window* (strips of metal foil now more universally referred to as chaff) into the air to obstruct radar detection, plus the development of electronic countermeasures, which at the time of drafting the requirements, in 1946, was placing a lot of faith in an embryonic science. In America, the current B-1 is the first multi-engined bomber designed not to carry a tail-gun position.

Four Rolls-Royce Avon RA.2 engines, each delivering 6,000lb (2,720kg) static thrust, were installed and by the beginning of 1951, VX158 had been completed. The move to Belfast in 1947 now produced another delay in the S.A.4 programme. The company's airfield at Sydenham, alongside Belfast Lough, had runways of insufficient length for the testing of such a large aircraft. Consequently, permission had to be sought from the Air Ministry for RAF Aldergrove to be used for the programme. This having been obtained, VX158 had to be dismantled and transported in sections along the 13-mile journey by road to what is today Belfast Airport. Once at Aldergrove, there followed reassembly, taxiing and systems trials, which occupied more than six months, so that it was August before the first S.A.4 was ready for a maiden flight.

More than a year prior to this, in May 1950, it had been decided that the S.A.4 would not go into production as the RAF's first four-jet bomber. In order to keep employment at the company, however, construction of the three airframes was continued and the two flying aircraft were designated for trials programmes relative to Bomber Command's requirements. These would prove to be very valuable in the overall V-bomber development and

For the 1952 Farnborough, VX158's colour scheme was overall matt silver. Author's collection

VX161, the second prototype SA.4, on its maiden flight, 12 August 1952.
Author's collection

later VX158 was to fulfil an engine test-bed requirement that no other aircraft of that era could have undertaken so readily.

S.A.4 Gets Airborne

On 10 August 1951, Chief Test Pilot (CTP) Tom Brooke-Smith lifted VX158, the company's heaviest aircraft to date, off Aldergrove's operational runway for its first flight. The aircraft was immediately found to be easy and pleasant to fly, although it was manually controlled.

There was a mandatory requirement for all new aircraft to have flown a minimum of ten hours, in order to qualify for a flying slot at the annual SBAC Display. 'Brookie', as the CTP was affectionately known, amassed these without any major

troubles and there was also time for the aircraft to acquire an impressive grey, red and black colour scheme before it landed on Press Day at Farnborough. A week of spirited high-speed, low-level runs and agile manoeuvres introduced the S.A.4 to the assembled gathering of the world's aviation representatives, before the return to Aldergrove to commence the many test schedules that make up a manufacturer's trials programme.

The static-test airframe was completed shortly after VX158 and placed in the company's new purpose-built testing facility, where it proved that Keith-Lucas had provided a rugged aeroplane. Wing load tests produced failures at 104 per cent of maximum, while the fuselage's figure was 108 per cent. Tests on the 9lb/sq in pressurized crew compartment showed minimal hatch distortion at 23lb/sq in, which in itself displays the strength of the capsule and the reason for it being adapted for ultimate V-bomber application.

With such a large and complex aeroplane, various small problems arose and had to be addressed, one of which the need to increase the pressure-balance airflow capacity, in order to prevent the fuel bag tanks collapsing during fast descents. The aircraft was cleared to descend at 18,000ft/min (5,485m/min), which was a very good performance for a large aircraft at that time. Aileron flutter was initially experienced at 42,000ft (12,800m), which limited the maximum speed to Mach 0.78. Frosting of the screwjacks at medium altitude also gave cause

The SA.4's impressive British Messier undercarriage is evident in this shot of VX158. Author's collection

for concern. Before modifications were made, they froze solid at above −65°C.

During the summer of 1952, the Avon RA.2s, which had been installed before the maiden flight, were replaced by four RA.3s, rated at 6,500lb (2,950kg) thrust. Small pointed fairings were fitted between each pair of jet pipe outlets to cure local buffeting around the nacelles and, for a while, a fairing was added to each wing trailing edge joint to the slab-sided fuselage, only to be discarded later.

VX161 Joins the Programme

Almost exactly a year after VX158's first flight, on 12 August 1952, the third S.A.4 airframe, VX161, made its maiden flight in the hands of Brooke-Smith. It had followed the pattern of the first prototype in being transported by road to Aldergrove, prior to the flight. Avon RA.3s were installed from the start and in general appearance, apart from the absence of the 'Farnborough colour scheme', the two aircraft were very similar. One subtle difference lay in the fitting of a wiper seal on the rudder leading edge on the later airframe, whereas VX158 employed a flexible sealing strip joining the fin. Both sealing methods had been tested on the Sunderland without either proving to be superior to the other. Careful examination of the two aircraft revealed that the large under-nose radome was slightly more streamlined on VX161.

In the first week of September 1952, VX158 was again displayed at Farnborough and about a month later the runway exten-

sion at Sydenham was completed. The two aircraft performed a formation fly-past on departing from Aldergrove and the manufacturer's trials were, from then on, conducted at the company's home base until the spring of 1953.

Separate Ways

With Short Brothers' testing completed, VX158 went to the RAE at Farnborough in May 1953, where it was used for a lengthy schedule of radar navigation and bombing trials in order to get operational procedures planned for the V-bomber force. This first S.A.4 was fitted with an air-operational radar system, but had no ability to drop bombs, and small markers were ejected through a panel in the bomb-

A Short Brothers' formation of SA.4 VX158, deploying full flap, followed by one of the small number of Seamew anti-submarine aircraft built, with the isoclinic-winged Sherpa off its port wing. Author's collection bay doors. These comprehensive RAE trials occupied a full twelve months and during this time service attrition was negligible. The installed electronics were more typical of the forthcoming centrimetric H_2S ground mapping/target location radar that had been tested in Avro Ashton Mk.3 WB492 for the past year, from the Royal Radar Establishment base at Defford in Worcestershire. The grey, red and black colour scheme had been removed from VX158 prior to delivery to the RAE and the radar trials were flown with an overall silver finish, with the radome left unpainted. It was at this stage that the glazed visual bomb-aiming position was fitted in a new nose cone above the radome. Just prior to the end of 1954, the aircraft returned to Sydenham for storage, pending further allocation for test flying. It was also around this time that the name *Sperrin* was conferred upon the S.A.4s, after the mountain range that straddles the Londonderry/Tyrone county border.

The second aircraft, VX161, was not fitted with a radar system and had a metal nose skin, but it did have a fully active weapons bay. On 11 April 1953 it became the property of the MoS and deployed to Woodbridge in Suffolk for a three-year period of weapons loading, releasing and aiming trials. Woodbridge was one of three special landing fields constructed in East Anglia during 1942, to cater for emergency landings by damaged or incapacitated Allied aircraft returning from operations over the European mainland. They each had a runway that was 250yd wide by 3,000yd long, with generous over- and under-shoot areas. The facility at Woodbridge was in fact an overspill airfield from the Armament and Instrument Experimental Unit (A&IEU) based at Martlesham Heath in the same county, the large runway proving more suitable for the operating of heavier A&IEU aircraft.

Considerable work had been put in by the Short Brothers' design team to perfect an inbuilt 4,000lb/sq in hydraulic-operated weapons loading system within the Sperrin's bomb-bay, but at Woodbridge it was found easier to pass cables from a Coles crane through two hatches in the fuselage roof to haul the weapons aboard. Since the original S.A.4 design, the length of *Blue Danube* had been reduced by 6ft (1.8m) and consequently there was plenty of space within the 30ft (9m) weapons bay when concrete dummies of

By now named 'Sperrin', VX158 carries de Havilland Gyrons in the lower engine bays, at the 1956 SBAC Display. Author's collection

the bombs were carried. These dummies were dropped over the Establishment's range at Orfordness, on the East Anglian coast. VX161 was also used for similar dropping trials of *Blue Boar*. This was the codename for a television-guided bomb being developed in the mid-1950s, but which did not go into production.

Operations for the Sperrin at Woodbridge were not always straightforward and schedules sometimes had to be modified or even abandoned on occasions. Although it was an enclave of the A&IEU at Martlesham Heath, administration of the base had been taken over on 5 June 1952 by the USAF. No.79 Squadron of the 20th Fighter/Bomber Wing, equipped with Republic F-84Gs as a part of the North Atlantic Treaty Organization (NATO), which had priority so far as the USAF was concerned, and A&IEU trials had to be dovetailed into the requirements of the Wing.

By the beginning of 1955, VX161 had been transferred to RAE Farnborough, from where it flew for many months on a variety of programmes, including an extension of its Woodbridge trials. During one of these flights the roof escape hatch came adrift and departed from the airframe, but the Establishment's luck held good and the errant hatch was recovered, having suffered remarkably little damage. Towards the end of the year the RAE trials were completed and the aircraft returned to Sydenham. It was not realized at the time, but this flight was to be VX161's final sortie.

The Engine Test-Bed

De Havilland Engines at Hatfield in Hertfordshire started producing indigenous centrifugal-flow turbojets in 1941, their Goblin and Ghost engines proving very successful both commercially and technically. In 1950 Major Frank Halford, the company's brilliant engine consultant, turned his attention to designing a private-venture engine employing a simple axial-flow compressor with seven stages, which would use the ram-air effect of supersonic flight to generate augmented compression. Type-named the H.4 Gyron, it had a proposed 6:1 compression ratio that would rise to 40:1 with intake compression in an airframe operating at supersonic speed when reheat was cut in.

The first engine, designated the D.Gy.1, started bench running on 5 January 1953, when the design thrust of 15,000lb (6,800kg) was achieved. The additional 5,000lb (2,270kg) reheat thrust attained later in the year suggested that the Gyron was the most powerful turbojet engine in the western world at that time. With a length of 13ft (4m), diameter of 4½ft (1.4m) and weighing only 4,270lb (1,937kg), Halford's new engine was showing a specific fuel consumption of 0.95lb/lb/hr. By September 1954, the first flight-standard Gyron, the D.Gy.2, developing 20,000lb (9,070kg) static thrust, was ready and design applications included Vickers Supermarine's Type 599 fighter, a Fairey fighter based on their F.D.2, Hawker's P.1121 interceptor, as well as the Avro Type 730 supersonic bomber. The Gyron was going to be an important engine and the need for a flying test-bed was urgent.

The unconventional engine layout of the Sperrin, plus the fact that VX158 was in store and readily available, made it an ideal selection. The aircraft was withdrawn from storage and flown to Aldergrove, where a conversion was put in hand for a D.Gy.2 Gyron to replace the lower port-side RA.3 Avon. Remarkably little structural redesign was required, apart from the stiffening of the area around the test engine's location. The major work involved the recontouring of the nacelle's lower section, changes to the fuel system and alterations to the original engine controls. The whole work was completed within a few months and on 7 July 1955, Short Brothers test pilot 'Jock' Eassie was at the controls when the reconfigured VX158 took to the air for the first time as an engine test-bed. It was possibly the aircraft with the most available power then flying anywhere in the world. The odd engine combination was quickly mastered, with the upper port Avon hardly being required. Eassie delivered the aircraft to de Havilland's Hatfield airfield, from where the majority of test flying was undertaken by de Havilland test pilot Chris Beaumont. In September, he demonstrated the Sperrin at the 1955 SBAC Show, after which a concentrated test programme was begun.

Twin-Gyron Sperrin

Early in 1956, VX158 returned to Aldergrove for a similar Gyron installation to be made on the starboard side and the first flight with two Gyrons took place on 26 June. It was instantly discovered that the pair of de Havilland engines delivered more power than the four Rolls-Royce engines originally fitted. This maiden flight with a pair of Gyrons was not without incident. The outer starboard landing-gear door parted company with the aircraft and vanished beneath the rollers of the Irish Sea. With nothing remaining in the way of the original S.A.4 jigs or assembly machinery, it was quite uneconomic to manufacture a new door. VX161 was in storage with no immediate plans for its further utilization, so it

Specification – Short Brothers S.A.4 Sperrin	
Powerplants:	VX158: four Rolls-Royce RA.2 Avon turbojets each producing 6,000lb (2,720kg) thrust;
	VX158: four Rolls-Royce RA.3 Avon turbojets each producing 6,500lb (2,950kg) thrust;
	VX161: Four Rolls-Royce RA.3 Avon turbojets each producing 6,500lb (2,950kg) thrust.
Weights:	Empty 72,000lb (32,660kg); loaded 115,000lb (52,160kg).
Dimensions:	Span 109ft 0in (33.2m); length 102ft 4in (31.2m); wing area 1,663sq ft (154.5sq m).
Performance:	Maximum speed 514mph at 36,000ft (827km/h at 10,970m); Mach 0.78 Maximum ceiling 42,000ft (12,800m) Maximum range 3,860 miles (6,212km) Maximum bomb load one 10,000lb nuclear bomb or sixteen 1,000lb iron bombs.

became benevolent and supplied the replacement. By so doing it ensured that it would not fly again.

In September 1956, VX158 appeared at the SBAC Show for the fourth time and its flying display on the power of just the two Gyrons was something to behold. At this time, it was definitely the most powerful aircraft aloft, with over 53,000lb (24,040kg) thrust available. Getting back into test-flying mode later in the month, altitudes exceeding 50,000ft (15,240m) were regularly attained and the Sperrin was proving to be the ideal test-bed for de Havilland's promising axial-flow engine, which was meeting all its design expectations. A pre-production engine was delivered to Hawker Aircraft at Kingston-upon-Thames, to assist them with their P.1121 mock-up. The Gyron's prospects looked good.

On 4 April 1957, Defence Minister Duncan Sandys presented his White Paper on defence to the House of Commons and in one fell swoop decimated the British aircraft industry. The Avro, Fairey and Vickers Supermarine Gyron-powered projects were all cancelled forthwith, while Hawker Aircraft continued with the prototype P.1121's construction for another year as a private venture and de Havilland carried on with Gyron development on the same basis. However, by August 1958 economics had to be recognized and work on the P.1121 ceased. Now, the Gyron had nowhere to go and despite it having been developed to the point of delivering 29,300lb (13,290kg) static thrust, engineering work on the engine terminated, as did all flight testing.

A total of eight years of design and development on the engine, assimilating over £3.4 million, had come to naught. Following its donation of a replacement undercarriage door to the first prototype, VX161 was scrapped by Short Brothers in 1957 and the following year, in August 1958, de Havilland had finished with VX158 and it was sold for scrap. However, the aircraft did not disappear from Hatfield for some time and photographic evidence exists placing it still on the de Havilland airfield as late as June 1960. Anecdotes from that era carried the information that VX158 was sold with a Gyron still in situ and de Havilland had to pay out substantially more to buy it back from the scrap merchant than they had initially received for it, but such stories have not been substantiated.

It is very easy to speculate in retrospect, but there is no doubt that had Air Ministry sights been set a little lower and the S.A.4 Sperrin, as a more basic four-jet bomber, been ordered in 1948, there would have been no need to acquire second-hand B-29s. Mind you, Vickers-Armstrongs would strongly disagree and who is to argue with them. Short Brothers' move from Rochester to Belfast had a profound effect on the timing of the programme, as did the company's lack of wind-tunnel facilities. Accepted that the Sperrin was less radical than the three V-bombers, it is pertinent to remember that two of them required design changes before becoming acceptable service aircraft, whereas the Belfast product performed all that was asked of it in its original guise.

CHAPTER FOUR

The 'Unfunny' Bomber from Weybridge

The fact that Vickers-Armstrongs' original offering to Specification B.35/46 had been rejected did nothing to convince the company's Chief Designer that they had got it wrong, but simply served to encourage him to prove his point to the MoS with his customary drive and verve. This Chief Designer was George (later Sir George) R. Edwards, whose affection and respect throughout the British aircraft industry is acknowledged by his always being known as 'GRE'.

GRE's Persuasive Powers

George Edwards saw the company's submission as being practical from the point of view that it was based on contemporary aeronautical knowledge. Its lack of sophistication meant that it could be available for RAF service much earlier than the designs with more advanced, but untried, aerodynamics, which were bound to require a lengthy time of research and development. GRE is quoted as saying that his design was an 'unfunny' aeroplane. It met a large proportion of the original specification's requirements, only really falling down on range, which both the MoS and RAF deemed to be acceptable if the aircraft could be available early enough.

George Edwards' powers of diplomacy and persuasion, coupled with his respected reputation of not promising the unattainable, carried enough weight for the MoS to accept his proposals. His promise to have a prototype in the air in three years and the first production aircraft flying two years after that, won the day. A new specification, B.9/48, was written around the Vickers-Armstrongs Type 660, with GRE's timescale embodied in it. Two prototypes were ordered on 15 April 1948, the first to be powered by four Rolls-Royce Avon RA.3 turbojets, the second by four Armstrong Siddeley Sapphires and the

official contract was placed on 2 February 1949. Serials WB210 and WB215 were allocated to the two aircraft.

GRE's promised timescale was based on his belief in his team at Weybridge. Ernie E. Marshall, who had shared the aerodynamic outline of the original design with GRE, headed the Project Office, structures was led by Basil Stephenson and stress by Henry H. Gardner, while Elfyn 'Sam' J. Richards was responsible for aerodynamics. The Experimental Manager in charge of prototype construction was A.E. 'Charlie' Houghton. Vickers-Armstrongs had their experimental establishment hidden within a copse of fir trees at Fox Warren, roughly midway along the minor road between Brooklands and the Wisley test-flying airfield. Many of the company's prototypes began life in this collection

of T4 hangars, with its geographical location making it an ideal site for work on secret projects. One could drive down the country road without realizing what the coniferous wood concealed – on my first visit to the site, I passed by and a hasty application of the handbrake was necessary!

The original submission to B.35/46 featured a high-aspect ratio wing with a constant 26-degree angle of sweep and four separate undercarriage legs, as on the earlier Windsor. Further studies by the company, after their design had been rejected, convinced them that a wing with compound sweep on the leading edge was a superior article and GRE's Type 660 had 42 degrees sweep on the inner wing, melding into 20 degrees on the outer section.

Seen at the Centenary Celebration in honour of Sir Thomas 'Tom' Sopwith, at Brooklands in 1988, Sir George Edwards, centre, shares a table with Sir Peter Masefield, left, and Sir Arnold Hall. *Aeroplane*

The Aircraft Works by the Racetrack

Established armaments maker Vickers, Son and Maxim Ltd started a flying school within the oval Brooklands motor racing circuit in 1912. Set a couple of miles from Weybridge in Surrey, the Brooklands track witnessed the establishment of the company's flying school shortly after Vickers had set up an aviation design and construction department in 1911. The company's earlier work on airships at Barrow in 1908 started with disaster, when the structure of their first example, the *Mayfly*, collapsed while being taken from its assembly shed. However, further airship design and construction was undertaken until 1929, by which time a total of ten different models had emerged, the last being the R.100, conceived by Barnes (later Sir Barnes) Wallis.

Frenchman Robert Esnault Pelterie (R.E.P.) agreed to Vickers manufacturing one of his designs under licence, and R.E.P supplied the rear fuselage for Vickers No.1 monoplane, which first flew on 28 March 1911, piloted by Capt Herbert F. Wood, the manager of Vickers' aviation department. The company's entry to the field of military aircraft was made with the Type E.F.B.1 (Experimental Fighting Biplane No.1) in 1913, from which a succession of forward-firing Vickers or Lewis gun-armed pusher-biplanes spawned, under the collective name of Vickers Gunbus, which saw service during the 1914–18 war.

Early in the war a factory was established at Weybridge, beside the Brooklands track, and in 1917 the Air Board detailed Vickers Chief Designer Rex Pierson to design a twin-engined bomber, using 200hp Hispano Suiza engines. B9952, the first prototype F.B.27, as the design was titled, had its maiden flight on 30 November of that year and in 1918 the name Vimy was conferred on the design, which had various prototypes powered by Sunbeam, Fiat and Rolls-Royce engines. Two Rolls-Royce Eagles developed the aircraft into a long-range bomber capable of carrying a 2,476lb (1,123kg) bomb load and it entered RAF service just too late to be used operationally in the war. After the Armistice on 11 November 1918, Vickers closed its factories at Crayford and Erith in Kent, keeping aircraft production centred at Weybridge, where commercial Vimy variants were built alongside the ninety-nine bombers that entered the RAF between 1918 and 1921.

A civilian Vimy hit the headlines on 14 June 1919, when the thirteenth production aircraft, crewed by Capt John Alcock and Lt Arthur Whitten-Brown, started the first non-stop transatlantic flight from St John's in Newfoundland. The following day they landed, rather ignominiously nose first in a peat bog, at Clifden, County Galway in Ireland. This was followed in November/December by a 135hr 55min flight from Hounslow (now swallowed up by London Heathrow), to Darwin, Australia. The company supplied the RAF with a succession of twin-engined aeroplanes – Vernon transports, Virginia bombers, Victoria and Valentia troop-transports – throughout the 1920s. The single-engined Vixen biplane fighter family won valuable export orders and various monoplane fighter designs passed through the Martlesham Heath trials establishment during the 1930s. The RAF maintained its penchant for the biplane and the first single-engined Vildebeest torpedo bomber arrived at No.100 Squadron in 1932, to be followed by its derivative, the Type 266 Vincent, which first joined No.8 Squadron two years later, in the winter of 1934. Both types were still in service, with overseas squadrons, when World War II started.

In 1928 the engineering facilities of Vickers Ltd and Armstrong Whitworth Ltd united to form Vickers-Armstrongs Ltd, prior to which the aviation section of Vickers Ltd had taken over the Supermarine Aviation Company to form Vickers Supermarine Ltd. Both companies were to provide history with outstanding aeroplanes for over fifty years and Vickers-Armstrongs' input was to be greatly enhanced by George R. Edwards (GRE), who joined the company at the end of 1934 as a stressman, to be moved into the drawing office as a draughtsman a few months later.

The first Vickers-Armstrongs' monoplane to enter service with the RAF was the single-engined Type 287 Wellesley bomber, designed to Specification 22/35 and 177 aircraft were built. It was unique in being the Service's first bomber to feature a retractable undercarriage and its bomb load was carried in panniers suspended below the wings on pylons. The first production aircraft made its maiden flight on 30 January 1937 and No.76 Squadron received its first Wellesley later in the same year. The RAF formed the Long Range Development Unit at Upper Heyford with five Wellesleys, and several long-endurance sorties were flown to the Middle East in preparation for setting a new record from Ismailia, in Egypt, to Australia. Achieved in November 1938, the officially recognized record non-stop flight of 7,157.7 miles remained intact for eight years. The Wellesley remained in Bomber Command service until the beginning of World War II (with some overseas squadrons operating with them well into the early months of the conflict), when new twin-engined monoplane medium bombers started arriving, among them the Type 290 Wellington, universally known as the *Wimpey* (after 'Wimpey Wellington', a contemporary cartoon figure). The Vickers-Armstrongs' bomber was built to Specification B.9/32 and was the company's first to feature power-operated gun turrets. In 1940, GRE was made Experimental Works Manager – he was on his way to the top.

The Wellesley had been the first to employ Barnes Wallis's geodetic construction, which transferred loads to intact areas of airframe when localized damage was received. This was a lattice-type metal structure that had a fabric outer skin and when the Wellington was designed to be built by similar construction, it was thought impractical for such a large airframe that was destined for large-scale production. However, the Weybridge production department had faith in Wallis's assurance that it would work. The grand total of 11,460 Wellingtons built proved that their faith was not misplaced. Eighty-eight RAF squadrons and forty-eight Operational Training Units flew the Wellington, which was finally pensioned off by the service in 1948. It is also pertinent to recall that the first British turbojet flying engine test-bed was a Wellington, Mk.II W5518/G, which had a Rover-built Whittle W.2B installed in place of its Nash & Thompson two-gun rear turret and had its maiden flight on 1 August 1942.

Produced parallel to the Wellington later in World War II, the Warwick was a slightly larger version of the *Wimpey* designed to Specification B.1/35, which also employed geodetic construction. 845 Warwicks were built and they were followed by Vickers-Armstrongs' first four-engined heavy bomber, the Type 447 Windsor designed to Specification B.5/41 for Far East operations. The end of the war brought an end to production plans for the Windsor after four prototypes, three of which flew.

During the autumn of 1945 Rex Pierson, who had been Chief Designer for twenty-eight years, was appointed Chief Engineer. GRE took over Pierson's former post, to which he added his undoubted great business acumen. This was proven with the company's first post-war civil aircraft, the Type 610 Viking, which met the Brabazon Committee's proposed blueprint for future British commercial aviation as the VC1, and 163 examples were

The Aircraft Works by the Racetrack *continued*

made. Military offshoots became the Valetta transport and trainer, built together with a first tricycle-undercarriage trainer design, the Varsity.

Chief Test Pilot Capt Joseph 'Mutt' Summers, who held the position for twenty-five years, was briefed to find an additional airfield site in close proximity to Weybridge and his selection of a grassed plateau at Wisley, less than a 5-minute flight from Brooklands, became Vickers-Armstrongs' flight-testing facility, which was at times shared by Vickers Supermarine. The flight sheds and concrete hard standings witnessed the company's products for many decades, the runway at Brooklands becoming purely a first-flight take-off strip, with many aircraft not even retracting their undercarriages, so short was the flight between the two sites.

Vickers-Armstrongs' – and British – civil aviation entered new realms of glory in 1945, when the Brabazon Committee allocated the designation Brabazon IIB to their recommendation for a propeller-turbine-powered passenger-carrying transport. Pierson's proposal for a twenty-four seater airliner, powered by four Rolls-Royce, Armstrong Siddeley or Napier engines, became the VC2 Type 630 Viceroy, which was quickly renamed Viscount. Four Rolls-Royce Darts powered the world's first prop-jet airliner to go into regular service and the total of 445 examples were jointly built on a new production line laid down at Weybridge, plus a further facility at Hurn in Hampshire. Export orders were received from over forty foreign airlines, of which the one from Capital

Airlines of Washington in 1954 was of great significance, as American airlines were not noted for purchasing aircraft from outside the United States. The Viscount is recorded as earning nearly £200 million, which did the company no harm.

History still abounded on the new Viscount production facility on the opposite side of Brooklands airfield from the main works, for it was a conversion of Sopwith's original workshops from which that company built vast numbers of fighters during the 1914–18 war. The conversion for Viscount production was necessary because bombers were again filling the main works' shop floor, these being Type 660 Valiants. A larger civil turboprop aircraft than the Viscount followed the Valiants, the Type 951 Vanguard, powered by four Rolls-Royce Tyne engines. A total of forty-four Vanguards came off the line before production ended.

The main works' assembly line at Weybridge carried the company's first production pure-jet civil transport when the Type 1100 succeeded the Vanguard. It was not, however, Vickers-Armstrongs' first multi-engined turbojet transport aircraft design for which metal was cut. The Type 1000 was a development of the Valiant, to be powered by Four Rolls-Royce Conways, aimed at the military transport and civil markets. The first prototype, XD662, was 80 per cent completed when the MoS cancelled the military requirement and a proposed British Overseas Airways Corporation (BOAC) order did not materialize. The cancellation had political overtones – not for the first time by any means – as Short Brothers were in a position to manufacture the Bristol

Model of the proposed Vickers-Armstrongs Type 1000, left, shows its lineage with the Type 660 Valiant. Author's collection

Britannia as a troop transport under licence and needed to keep the workforce, in order to prevent further unemployment in Northern Ireland. Furthermore, BOAC directors had interest in the Boeing 707. The author remembers seeing the cut-up sections of XD662 awaiting collection by a scrap-metal company and thinking that it was all a great waste. This was before it was known that £4 million had been spent on the project, which only goes to compound the thought.

The Type 1100 VC10 had its origins in a large three-engined variant of the Vanguard called the Vanjet and BOAC received a brochure of the design. However, they showed little interest, deeming that a tri-jet aircraft was not for transatlantic routes. Somehow, Boeing Aircraft did not subscribe to the same opinion! The four-Conway-powered VC10 and its stretched variant, the Super VC10, finished production after the fifty-fourth example had flown out of Brooklands. Today, more than twenty operate out of RAF Brize Norton on a regular basis, some of them having been converted to a flight-refuelling tanker role.

The final aircraft to be assembled at the Weybridge plant was possibly the most contentious political football in Vickers-Armstrongs' history. Joint discussions about a collaboration between the company and English Electric Aviation for a projected Canberra replacement began in April 1958. Operational Requirement 339 had been issued two months earlier and the project was designated TSR.2 in January 1959. One year later, on 1 January 1960, the two company names, together with Vickers Supermarine, disappeared in the formation of the British Aircraft Corporation (BAC). With TSR.2 design integrity shared between the original companies, assembly of the first two prototypes was laid down at Weybridge, with plans made for the rest of the development aircraft to follow, while pre-production aircraft were to be built at the former English Electric plant at Samlesbury in Lancashire.

The first prototype, XR219, was transported by road to the A&AEE at Boscombe Down on 6 March 1964 and on 27 September it made its first flight, in the hands of the former English Electric company's Chief Test Pilot, Roland 'Bee' Beamont. There followed twenty-four test flights, totalling 13hr 14min, and the second aircraft, XR220, arrived at Boscombe Down from Weybridge on 9 September 1964. It was ready for initial test-flying at the end of March 1965.

The Chancellor's Budget Speech in the House of Commons on 6 April 1965 pronounced the cancellation of the whole TSR.2 project, after an expenditure of something between £125 million and £190 million. Two more aircraft, XR221 and XR222, were almost completed and further components were being assembled at Weybridge when the cancellation was announced. The contract was officially terminated on 6 July and the plants involved were ordered to destroy all jigs forthwith. Two airframes, neither of which flew, exist today. XR220 is at the Aerospace Museum at Cosford, while XR222 is at the Imperial War Museum at Duxford. The rest were destroyed at Salmesbury and the Proof and Experimental Establishment at Shoeburyness.

So closed over fifty years of historic aviation within the acreage of the Brooklands track, which first witnessed four-wheel activity in 1907 and flying the following year. The finale was certainly more ignominious than was deserved, but then, history is often like that. Today, the thriving Brooklands Museum is all that remains on the site to treasure the memories. The single runway hears the squeal of landing wheels occasionally, when a new exhibit arrives or when the museum holds one of its special events, which is when the dulcet tones of the museum's commentator informatively waft from the public address system, to eulogize over the well-preserved aeroplane performing before the gathered spectators.

When detail design got under way in May 1948, leading edge sweep on the inner wing section was reduced to 37 degrees, which gave it a 12 per cent t/c ratio. Provision for fuel tanks to be carried on pylons at roughly half span of each wing was also implemented. The fuselage was a beautifully clean aerodynamic shape of circular section, the lines only being broken by the raised dome of the crew compartment and the smaller ventral blister of the visual bomb-aiming station. A broad chord fin had a short dorsal fairing at its junction with the tapering rear fuselage and a moderately swept, variable-incidence tailplane was mounted nearly halfway up the fin, to keep it clear of the turbojet exhaust efflux.

Four Rolls-Royce Avon RA.3s, each developing 6,500lb (2,950kg) static thrust were buried in the wing centre section, with the tailpipes emerging from the wing upper surface forward of the trailing edge. The wing centre sections each had a single narrow slot air intake in the leading edge to feed each pair of engines. Troubles encountered during engine running prior to the first flight were cured by the addition of fourteen narrow vertical supports being installed in each intake. Outboard of the engines, large bays in the shoulder-mounted wing housed the outward-retracting tandem-wheeled, more conventional main undercarriage, and the twin-wheeled nose unit aft of the bomb-aimer's housing retracted rearwards into the lower fuselage. A large electronics bay in the lower half of the nose section forward of the five-crew compartment, which was a pressurized capsule manufactured by Short Brothers, was to house the H_2S radar. The two pilots were equipped with Martin-Baker Mk.1 ejector seats and the three observers sat facing rearwards, as in the Sperrin, except that in the Type 660 they made their emergency exits via the elliptical crew entry door on the port side, which had a built-in slipstream deflecting panel ahead of the door when open.

All-Electric

The dual-level pressurized capsule, actuated by air bled off the engine compressors, had a low equivalent altitude level for routine flying and a higher one for combat sorties, while an emergency system maintained moderate pressure should a windscreen panel get punctured.

All other services on the aircraft were electrically powered by eighty-five different electric motors. Four 112-volt DC generators, driven by the engines, operated the power controls, undercarriage, flaps, trim tabs, airbrakes, tailplane incidence, bomb doors, fuel and hydraulic pumps, plus much of the instrumentation. A 28-volt system driven by a rotary transformer from the main system actuated all secondary electrics. The electro-hydraulic power controls had an artificial feed system, fed by air taken in by an intake positioned at the base of the fin leading edge.

The beautiful first Type 660 prototype, WB210, shows its narrow air intakes for the Avon RA.3 engines. Author's collection

The Prototype Takes Shape

The manufacture of assemblies for WB210, the first prototype Type 660, gathered pace at Fox Warren throughout 1950. On completion, the sections were taken the couple of miles by road to Wisley, where final assembly was scheduled to finish by spring 1951. The measure of this achievement can be gathered when it is appreciated that the jigs at Fox Warren had to be constructed from builder's scaffolding, due to the shortage of raw materials and finances that existed at that time. It was less than five years since the end of World War II, which had drained British resources to the bottom of the barrel.

By early April 1951, WB210 was completed. Systems testing, together with engine runs, occupied the rest of the month and into May, but by the second week the first Type 660 was ready for flight testing. Apart from the national markings and stencilled instructions, there was no paint on WB210. It was in natural metal, gleaming from the overall polish applied by a proud workforce. 'Mutt' Summers was coming up for a well-earned retirement, but he was determined to add the Type 660 to his impressive tally of first flights.

The company's flight-test airfield at Wisley, which still had a grass runway in the spring of 1951, was notorious for getting waterlogged on occasions. One day near to when WB210 would be ready to fly and the Wisley grass squelching underfoot, it was mentioned to GRE that the flight might have to be made from the vast concrete tract at Boscombe Down. Recognizing the fact that this would require the prototype being dismantled for transportation by road, the Chief Designer opined in no uncertain terms that he would have built it differently if he had thought along those lines!

However, being on a plateau, Wisley dried out well and 18 May 1951 found the grass runway ideal, following the stiff breeze that prevailed that day. 'Mutt' Summers, accompanied by Assistant CTP Jock Bryce, lifted WB210 into the air for the first time with the flaps set at 20 degrees, to make a 5-minute circuit of the airfield at under 1,000ft, keeping the undercarriage locked down. Summers was noted for not making maiden flights into cross-country sorties! He landed and it has to be stated that this was exactly twelve weeks before the S.A.4 Sperrin first got airborne. GRE was running to schedule.

Official faith in the aircraft and its importance in RAF forward planning were proved even before the first flight had been made, when the company received an order for twenty-five aircraft in April 1951.

Test-Flying Begins

Although the grass runway at Wisley was drier than it had been a few days earlier, over 75,000lb of aeroplane leaves an impression and when WB210 had returned to the concrete apron outside the flight-sheds, it had left behind large, deep ruts, which, if repeated as in a normal flight-testing programme, would soon leave the airfield only fit for sowing crops. An alternative site had to be found quickly while a tarmac runway was laid at Wisley. The company had a large stroke of luck here, as BOAC was in the throes of moving from their maintenance base at Hurn, outside Bournemouth, which is now Bournemouth Airport.

The second flight of WB210 was its last from Wisley, as Summers terminated the sortie at Hurn, and the rest of its flying career was conducted from the Hampshire base. Following the third flight, 'Mutt'

The Many Faces of Hurn

The year following the outbreak of World War II, construction was started on an airfield four miles north-east of Bournemouth, which was then in the County of Hampshire but, following the changes of county boundaries in the 1960s, now resides in Dorset. By July 1941, the airfield was ready to be a satellite of the New Forest base of Ibsley, which itself was a satellite of Middle Wallop.

Spitfire IIBs and VBs of Ibsley's No.118 Squadron intermittently used Hurn during 1941, but in November the Special Duty Flight arrived from Christchurch, with its collection of Ansons, Battles, Blenheims and Harrows. The Flight was engaged on radar trials for the Telecommunications Research Establishment at Swanage and in December it was joined by a detachment of No.1425 Flight from Honeybourne, operating Consolidated Liberators. The units remained until the spring of 1942, when Hurn became a No.38 Wing base and No.297 Squadron arrived in June, to be joined in August by No.296 Squadron, both equipped with Whitley Mk.Vs. Leaflet dropping sorties, codenamed *Nickels*, were flown over France and the airfield was one of the bases used for the North African invasion, Operation *Torch*.

No.1458 Flight, flying Lysanders, was formed on 19 December 1942 and two months later, Armstrong Whitworth Albemarles (the medium bomber that did not go into service as such, but became an excellent glider tug) started joining No.296 Squadron. In June 1943 the squadron deployed to Froka in Algeria, to work up for the invasion of the Mediterranean island of Sicily, under the codename Operation *Beggar*. Halifaxes were adapted at Hurn for glider towing by a detachment of No.13 Maintenance Unit and aircrews from No.295 Squadron collected them, together with a number of Horsa gliders, for the Sicilian operation.

On the return of Nos 295 and 296 Squadrons in the autumn of 1943, No.570 Squadron joined them, all three units flying Albemarles, for a concerted training programme in preparation for Operation *Overlord*, the invasion of mainland Europe. This lasted until March 1944, when the units were posted, Nos 295 and 570 Squadrons to Harwell, while No.296 Squadron went to Brize Norton. Their place at Hurn was taken by No.125 Squadron, equipped with Mosquito NF.XVIIs, to be joined days later by No.143 Wing's Nos 438, 439 and 440 Squadrons of the Royal Canadian Air Force (RCAF), freshly equipped with Hawker Typhoon Ibs. Almost daily sorties were flown against targets in France, until the Wing transferred to Funtington, near Chichester in Sussex, for training in the dive-bomber role. In their place, Hurn received Typhoon-operating Nos 181, 182 and 247 Squadrons of No.124 Wing.

In April 1944, No.143 Wing returned from Sussex and all six squadrons flew sorties over mainland European targets attacking V-1 flying-bomb sites, when No.438 Squadron was the first to use the Typhoon with 1,000lb (450kg) underwing bombs. No.604 Squadron from No.83 Group brought its Mosquito NF.XIIIs in May to join No.125 Squadron and several enemy aircraft were shot down by the Mosquitos during Luftwaffe night raids on southern coastal towns during the month.

Following Operation *Overlord* on 6 June 1944, No.124 Wing deployed to captured airfields in France, while three Typhoon Wings, Nos 123, 136 and 146, operated from Hurn until they too moved to ex-Luftwaffe bases in the Low Countries. No.418 Squadron of the RCAF had temporary tenure of Hurn with their Mosquito FB.VIs until 5 August, when the USAAF arrived in the form of the 397th Bomb Group with their B-26 Marauders. USAAF operations ceased in October 1944 as bases in France became liberated and after the B-26s had departed, that was the end of military operational flying from the airfield for several years.

BOAC took over on 1 November 1944, to make Hurn its principal landplane base and ownership was transferred to the Ministry of Civil Aviation. After World War II ended, the Belgian airline Sabena and Holland's KLM joined BOAC, with American Overseas Airways, plus Pan American, all commencing regular services from the Hampshire base. These services continued until 1 January 1946, when London Airport (Heathrow) was opened and the airlines gradually moved to the London site.

Crew training and maintenance work was continued by BOAC until the summer of 1950, when Hurn slowly became less active, but in May 1951 Vickers-Armstrongs moved into the former BOAC hangars for test-flying of WB210, the Type 660 first prototype, while a tarmac runway was being laid at Wisley. The facilities at Hurn suited Vickers-Armstrongs, who saw production potential there and they transferred the building of their Varsity navigational trainer from Weybridge after the seventeenth aircraft. A total of 146 Varsities came off the Hurn production line. With Viscount orders flooding in, a further line was laid down for the production of the prop-jet airliner at the Hampshire site. By the time the last Viscount had been built, Hurn had accounted for 279 of the total of 445 that had been produced.

Airwork Services Limited took over some of the former RAF/USAAF sites before Viscount production got under way, to form a Fleet Requirement Unit (FRU) for the Admiralty and military service aircraft returned to Hurn – the Type 660 prototype being a test aircraft did not really qualify. The FRU was a unique unit, in which civilian pilots flew Service aeroplanes, with most of the post-war Fleet Air Arm types passing through the Unit. On 1 December 1972, the FRU left Hurn when it combined with the Fleet Requirement Air Direction Unit at Yeovilton, leaving the way for the site to become Bournemouth Airport.

Summers retired and development of the Type 660 was placed in the hands of Jock Bryce and Brian Trubshaw, the latter having joined the company from the RAF on 1 May 1950. Both pilots had served together in the King's Flight at Benson in the late 1940s, where they had first encountered Vickers-Armstongs' aircraft, as the Flight was then equipped with four brand-new Vikings. The two made their first flight together in WB219, on 20 June 1951.

Following the maiden flight on 18 May, the employees at Weybridge were invited to choose a name for the Type 660. The official RAF policy had been to name bombers after cities in Britain and the Commonwealth, but this had become a bit tenuous with the Warwick, as well as the Windsor, although the latter did not go into service. The turbojet heralded a new epoch in Bomber Command and the action of giving those who made the first of the new generation of bombers the chance to name it was typical of GRE's approach to his workforce. The name Valiant was chosen, this reiterating a Bristol Jupiter-powered biplane of 1928 and returning the company to the alliterative policy that had begun with the Vimy in 1918, running, with very few exceptions, through to the Wellesley in 1935. The 'V's returned post-World War II with the Viking, so the choice of Valiant was very apposite. It also became the benchmark for the naming of the subsequent

Specifications – Valiant

Dimensions:	B.1: span 114ft 4in (34.84m); length 108ft 3in (33.0m); wing area 2,362sq ft (219.45sq m). B.2: span 114ft 4in (34.84m); length 112ft 9in (34.36m); wing area 2,362sq ft (219.45sq m).
Powerplant:	Prototypes: four Rolls-Royce Avon RA.3 turbojets each producing 6,500lb (2,950kg) static thrust or four Rolls-Royce Avon RA.7 turbojets each producing 7,500lb (3,400kg) static thrust. B.1: four Rolls-Royce RA.14 turbojets each producing 9,500lb (4,300kg) static thrust or four Rolls-Royce Avon RA.28 turbojets each producing 10,000lb (4,500kg) static thrust. B(PR).1: four Rolls-Royce Avon RA.14 turbojets each producing 9,500lb (4,300kg) static thrust. B(PR)K.1 and B(K).1: four Rolls-Royce Avon RA.28 turbojets each producing 10,000lb (4,500kg) static thrust. B.2: four Rolls-Royce Avon RA.14 turbojets each producing 9,500lb (4,300kg) static thrust.
Weights:	From 75,880lb (34,410kg) empty to 159,042lb (63,490kg) maximum loaded.
Performance:	Maximum speed (B.1) 567mph (912km/h) at 30,000ft (9,000m); (B.2) 552mph (888km/h) at sea level; service ceiling 54,000ft (16,000m); maximum range 4,500 miles (7,250km).
Armament:	One 10,000lb nuclear weapon or twenty-one 1,000lb iron bombs.

The generous flap area available to WB210 is shown on the Wisley tarmac. Brooklands Museum

The beautiful shape of WB210 became evident once it was in the air. Author's collection

WB210 on its way to the 1951 SBAC Display. Author's collection

edge identified the cause of their predicament. The aircraft had been on fire for some time and there was every chance that the starboard wing was about to be burned through.

The pilot on this sortie was Jock Bryce, with Squadron Leader Brian Foster, Bomber Command's Liaison Officer, as co-pilot. At the observer's table were company technicians Roy Holland, Jan Montgomery and John Prothero-Thomas, who made good their exits via the crew entrance door on the port side. Bryce and Foster ejected but the Liaison Officer hit the fin and, although alive when found, he died shortly afterwards. WB210 crashed outside the village of Bransgrove, less than five minutes' flying time from Hurn.

bombers being built at Avro and Handley Page, as it was decided to give their aircraft names beginning with 'V'. The V-bomber force was born.

Development flying with WB210 progressed throughout 1951, as did the laying of a tarmac runway at Wisley. A week's break in the test-flight programme allowed the Valiant to appear at the SBAC Display at Farnborough. From Short Brothers' point of view, it was rather unfortunate that they exhibited their S.A.4 at the same event, although it was bedecked in the striking special red, grey and black colour scheme. Alongside the aerodynamically graceful Valiant, whose polished natural metal finish simply exuded beauty with power, the Belfast-produced aircraft looked distinctly mundane. The agility it displayed in the hands of Jock Bryce proved that the Valiant was not only beautiful to look at, it was beautiful to fly. Shortly after Farnborough, the aircraft's RA.3s were replaced by Avon RA.7s, each developing 7,500lb (3,400kg) static thrust.

Tragedy

The pessimist's maxim that 'things are going *too* well' was exemplified on 12 January 1952, and it was ironic that the test sortie being made was not solely connected with Valiant development. WB210 had taken off from Hurn to undertake engine shutdown and relight trials in flight, in connection with internal noise-level tests for the Type 1000, which was still on the drawing board at the time but

was scheduled to start being built at Fox Warren the following year. During the flight, an unsuccessful relight of a starboard engine had resulted in leaking fuel gathering within the wing flap shroud around the engine tailpipes and igniting. Being within the wing structure and aft of the crew's field of vision, the fire burned unnoticed, melting a main fuel line coupling and becoming a major conflagration that burned through the aileron control rod. This produced an uncontrollable roll of the aircraft, which informed the crew that they were in real trouble and the sight of flames emitting from the wing's leading

Second Valiant Flies

The loss of the first Valiant could have badly affected the development programme, had not WB215, the second prototype, been nearing completion at Wisley. In keeping with Vickers-Armstrongs policy of giving a new type number to every aircraft that embodied any change, WB215 was the Type 667 and its principal difference from WB210 was the change in intake shape, to cater for the increased airflow required for its Avon RA.7s, the original proposal to fit Sapphires in the second prototype having

Everything down as WB210 comes in to land after its display flight at the 1951 Farnborough. Author's collection

By now named Valiant, the second prototype WB215 lines up on Farnborough's
main runway, at the 1952 SBAC Display. Author's collection

the rest of its flight testing. The revised intake shape was applied to production aircraft on the line.

Trials with dropping 10,000lb *Blue Danube* test rounds during the summer of 1952 were administered by RAE Farnborough for security reasons. The trials weapons were loaded in a secluded area and the aircraft towed out to the runway. Early trials, coupled with wind-tunnel tests, confirmed that after release from its attachment points, the weapon was reluctant to leave the aircraft and floated within the bomb-bay area due to the slipstream. A series of small ventral spoilers, referred to as 'dragon's teeth', was fitted ahead of the bomb-bay and they did much to cure the problem. On WB215 they were fixed, but on production aircraft the spoilers retracted into the underside of the fuselage, their actuation being coupled with the bomb door mechanism so that they came out when the doors were opened.

During the test sortie flown on 30 July 1952, the dummy round became detached from its shackles in the bomb-bay roof and rested on the closed doors while WB215 was flying over Dorking in Surrey. The errant weapon could be felt moving on the doors and Trubshaw set a course for the Thames Estuary, where he opened the doors once over open water. With the

been abandoned. The new intakes of greater area resembled spectacles in appearance and, while not being as aesthetically neat as WB210's narrow slots, they blended in well with the wing thickness. Furthermore, they were necessary for the more powerful Avon variant, which, although installed in WB210 at the time of its loss, were not running at full potential due to the intake design.

Jock Bryce, with Brian Trubshaw as co-pilot, lifted WB215 off Wisley's new paved runway for the first time on 11 April 1952, so that there was only a three-month break in Valiant test-flying. It too had a polished natural finish, although later in its life the aircraft was sprayed an overall matt silver. Bryce became heavily involved in the Viscount flight-test programme, so Valiant development became the province of Brian Trubshaw. Following the sad death of Sqn Ldr Foster, the co-pilot's seat was filled by Sqn Ldr Rupert Oakley, while the surviving trio of technicians from WB210 resumed their duties with the second prototype. It is not surprising to know that the memories of 12 January lingered with the three for some time, but their professionalism eventually won the day and at no time was the Valiant test programme ever jeopardized.

Flame-Outs, Buffets and Floating Bombs

When the aircraft was initially taken to 40,000ft (12,200m), the first real problem was encountered. Engine control balance became erratic during the climb and the throttles had to be juggled to maintain engine speed. On levelling out, Trubshaw

elected to throttle the Avons back in pairs, one either side, but the first two had flame-outs and the aircraft returned to Wisley on the power of the two remaining engines. Several subsequent flights were made with tufting on the intake lips, which showed that their contours at the inner edges had to be modified. Lumps of putty were shaped and covered with fabric, for new evaluation tests to be flown, but after a few changes, the optimum shape was achieved. WB215 was fitted with wooden inserts to the final shape and they stayed on the aircraft for

WB215's polished finish reflects Farnborough's trade marquise along its front
fuselage, as it displays down the flight line. Author's collection

weapon rolling on the doors, considerable damage was inflicted on them during their opening sequence and, due to the pilot's uncertainty as to how much damage had been done, he elected to make an emergency landing at the first suitable airfield. Manston, on the Isle of Thanet in Kent, proved to be nearest and inspection of the bomb doors after landing showed that the damage was great enough for them to need to be removed before the aircraft flew back to Wisley.

WB215 was displayed at the 1952 SBAC Show and then it was back to the test programmes. During high Mach number trials at high altitude, heavy buffeting had been experienced and when the aircraft went to the A&AEE at Boscombe Down for assessment, one pilot's dive at a lower altitude produced a split in the leading edge of a wing. Strong buzzing of the ailerons due to the buffets was cured by fitting steel aileron rods and adding a row of vortex generators on each wing upper surface, ahead of the ailerons.

In October, an emergency landing was made at Farnborough with the port side main undercarriage unable to be locked down due to a clutch failure on the landing gear actuator. Brian Trubshaw held the port wing up during the touch-down and the undercarriage on that side slowly collapsed when loads were placed on it as the aircraft's speed diminished. Forward speed was minimal when the wing finally touched the runway, with the extended

WB215 was painted overall matt silver before it started trials with external fuel tanks. *Author's collection*

flaps taking the brunt of the impact. Repairs were made in a very short time and Trubshaw flew the aircraft back to Wisley.

External Tanks

The Valiant design had catered for the carrying of underwing, pylon-mounted, additional fuel tanks, with the original thinking being that they would be capable of being jettisoned. However, each tank had a capacity of 1,500 gallons (6,820 litres) and it soon became apparent to many at Weybridge that the releasing of tanks that size from a height constituted considerable dangers. These concerns were transmitted to the Air Ministry, who agreed and consequently the external tanks were installed as fixed members. This resulted in a further series of trials to evaluate the flight envelope of the Valiant in its new configuration and they proved that Wisley's new tarmac runway was not long enough for the aircraft at its increased maximum take-off weight. Consequently Boscombe Down was used and the Establishment's 'B' squadron assisted in the testing programme.

It was at the time of the external tank trials that the idea was broached about flying the Valiant as a Bomber Command entrant in the speed section of the Christchurch Centenary Air Race. Several Canberras had already been entered, but the Valiant programme was reaching its final stage, which included tropical trials, and GRE was quite relieved when it was decided that the aircraft would not be ready for the race. Furthermore, it was required for engine trials in order to guarantee that there would be no delay once production aircraft came off the Weybridge line. Interim Rolls-Royce RA.8s, each delivering around 9,000lb (4,080kg) static thrust, were installed, as the intended Avon RA.14 was still being test-flown in the second production Canberra B.2, WB930. In its configuration with underwing tanks, WB215 became the

WJ954, the sole Valiant Mk.2, taxies on its four-wheel bogie undercarriage along Farnborough's operational runway and shows the longer nose. *Aeroplane*

Vickers-Armstrongs Type 709 and this number was carried over to the production Valiant B.1.

The 'Black Bomber'

On 15 August 1942, the Path Finder Force (PFF) of Bomber Command was inaugurated under the command of Group Captain (later Air Vice-Marshal, CB, CBE, DSO) Donald Bennett. Its purpose was to spearhead night-time bomber operations by locating and accurately marking the target prior to the arrival of the main bomber stream. Avro Lancasters equipped the first PFF squadrons, being joined in 1943 by the de Havilland Mosquito.

The pathfinder principle was carried forward to the new generation of turbojet-powered bombers; it was by then rather outmoded, but the Air Ministry's thinking was still inclined to be a little hidebound. Bomber Command, with a sky-full of heavy bombers night after night during the last two years of World War II, was a formidable force and it was difficult to abandon in principle, despite the fact that one of its new aircraft, with a nuclear bomb, could do more damage than a hundred of its predecessors.

English Electric was instructed to supply a pathfinder prototype Canberra and the sole Mk.5, VX185, was built. It was later reconfigured to become the prototype B(I).8. Vickers-Armstrongs too received an order to provide a Valiant for a similar role, but as the requirement called for a very low-level, high-speed ability, amendments to the basic Valiant design were required. This, the last Valiant prototype to be built at Fox Warren, was first laid down in 1952. Given the company type number 673, it was the Valiant Mk.2, with the serial WJ954. The fundamental changes compared with other Valiants were a 4ft 6in (1.37m) increase in fuselage length, a new undercarriage and a redesign of the inboard wing section.

The increased fuselage length was necessitated by the requirement to house additional avionics and the bomb-bay was slightly lengthened. It was the high-speed, low-level role that dictated changes to the wing, which in turn led to the need to redesign the main wheels of the undercarriage. The large gaps in the standard wing's structure, which accepted the main wheels when retracted, meant that this wing was unsuitable for the aerodynamic loads of the new role. Consequently, the area was redesigned to be considerably stronger by keeping the wing torsion box intact, as well as employing localized reinforcing, and this meant there was no room for the standard main wheel units. A new four-wheel bogie was designed, which retracted rearwards into large Küchemann pods extending aft from the wings adjacent to the outboard engine jet pipes, which also had the added benefit of reducing airflow separation at high subsonic speeds. Additional fuel tanks were built into the new wing section.

Like its two predecessors, the Mk.2 prototype was transported in sections from Fox Warren to Wisley, where it was assembled and ready for test-flying at the beginning of September 1953. It was bedecked in an overall gloss black paint finish. Jock Bryce and Brian Trubshaw made the first flight on 4 September and amassed the necessary flying time of ten hours to qualify for display at that year's SBAC Show, where it was the sole Valiant, as WB215 was heavily committed on testing. Jock Bryce flew WJ954 at Farnborough, following which the aircraft had to be cleared for its higher speed limits, which had been estimated as about 33 per cent higher than the standard Valiant.

It was essential to have smooth air at low altitude to get true readings of the aircraft's structural behaviour, and so 'dawn patrols' were flown at 1,000ft over the English Channel, starting as early as 04.00hrs. Speeds were built up to 640mph (1,030km/h) and 580mph (933km/h) was set as the normal operating limit. This compared with the 567mph at 30,000ft (912km/h at 9,140m) of the standard Valiant, but Air Ministry requirements had changed and the pathfinder role in Bomber Command was dropped. The Valiant Mk.2 remained a one-off prototype.

This did not stop the company from entering WJ954 for display at the 1954 SBAC Display. On Monday's Press Day, Trubshaw flew it under a 500ft moisture-laden cloud base at a high Mach number, with the aircraft swathed in its own condensation cloud. In its glossy all-black finish, it presented an exciting but menacing spectacle.

The Küchemann pods containing the main undercarriage are well shown in this view of WJ954, as Jock Bryce brings the aircraft in close for another Charles E. Brown air-to-air portrait. Author's collection

Despite its not going into production, the Mk.2 was used for Valiant development programmes, one of which was to investigate the use of rocket assistance for take-off at overload weights or from airfields in hot climes and higher altitudes. De Havilland Engines had been conducting rocket-assisted take-off trials since 1947, when a pair of German Walter 109/500 rocket motors had been installed in a ventral position on Avro Lancastrian C.2 VM703, which they were using as a flying test-bed for their Ghost turbojet. Encouraged by these trials, they designed their first indigenous rocket motor, the Sprite, to be incorporated in the D.H.106 Comet for take-offs on tropical routes.

From the Sprite, de Havilland developed the 4,200lb (1,900kg) thrust Super Sprite, which could be operated at full power for 40 seconds. It was a hot motor, fuelled by kerosene injection with combustion throat cooling, and it met Air Ministry type approval for the Valiant. WJ954 was allocated to clear the Super Sprite, but the attachment of the motor, in a triangular frame, by just one bolt to the side of the aircraft was amazingly crude. Brian Trubshaw is on record as expressing his doubts about this installation, doubts that were fully vindicated when the whole unit, complete with Super Sprite, parted company with the aircraft even before the undercarriage was retracted. Considerable damage was inflicted on the underside of the wing, as well as the undercarriage pod, and no further rocket trials were conducted with the aircraft.

Strong juddering of the undercarriage had been experienced when braking was applied to the bogie units and a member of the company's test pilot team liaised with the drawing office for them to come up with a modification that would cure the problem, which, in view of the fact that the aircraft was not going into production, does seem a little surprising. Considerable time was spent on taxiing trials to evaluate modifications and the outcome was maybe rather predictable. The main leg attachment point fractured due to fatigue, resulting in the collapse of the affected landing gear. WJ954 was towed to a hardstanding behind one of the Wisley hangars, where it remained until eventually being broken up in 1958. That the requirement for a low-level operating Valiant would arise within six years could

WJ954 squeezes the moisture out of the Farnborough air, as it powers down the flight line at the 1954 SBAC Display. Author's collection

not be known. However, there is no doubt that had the 'Black Bomber' been ordered into production, the Valiant would have been in RAF service much longer.

The Timescale is Met

GRE's guarantee made in 1948, to have a production Type 660 ready before the end of 1953, was upheld. Type 674 Valiant B.1, WP199, the first of a pre-production batch of five aircraft ordered under Contract No. 6/Air/6313/CB6(c), had its maiden flight from Brooklands on 21 December 1953. The Chief Designer had ten days in hand!

To achieve this, numerous new production methods had been developed and new close tolerances adhered to. A Hufford stretch former was installed for fuselage and wing panels – I well remember watching the incongruity of a shop-floor member of below average height operating the console of this enormous piece of equipment, as it formed the required panels. A Cincinnati milling machine formed spar web plates and Redux bonding was employed for the

attachment of double plating on all the flying control surfaces. New fibreglass techniques had been evolved for the large nose radome cover and suppressed aerials, while a national steel shortage was overcome when the jigs were designed. Interchangeable pillars were manufactured from pre-stressed concrete, which were rag-bolted to the floor, with the assembly jig attachment mounted atop. The whole Valiant production programme employed far better materials than had been used previously, for every aspect of operations, and, although the company was stretched to new limits, output never fell behind schedule. GRE is quoted as saying that the aircraft was designed in only 486,000 drawing hours and, with the timescale precluding the use of flying models, everything had to be right first time. He said in the April 1974 issue of *The Aeronautical Journal* that the Valiant was 'far and away the hardest aeroplane that I ever did'. Furthermore, both Avro and Handley Page benefited from Weybridge's experience in the new technologies that were met in producing the RAF's new generation of bombers.

CHAPTER FIVE

Testing the Shapes

While Vickers-Armstrongs were beavering away on the Valiant, with no leeway in their timescale to allow for aerodynamic or systems test models, Avro and Handley Page had the comparative luxury of being able to confirm their respective design approaches. That this did not work out exactly as originally envisaged is due to a number of factors and the net value of the two companies' test models is, to a certain extent, open to debate.

Avro's Greek Models

When Roy Chadwick received Specification B.35/46 in January 1947, he was only two months away from becoming the company's Technical Director and

handing the Chief Designer reins to Stuart Davies, who had joined Avro in January 1938 as Assistant Designer. The two appreciated that the requirements of the specification were some way ahead of contemporary aeronautical thinking in Britain and would necessitate a radical approach to meet the demands. A certain amount of data had been procured from German sources after World War II, but experience of high-speed, high-altitude operations was very limited.

The company's design team explored swept-wing layouts, progressively reducing the fuselage and filling in the wing trailing edge to maintain the wing area. Armstrong Whitworth and de Havilland had experience with flying wings and in the United States, Northrop was flying the

piston-engined YB-35, but the weight of a flying wing capable of meeting Specification B.35/46 was far greater than RAF airfields could handle and the delta became the natural progression. Coupled with a sketch that Chadwick had produced earlier, along the lines of workings made by the Chief Aerodynamicist, Eric Priestley, the delta wing's advantages outweighed the daunting task of translation into an operational bomber. The basic outline had hardened by May 1947 and the company's Type 698 was submitted to the MoS.

Faced with the lack of experience of delta-wing aerodynamics, Avro considered that a glider modelled to the configuration could prove useful, by limited, data. The MoS considered that powered

At the time that this first photograph was taken, in August 1948, the first Avro 707 VX784 was officially known by the MoS as the E.15/48. Derek N. James

In September 1949, VX784 was on static display at the annual Farnborough show. Author's collection

one-third, scaled-down trials aircraft would be a better option and the Avro Type 707 was ordered early in 1948, with Specification E.15/48 written around it. Type 710 was allocated to a twin-engined high-speed, scaled-down test aircraft, to investigate a flight envelope up to Mach 0.95 and an altitude of 60,000ft (18,300m). However, Avro had second thoughts, considering that such an aircraft would not provide enough additional data to merit the work required to produce it, so the project was dropped before any construction was put in hand.

To replace the 710, two low-speed and one high-speed Type 707s were ordered and metal for the first aircraft was cut in the autumn of 1948. Power was to be supplied by one 3,500lb (1,590kg) static thrust, centrifugal-flow Rolls-Royce Derwent 5 turbojet. In the interests of economy and speed of construction, assemblies of existing aircraft were utilized where possible. The purpose of the aircraft was purely to provide design data for the Avro 698 and not to investigate the delta-wing configuration *per se*. Neither was there a requirement for high performance.

Avro submitted their Type 701 Athena to Specification T.7/45 for a three-seat, advanced prop-jet-powered trainer, which was later amended to be powered by a Rolls-Royce Merlin 35. Construction finished after only fifteen examples had been built and Athena undercarriage assemblies

were impressed into the 707 programme as main wheels, while the nose-wheel and cockpit canopy came straight off the Gloster Meteor F.8 production line. No ejector seat was installed in the cockpit, which was sited well forward on the fuselage, giving an excellent forward field of vision. Retractable air brakes were installed on top of the rear fuselage skin, either side of the engine outlet, with another pair fitted flush with the wing underside.

The Derwent, mounted in the rear fuselage, was fed by a dorsal air intake, which was divided by an extension of the fin leading edge and a spin-recovery parachute housing was sited at the base of the rudder. The aircraft was of all-metal stressed-skin construction, with controls supplied by four surfaces hinged to the wing trailing edge, combined with the rudder. The inboard pair of surfaces acted as elevators, with the outer pair being ailerons.

First British Delta Flight

Construction was completed within ten months and the serial VX784 was allotted to Britain's first delta-winged aircraft. Preliminary checks and taxiing trials were conducted at Avro's Woodford facility, after which the first 707 was dismantled to be taken by road on 26 August 1949,

to the A&AEE at Boscombe Down. Eight days later, VX784, resplendent in an overall silver finish, was ready to become airborne. But the British weather intervened in the form of a crosswind, which was much too strong to risk the maiden flight of a virtually unknown configuration and it was not until 19.30hr on the evening of the following day, Sunday 4 September, that conditions were conducive to the important event.

The pilot for the flight was the company's Assistant CTP, Flt Lt Eric 'Red' Esler, the sobriquet hailing from his RAF service days after Eric the Red, the Danish Viking who led the colonization of Greenland in 982AD. He lifted VX784 off Boscombe Down's acres of runway, to commence a successful 35-minute flight and over the next two days a further 2.5hr flying revealed that the little delta-winged aircraft handled very similarly to a conventional turbojet aeroplane. It was found, however, that it required a considerably longer take-off run. At the end of 6 September, Esler flew the 707 across country to Farnborough, where it was a static exhibit at the years' SBAC Display.

Post-Farnborough, VX784 returned to the A&AEE, where additional data-measuring equipment was installed and the aircraft resumed flying during the last week of the month. Because it handled so well and gave no grounds for concern, it was a great shock to everyone concerned when the little delta crashed near Black-bushe on 30 September, only twenty-six days after the maiden flight, killing 'Red' Esler. The true cause of the accident has never been accurately established, but the consensus of opinion lays the blame on a fault in the airbrake control circuitry, which locked them in the extended position during low-speed, low-altitude testing, creating a stall with insufficient height for recovery.

The Type 707B

The second 707, designated the 707B, was at an advanced stage of construction when VX784 crashed and, although everyone was anxious to get the aircraft finished, it was decided to defer completion, in order to incorporate a number of fundamental changes, not the least being the installation of a Martin-Baker Mk.1 ejector seat. This entailed the design and construction of an entirely new front fuselage section, with a revised cockpit canopy. The 12ft (3.7m) longer front fuselage improved both the aerodynamics and centre of gravity of the aircraft in general. The 707B was intended to explore the low-speed handling characteristics of delta wings in general, rather than being related wholly to the Type 698.

Not unnaturally, the complete airbrake system was redesigned, with the rear fuse-lage installation being replaced by an upper-wing surface unit on either side that retracted flat with the outer skin. The underwing airbrakes of the first prototype were retained, but reconfigured, while modifications were incorporated in the

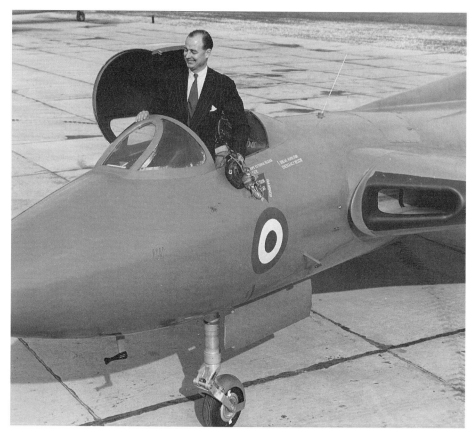

'Roly' Falk enters his 'office', the 707A WB280, dressed in his customary lounge suit. Author's collection

elevators and a 12in (30.5cm) extension added to the fin. The use of existing units prevailed and the 707B's nose-wheel came courtesy of the Hawker Sea Hawk production line – but as Avro and Hawker were both members of the Hawker Siddeley Group, things were kept in the family.

Given the serial VX790 and painted an overall blue, the 707B was transported to Boscombe Down at the end of August 1950 and, on 6 September, Wg Cdr R.J. 'Roly' Falk, the company's CTP, introduced the aircraft to its natural habitat, although a short hop had been made during high-speed taxiing trials the previous evening.

'Roly' Falk was a very experienced RAF test pilot, who had been the Experimental Flying Department's CTP at the RAE, where he carried out handling and performance trials of captured *Luftwaffe* aircraft, including a Messerschmitt Me 163B-1 as a glider in July 1945, having been towed to release height by a Spitfire Mk.IX. Among other ex-enemy types that he evaluated at the RAE was a 'push-me pull-me' Dornier Do 335A-10. Before World War II he flew for the Press during the Abyssinian and Spanish Civil Wars, as well as the London/Aberdeen newspaper air service. He joined Avro in 1950 as superintendent of flying, under Jimmy Orrell. VX790 was the first Avro aircraft that he had flown on its maiden flight.

The low-speed Avro 707B, VX790, showing its original dorsal air intake shape.
Author's collection

Following the turbulence generated by the canopy, VX790's dorsal air intake was redesigned. *Aeroplane*

'Roly' Falk OBE, AFC and bar, was noted for his idiosyncratic habit of always wearing a lounge suit when flying.

With the sad loss of Eric Esler, the whole Avro delta programme was now in Falk's hands and the enthusiasm that he exhibited after the first 15-minute flight encouraged the company's Managing Director, Sir Roy Dobson and Controller of Supplies (Air), Air Marshal Boothman, to request that the aircraft be included as a static exhibit at the 1950 SBAC Display, which had started the previous day. Permission was granted and VX790 flew in to Farnborough the following day, spending the rest of the week in a mixture of sunshine and drizzle.

After Farnborough, Falk commenced the serious business of test-flying the 707B and it went to Boscombe Down for general assessment on 24 October 1950. The first prototype had not done much test-flying. Only twenty-seven days had elapsed between its maiden flight and its demise, six of which it spent on static display at Farnborough, so, apart from Esler having proved that the delta configuration held no unpleasant surprises, a true trials programme had not been conducted. Falk tested the aircraft in a speed range of 95 to 410mph (153 to 660km/h), and at the higher end of the performance envelope air starvation to the dorsal intake was encountered. Wind-tunnel tests by Rolls-Royce showed this to be caused by turbulence from the canopy and modifications to the intake geometry were made in

February 1951 by making the airflow guide channel deeper and increasing the depth of the air intake itself, which together cured the problem. The length of take-off run was still considered too long and it had been noted on the first prototype that the elevators were not active until the aircraft had nearly reached lift-off speed. A cure was found by lengthening the nose-wheel leg by 9in (23cm), thereby improving the aircraft's angle of incidence on take-off.

The blue VX790 put in more than 100 hours of test-flying associated with the Type 698 over a twelve-month period, which included using the anti-spin parachute as a brake, and thrust experiments were conducted, which proved that angling of the jet pipes on the 698 would improve longitudinal stability. In September 1951 the aircraft was transferred to the A&AEE's inventory, for general delta-wing stability research, where it flew with a smoke generator under the starboard wing for some time. It was damaged in an accident shortly after arriving at Boscombe Down, but was repairable and flying was resumed on 16 May 1952. The Establishment flew another 30 hours with VX790, before passing it to the RAE who, on 26 January 1956, transferred the aircraft to the Empire Test Pilot's School (ETPS) for test pilot experience of delta-winged aircraft. The ETPS had been formed at Boscombe Down in June 1943, but was moved to Cranfield in 1946. However, the growth of the College of Aeronautics at

the airfield necessitated another move and in 1949 the School transferred to RAE Farnborough, where it was based when VX790 arrived. In 1968 the ETPS returned to Boscombe Down, where it still resides today.

Utilization of the 707B by the School was not very high, but on 29 September 1956 it suffered a landing accident, sustaining damage that was considered uneconomic to repair and the aircraft was transported by road to No.71 MU at Bicester for storage. On 22 October 1957, VX790 went to RAE Bedford and became a 'hangar queen', providing spares for the third 707, before eventually being consigned to scrap.

Type 707 Number Three

The little 707 deltas had provided much data for the Avro Type 698, but by 1951 this had more or less reached its zenith. Full-size models of the bomber were being tested in the RAE wind tunnel and metal was being cut for the first prototype while a third Type 707, the 707A, was being constructed. Given the serial WD280, it was covered by Specification E.10/49 and, as the nose had already been used in the building of VX790, there were doubts as to whether the 707A was really necessary. Much of the data supplied by VX790 had been fed into the Type 698 design, but wind-tunnel trials of the full-size model had suggested the benefits of wing-root intakes and a greater wingspan, so these aspects were scaled down to one-third size, in order to be incorporated in WD280.

In keeping with the overall colour scheme adopted on VX790, the third Type 707 was finished in a vivid vermilion, which contemporary writers quoted as red or orange, with the area immediately outboard of the wing-root intakes being painted black. Like its two predecessors, the Type 707A was taken by road to Boscombe Down and 'Roly' Falk handled it for its first flight on 14 July 1951.

WD280 Gets a Twin

Because WD280 bore a closer relationship to the Type 698 design than previous 707s, Avro decided to construct a second 707A, which was the fourth of the Type 707 series. Allocated the serial WZ736, the second 707A was built at Avro's over-

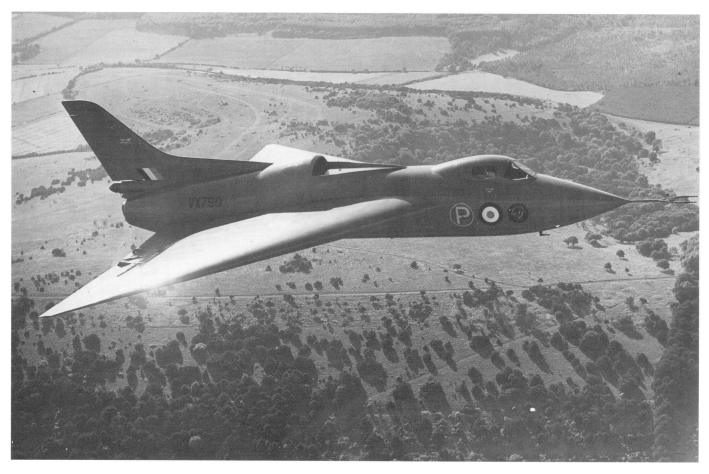

Wearing a prototype 'P' and Hawker Siddeley logo, VX790 is shown on its way to the 1951 SBAC Display.
Aeroplane

haul and repair facility at Bracebridge Heath, south of the beautiful city of Lincoln. Like WD280, it was powered by one Rolls-Royce Derwent 8, producing 3,600lb (1,630kg) static thrust and when finished, again in overall vermilion, it was towed two miles along the A15 trunk road to RAF Waddington, from where it was first flown on 20 February 1953 by Avro test pilot J.C. Nelson.

The Phase 2 Wing

Whereas the two 707As provided very little to influence the original basic design of the Type 698, apart from confirming the wing-root intakes – in fact the first prototype bomber had flown six months before WZ736 – they were destined to discover and evaluate the main change to the larger aircraft's configuration more than any other 707. The wings were true one-third scale of the 698 and early in the 707A flight programme, the unpleasant

fact that the wings 'buzzed' became apparent, with the severity increasing as speed was built up. It was also noted that increased altitude presented a greater buzz; it was eventually diagnosed as being caused by airflow over the wing-tips. Large wing fences were fitted on WZ736, positioned well down the span, but, while they did slow down the airflow to a certain extent, it was no cure to the problem.

It was literally 'back to the drawing board' in order to rectify the phenomenon and a solution was found by reducing the leading-edge sweep of the inner section of the outer wing, then increasing the sweep of the outermost section. Wind-tunnel tests verified that this shape of leading edge would provide a cure and the configuration was fitted to WD280 at Bracebridge Heath for air testing. The new wing form eliminated the buzz and was referred to as the Phase 2 wing in Type 698 production.

The production rate of 698s, coupled with the time taken to rectify the buzzing,

meant that sixteen sets of wing leading edges had to be scrapped, some of them already installed on production aircraft that had been completed. This was the kind of unpalatable delay that the 707s should have prevented, had their programmes been properly co-ordinated with the 698 production schedule. Nevertheless, one positive aspect to come out of the 707s was the reassurance given to everyone, from the MoS downwards, that the delta wing was sound. It should be appreciated that several times the whole 698 programme might have been cancelled on the grounds of financial risk, had it not been for the 707s proving satisfactory test results along the way.

On completion of Avro test-flying, both 707As joined the RAE's trials fleet, continuing research into power controls and general delta-wing investigations. Prior to this, both aircraft had appeared in one of the visual highlights of all SBAC Displays, when the two Type 698 prototypes, by now christened the Vulcan and painted an overall brilliant white, performed a formation fly-past in line astern, flanked by four colourful Type 707s, in September 1953.

A 707 Goes 'Down Under'

On 12 March 1956, WD280, complete with the test Phase 2 wing, was shipped to Australia. It was loaded aboard the Royal Australian Navy aircraft carrier HMAS *Melbourne* at Glasgow and arrived at Sydney Harbour on 11 May. The unloading itself was not without incident, as the vehicle onto which it was being transferred collapsed under the weight and WD280 had to be loaded onto another truck. It first flew in Australia on 13 July 1956, from the RAAF base at Laverton in Western Australia, following which the aircraft was employed on aerodynamic research for the Australian Aeronautical Research Council (AARC). These trials included the evaluation of airflows over delta wings at low speed, for which the aircraft's port wing and fuselage were painted black, prior to which the vermilion colour scheme had been replaced by an overall silver finish. A kaolin mixture was sprayed over the black surface and its flow pattern observed. It served with the AARC for

---

Specification – Avro Type 707 (VX784)

Powerplant:	One Rolls-Royce Derwent 5 turbojet producing 3,500lb (1,588kg) static thrust.
All-up weight:	8,600lb (3,900kg).
Dimensions:	Span 33ft 0in (10m); length 30ft 6in (9.3m); height 10ft 7in (3.2m); wing area 366.5sq ft (34.5sq m).

Specification – Avro Type 707A (WD280 and WZ736)

Powerplant:	One Rolls-Royce Derwent 8 turbojet producing 3,600lb (1,633kg) static thrust.
All-up weight:	9,500lb (4,309kg).
Dimensions:	Span 34ft 2in (10.4m); length 42ft 4in (12.9m); height 11ft 7in (3.53m); wing area 408sq ft (37.9sq m).

Specification – Avro Type 707B (VX790)

Powerplant:	One Rolls-Royce Derwent 5 turbojet producing 3,500lb (1,588kg) static thrust.
All-up weight:	9,500lb (4,309kg).
Dimensions:	Span 33ft 0in (10m); length 42ft 4in (12.9m); height 11ft 9in (3.58m); wing area 366.5sq ft (34sq m).

Specification – Avro Type 707C (WZ744)

Powerplant:	One Rolls-Royce Derwent 8 turbojet producing 3,600lb (1,633kg) static thrust.
All-up weight:	10,000lb (4,535kg).
Dimensions:	Span 34ft 2in (10.4m); length 42ft 4in (12.9m); height 11ft 7in (3.53m); wing area 408sq ft (37.9sq m).

The prototype two-seat 707C, WZ744, showing a cine camera installation on the fin leading edge. Author's collection

WZ744 shown on its way to the 1953 SBAC Display. Author's collection

seven years, during which, in September 1958 and again in 1962, it participated in an RAAF air display at Laverton, before eventually being struck off charge on 10 February 1967. After thirty-two years of static display in the garden of a Mr Mallett, of Williamstown in New South Wales, the aircraft was moved to the RAAF Museum at Point Cook, Victoria, on 17 April 1999.

The RAE continued to use WZ736 for automatic throttle development programmes aimed at delta-winged aircraft. It had been found that the great drag rise on delta wings in the high-incidence angles adopted during the landing approach needed to be compensated by throttle responses that were easier to handle in an automatic mode. These and further RAE research programmes were flown until 1967, when the aircraft was grounded and, given the Instructional Airframe Number 7868M, was sent to RAF Finningley in Yorkshire for refurbishment. WZ736 was finally given to the Museum of Science and Industry in Manchester, where it is displayed alongside two other Avro types, Shackleton AEW2 WR960 and Avro

504K G-ABAA, representing a production span of more than fifty years.

A 707 for Two

The fifth and final Type 707 was WZ744, the sole survivor of an order for four 707C two-seat trainers, placed at the same time as the second 707A. The trainers were to have side-by-side seating and be dual-controlled, in order to convert pilots to the handling of delta-winged aircraft. But their requirement proved to be unnecessary, so three were cancelled before any construction was started and WZ744 was built at Bracebridge Heath. Completed in June 1953, it followed the path of WD280 in being towed to RAF Waddington and had its maiden flight on 1 July, in the hands of Avro test pilot J.B. Wales. Manufacturer's trials were conducted at the company's home base of Woodford, south of Manchester.

Painted an overall silver, the 707C proved to be a very claustrophobic aeroplane, with the side-by-side bucket seating – no room for ejector seats! – being

squeezed into the same fuselage width as the previous single-seat aircraft, with just a small circular window fitted on both sides of the bulbous metal canopy. It, too, like the 707As, was powered by one Derwent 8.

The 707C made no contribution to the Vulcan programme, but it was used by the RAE at both Farnborough and Bedford for fourteen years, on the development of electronic and powered controls. These were, in modern parlance, 'fly-by-wire' systems, although rather rudimentary by current standards. As WZ744 was dual-controlled, trials were able to be conducted with manual control on one side and electronic control on the other, thereby making comparative assessments easier.

In 1967, the controls programme came to an end and the 707C was allocated Instructional Airframe number 7932M. Like WZ736, it went to Finningley, from where it travelled to Colerne and Top-cliffe, before arriving at the Cosford Aerospace Museum, restored with its original WZ744 serial.

The contribution of the five 707s to the

Taxiing past Farnborough's control tower in September 1953, 707B VX790 leads 707A WD280 and 707C WZ744, with 707A WZ736 bringing up the rear. Author's collection

Vulcan development programme was rather limited, apart from the Phase 2 wing episode. However, they confirmed Avro's belief in the delta-wing layout as being a sound approach to Specification B.35/46. From a purely visual point of view, I know many who consider that the 1953 Farnborough formation fly-past with the first two Vulcans and four 707s made them worth every penny of taxpayers' money that they cost. But then, aeronautical enthusiasm and the financial aspect never go together very well!

Handley Page's Crescent

Just as Avro's delta design approach to B.35/46 was considered so aerodynamic-

ally advanced that it required testing in a scaled-down form, so it was with Handley Page. Their original thoughts of the H.P.80 being tailless, with the wing-tips swept up through 90 degrees to form endplate fin and rudders, gave way in January 1948 to a conventional fuselage-mounted tail assembly, but with the three different angles of sweep along the wing leading edge remaining. It was this multiple-angled sweep, or 'crescent', that it was felt required flight testing, as the design team considered it to be the ideal way to obtain the large root thickness needed to accommodate the engines and take the main bending loads. The progressive reduction of sweep towards the tips, with its corresponding lowering of the t/c ratio to keep the critical Mach number constant,

helped to reduce tip stall, which was found to be more prevalent on highly swept wings.

One of the Allied Technical Intelligence Missions made to Germany after World War II was made aware of developments made by Arado in this field. They were considering applying a similar principle to their Ar234 turbojet bomber, but Godfrey Lee, who was a member of one mission, maintains that the crescent wing was evolved by Handley Page rather gradually, with input coming from several members of the company's design team, and Charles Joy, the Assistant Chief Designer, putting it all together.

Specification E.6/48 was issued on 12 March 1948, to cover a scaled-down flying model of the crescent wing and the company designation H.P.88 was applied to the project, which was allocated the serial VX330. Records show that the serial VX337 was reserved for a second H.P.88, but the requirement was cancelled and the number never reallocated. Thoughts were also given to a glider, with the type number H.P.87, but these were discarded in favour of a powered trials aircraft, which was considered more able to evaluate properly the behaviour of the control surfaces at all attitudes.

The design office of the Supermarine division of Vickers-Armstrongs, based at Hursley Park between Winchester and Southampton, suggested to Handley Page that a basic fuselage off their Type 392 Attacker production line, which was building 149 of them for the Royal Navy, would make a good foundation for a trials aircraft to flight test a scaled-down wing. The fuselage suggested had already been modified to Type 510 standard, which, having swept wings, had their attachment points further forward than on the standard Attacker.

What's in a Name?

It is at this stage that the type designation of the crescent-wing test aircraft becomes a little confusing. With the workload that Handley Page's drawing office had in hand on the H.P.80, there was no chance of it getting down to design detail on a 40 per cent flying scale wing and tail unit. Consequently, the work was farmed out to General Aircraft Ltd at Feltham in Middlesex, who entered it into the company's design type numbering system as the GAL 63.

On 1 January 1948, General Aircraft Ltd merged with Blackburn Aircraft Ltd of Brough in Yorkshire. By the time that the GAL 63 was born, the mechanism of the merger was well under way and the Feltham design office had moved to Brough. With it went the H.P.88/GAL 63, which was promptly transferred to Blackburn's own type list. The new SBAC system of allocating letters to companies had recently been introduced, under which Blackburn received the letter

'Y'. VX330 became the Blackburn Y.B.2 and the Yorkshire company received a contract for the manufacture of the aircraft. So the bizarre situation existed that the airframe had received four different titles, before it had left the drawing board!

Construction Begins

Supermarine's fuselage was delivered to Brough on 25 November 1950, only to be knocked while being off-loaded from the 'Queen Mary' trailer but, being slight, the damage was repaired on site. Construction of wings and tail unit had begun at Brough, but in the meantime back at Handley Page the H.P.80 wing planform had been altered. In order to raise the critical Mach number from 0.83 to 0.86, the wing-root section had to be altered, giving a t/c ratio of 16 per cent. As this modification would reduce stability, the trailing-edge sweep-change point had to be repositioned further

The H.P.88 VX330, after its assembly and roll-out at Carnaby. Handley Page Association

Not many air-to-air photographs were taken of VX330, during its total of 14 flying hours. Handley Page Association inboard in order to restore the status quo.

Therefore, before the aircraft got off the ground, it was not a true test vehicle for the H.P.80 wing – its raison d'être. Furthermore, the bomber design had incorporated an all-moving tailplane and elevons but this was discarded on the test aircraft, to be replaced by conventional ailerons, together with elevators. It was too late to alter the H.P.88's tail assembly of a slab tailplane with elevons and it can be argued that the whole aircraft would only prove to be an academic exercise. Nevertheless, Handley Page engineers hoped that they would obtain some data on how the H.P.80 would handle, which justified continuation, so the trials aircraft was finished by the end of 1950.

VX330 is Completed

There was not a great sense of urgency about the project and even when it was finally painted, in an overall royal blue gloss for a photographic session in June 1951, the Martin-Baker Mk.1A ejector seat had not been installed, although this was rectified a day later. The aircraft was unusual in having large national roundels on its nose, ahead of the air intakes, the more common position being occupied by the airbrakes and it had no roundels on the upper surface of the wings. With the aircraft being overall royal blue, each individual national marking was surrounded by a thin white line. Incidentally, only side views were taken in order not to reveal the true wing shape and even its shadow on the ground was retouched to look like a straight-edged swept wing. The dominating features of the wings, apart from the leading-edge angles of sweep, were two prominent fairings on each inboard trailing edge top surface covering the actuators for the generous Fowler flaps, plus a long mass-balance arm above and below each aileron. These 2ft 6in (76cm) long arms protruded forward at an angle of 40 degrees. The all-moving tailplane was sited high on the fin, with the joint covered by an enormous waisted bullet fairing projecting forward and aft of the swept fin. A long yaw-vane boom protruded from the front portion of the bullet fairing, while the rear section contained a dual-purpose anti-spin/braking parachute. Generous retractable airbrakes, which operated to three set angles of 20, 45 and

80 degrees, were attached to the fuselage outer skin, behind the wing joint, each of the three positions having its own operating button in the cockpit.

The undercarriage was basically Type 510, with adjustments made for retraction into the new wing and the fin attachment to the fuselage was further aft than Supermarine carried theirs. The Type 510 Rolls-Royce Nene 2 centrifugal-flow turbojet (Nene number 259) was retained, as were the four fuselage fuel tanks together holding 236½ gallons (1,075 litres), but no tanks were fitted in the wings.

It has been reported that Blackburn test pilot Gartrell 'Sailor' Parker did some fast taxiing prior to the aircraft being painted, but the official date given for the commencement of taxi trials is June 1951, and these soon established that Brough's 1,430yd runway was certainly not long enough for the maiden flight of a trials aircraft fitted with an untried wing.

The H.P.88 Gets Airborne

The three Bomber Command Emergency Landing Grounds (ELG) built during World War II have already been referred to in Chapter 3, as one of the Short Sperrins operated for a while from Woodbridge in Suffolk. Another of the trio was Carnaby, outside Bridlington in Yorkshire, which, like the two other ELGs, had a 3,000yd runway, plus long over- and undershoot extensions. In the case of Carnaby, these extensions amounted to an additional 4,000yd and if the H.P.88 did not get airborne from that, it would not fly!

VX330 was dismantled, to be transported the 30-plus miles by road from Brough to Carnaby, arriving on 14 June. The ELG was actually non-operational, but the condition of the runway was considered acceptable for use. Following reassembly and systems checks, the aircraft made a 5-minute maiden flight on 21 June, in the hands of 'Sailor' Parker. The next fifteen days were occupied with an assortment of adjustments, not helped by the distance between Carnaby from the home base, and it was 7 July before the aircraft made its second flight.

Parker became aware very quickly that there was a marked over-sensitivity in the tailplane, with the aircraft pitching at the slightest atmospheric pressure variation. His natural reaction to correct the pitching only made matters worse, as low-

amplitude porpoising set in, which could only be damped out by his adopting a fixed hold on the control column. Two further flights were made to establish that the cut-in speed for the pitching was 270mph (434km/h), and during the fifth flight, on 25 July, Parker took VX330 to 300mph (483km/h), when things became quite dangerous, as the oscillations increased with the aircraft's speed.

Curing the pitching became a little problematic and was taken in stages. An angle bracket strip was fitted to the upper surface of the tailplane trailing edge, which enabled close to 320mph (515km/h) to be reached fairly smoothly. Encouraged by this, the bracket strip was lengthened and a similar strip installed on the under surface. 'Sailor' Parker made a flight on 5 August, which was the aircraft's seventeenth sortie, and reported a marked improvement, with 530mph (853km/h) being reached without any problems. This represented Mach 0.82 and further flights confirmed that, by using gentle backward pressure on the control column, pitching could be damped out after a couple of cycles. This was considered enough and Parker made no further attempts to increase speed above Mach 0.82.

Handley Page's Deputy CTP, 'Duggie' Broomfield DFM, flew up to Brough from Radlett to make an extensive test flight of the aircraft. He was in full agreement with Parker's findings and proposals, relative to keeping the speed to the limits that had been safely achieved. On 23 August, Broomfield accepted the H.P.88 on behalf of Handley Page and made its twenty-seventh flight in ferrying it to Stansted in Essex, for a series of airspeed calibration flights. During these, the aircraft was cleared to make progressively staged increases up to Mach 0.85, preparatory to being flown at the 1951 SBAC Display.

Further Test-Flying Tragedy

Broomfield took off from Stansted on 26 August, to begin rehearsing a routine for Farnborough; 15 minutes into the sortie, he received permission from the tower to make a straight high-speed flight down the runway, at an altitude of approximately 300ft. Halfway through the run, VX330 broke up without warning. 'Duggie' Broomfield was too low for a successful ejection and his body was found in the ejector seat, clear of the wreckage.

The inquest held at Stansted four days later, on 30 August, heard from Mr B.A. Morris, senior investigating officer to the Accident Investigation Branch of the Ministry of Civil Aviation (Stansted, being a civil airport, was administered by the Ministry), that he found a failure of the aircraft's construction had occurred, causing it to crash. He was satisfied that the H.P.88 had been airworthy before the accident and stated that the fuselage had failed aft of the wing trailing edge, with the pilot's seat becoming detached from the cockpit. These two statements did not really tie up.

Mr William MacRostie, the Handley Page works foreman at the time, vehemently disagreed with the finding of structural failure, stating that he considered very high accelerations could have arisen from instability in the hydraulic flying control system. A local farmer, one Mr George Brown, related how, when VX330 passed over him, the nose had pitched up, then the aircraft levelled off before rising steeply once more. The starboard wing appeared to come off, the aircraft turned to port and the port wing broke away. Examination of the wreckage and flight recorder indicated very high oscillations on a trace showing 618mph (994km/h). This meant that although the H.P.88 had flown faster at altitude, this was the fastest that it had achieved at such a low level. Later opinion concluded that an inertia coupling between the powered controls and the elevator produced a greater load than the airframe could absorb, causing structural failure.

Rather like Avro's first Type 707, VX330 did not last long. It was just over two months since the first flight and in twenty-eight sorties it had only achieved 14 hours of flying time. Virtually nothing was attained from the aircraft that would be of value to the H.P.80 and the majority of the flight testing related to curing its own problems. Some hold the opinion that 'Duggie' Broomfield's life was a pointless sacrifice, which, in the broad picture of Handley Page's turbojet-powered bomber, is rather hard to dispute. The death of Eric Esler could not be similarly considered, as he demonstrated that Avro's delta planform worked, but the losses certainly proved that the learning curve of aviation in that era carried a heavy price.

Specification – Handley Page H.P.88/GAL63/Y.B.2.

Powerplant:	One Rolls-Royce 2.RN.2 Nene turbojet producing 5,000lb (2,268kg) static thrust.
All-up weight:	13,197lb (5,986kg).
Dimensions:	Span 40ft 0in (12.2m); length 39ft 10in (12.1m); height 12ft 8in (3.9m); wing area 285.7sq ft (26.5sq m).

CHAPTER SIX

Avro's God of Fire

No one could foresee in March 1947 that the preliminary sketches of a delta-winged aircraft made by Roy Chadwick in 1945 would blossom into one of the most endearing aeroplanes that the British aircraft industry has ever produced. It ranks with the Supermarine Spitfire and Chadwick's World War II masterpiece, the Lancaster. It gave the RAF twenty-five years of unbroken service, during which it undertook the geographically longest sorties in the Service's history, and even as these words are being written, the aeronautical fraternity is eagerly anticipating that one will fly again within a year or two.

With the calculations confirming his original ideas, Chadwick had settled by the spring of 1947 for the Avro tender to B.35/46 to be a large delta-wing aircraft, and the Type 698 was in the hands of the Air Staff, together with the MoS, in May of that year. It was admitted that the former Chief Designer's tragic death created concerns as to whether the mandarins at Whitehall would have reservations about the company's ability to proceed on the project without his drive. However, Stuart Davies had survived the accident, and with him at the helm it was considered that the design team was capable of continuing. Furthermore, Bob Lindley, as head of the Project Office, had kept abreast of Roy Chadwick's thinking.

The early proposal of a large circular air intake on either side of the pressurized crew capsule had been changed to deep slit apertures in the leading edge of the wing section, deep enough to take a buried side-by-side pair of engines on each side. Wind-tunnel tests at RAE Farnborough had demonstrated that air pressure distribution over the circular intakes and wing would induce unacceptable compressibility drag. Therefore, a team of nearly 200 draughtsmen had laboured for three months on an almost complete redesign of the wing; however, in so doing, they ensured that future larger engines could be accommodated. A large central fin replaced Chadwick's earlier notion of wing-tip fins and later research by the RAE confirmed that the new configuration would meet the specification's requirements.

Power for the Type 698 had always been envisaged as four of the promising Bristol B.E.10 twin-shaft axial-flow turbojets. Development of the B.E.10 was now producing the BO.11, given the name Olympus. On its initial bench run on 6 May 1950, the engine, weighing only 3,600lb (1,633kg), produced 9,140lb (4,146kg) static thrust and within a year, a 9,750lb (4,423kg) thrust flight engine was ready. The engine had to be derated to 8,000lb (3,629kg) thrust for initial flight testing in English Electric Canberra

Roy Chadwick stands beside K-131, the first Avro 534 'Baby'. Avro Heritage

Stuart Davies, Avro's Chief Designer, who took over the delta programme after Roy Chadwick's tragic death. Harry Holmes

B.2 WD952, which first took it aloft on 6 August 1952, piloted by Bristol's assistant CTP Wg Cdr 'Wally' Gibb.

However, that was in the future, and when Avro received the Instruction to Proceed on 27 November 1947, followed by Contract No.6/ACFT/1942/CB.6(a) in January 1948 for two prototypes, the only available engine in production capable of powering a Type 698 prototype was the Rolls-Royce Avon R.A.3, developing 6,500lb (2,948kg) thrust. Avro was well aware that Handley Page had received a similar prototype order for their H.P.80 design to Specification B.35/46, powered by four Metrovick F.9/Armstrong Siddeley Sapphire engines, so it was accepted that at least the first aircraft would have to be fitted with Avons as, due to the wing redesign, the schedule was already running slightly behind time.

But the company's enthusiasm for the new bomber, from Design Office to shop floor, was virtually unlimited and the fact that they were more or less in competition with Handley Page provided additional impetus. The Project Engineer on the Type 698, Gilbert Whitehead, is on record as having arrived at Chadderton in the morning during one hectic period of development and not departing for home until fourteen days later. Final assembly jigs, working to closer tolerances than ever before, were installed at Woodford, where the wings were also fabricated. Chadderton produced all other major assemblies, apart from the crew's pressurized capsule, built at Saunders Roe, and the undercarriage components, which came from Dowty. The forward fuselage, nose, centre section and rear fuselage assemblies were conveyed by road to Woodford from Chadderton, cocooned in tarpaulins. Special arrangements were made along the 17 mile route between the two sites for lamp posts to be hinged at congested points, in order to allow the large sections, that were mostly transported during the hours of darkness, an unobstructed journey.

The Prototypes take Shape

The two prototypes had been allocated serials VX770 and VX777, with the second aircraft to be manufactured about a year behind the first. All-metal, stressed skin construction was used, with the wing/fuselage centre section housing all four engines, four fuel tanks, the bomb-bay, the four-wheeled, eight-tyred main undercarriage bogie units, which retracted forward, plus retractable airbrakes on top and lower skin surfaces. The wing was structurally conventional in having two-spar mainplanes that attached to the

The first prototype Type 698, VX770, being prepared for an early test flight. Author's collection

At the Sign of the Shed Roof

Edwin Alliott Verdon Roe came into this world on 26 April 1877, the fourth child of Dr Edwin Roe and his wife Sofia, whose maiden name had been Verdon. Early in his life he let it be known that he did not like his forename Edwin and by the age of eight years he went to Haliford House boarding school, near Brooklands, as Alliott Verdon Roe.

In March 1892, Alliott sailed from Liverpool on the steamship *Labrador*, bound for a civil engineering company in British Columbia in Canada, but his arrival coincided with a slump and by the following year he was back in England, to start an apprenticeship at the Lancashire and Yorkshire Railway Works at Horwich, in Lancashire. Five years later, with a Mechanical Institute certificate, he obtained employment at Portsmouth Dockyard and, having decided to make a career in the Royal Navy, went to King's College London to study marine engineering. He failed the Royal Naval College examination at Greenwich so enlisted in the Merchant Navy, but in 1902 he returned to dry land, to become a draughtsman in the motor industry. He joined Brotherton and Crockers Ltd, where he designed the company's first gear-change mechanism.

But Alliott Roe's interest in things aeronautical had taken seed and the 24th January 1906 edition of *The Times* carried his letter bemoaning the lack of British progress in heavier-than-air flying. *The Times'* response typified just what Roe was writing about – they said that aviation was dangerous to human life and doomed to failure on engineering grounds!

Undeterred, he took out British Patent number 26009 in 1906, for the world's first single control column for an aeroplane. The following year he built a model aeroplane that soared to a height of 100ft and in 1907 he won a prize in the *Daily Mail* model aeroplane flying contest. Meanwhile he was constructing his first full-size biplane in his brother's coach house at Putney, and by the end of the year had it at Brooklands for test-flying. At Brooklands he worked in a shed where, with *Avroplane* written above the door, the name AVRO first appeared. The shed roof had a steep pitch, which inspired the shape of the logo for A.V. Roe and Company, formed on 1 January 1910 in Great Anscoat Street, Manchester, with his brother Humphrey's financial backing.

The new company's first product was the Roe II triplane *Mercury,* two of which were built in 1910, followed by another triplane, the Roe III, built in the same year, which had a veritable production line, as four were made, with one going to the Harvard Aeronautical Society at Boston, USA.

A significant step was taken in 1911, when the company took on the services of Roy Chadwick who, a year later, had a hand in designing the first aeroplane that really stamped the name Avro on aviation history, the Type 504. It saw service with the RAF until 1933, was built under licence in several countries and was exported to twenty more. Another important step was taken in 1914, when R.H. Dobson (later Sir Roy Dobson CBE) joined the company and both men became instrumental in fashioning its prosperity.

The post-World War I years brought cutbacks in production to the whole aircraft industry, but Avro was fortunate in still having Type 504 orders for the RAF, as well as the refurbishing of existing aeroplanes so, although finances were difficult, the company survived. It took over land at New Hall Farm in 1924, to make an airfield for testing their products and it was renamed Woodford, which is still operational today. Alliott Verdon Roe sold his interests in the company that he had founded, in 1928, to Sir John Siddeley, Managing Director of Sir W.G. Armstrong Whitworth Aircraft Limited. A year later, he was knighted as Sir Alliott Verdon-Roe and took a controlling interest in the Isle of Wight marine company S.E. Saunders Ltd. The company had been involved in aviation for some years, and in 1929 Saunders Roe Ltd was formed. Sir Alliott was still the company's President when he died on 4 January 1958.

In 1928, A.V. Roe and Co., now being a member of the Siddeley Group, moved their design office from Hamble, on Southampton Water, to where they had expanded in 1916. Their new home was in Manchester and the Hamble facilities were fully taken over by Air Service Training Ltd in 1931. Four years later, in July 1935, Avro became a member of the newly formed Hawker Siddeley Aircraft Co. Ltd, but retaining the company name. Both Chadwick and Dobson became members of the Board in 1936.

The expansion of the RAF in the mid-1930s generated a spate of new aircraft factories, sponsored by the government of the day. One such factory was in the northern Manchester suburb of Chadderton, and by 1937 it was producing the Chadwick legend, the Type 652A Anson, the first prototype of which had flown on 7 January 1935. Designed as a coastal patrol aircraft, it became the type in which a large proportion of RAF Bomber Command's aircrew learned their trades in World War II. Having earned their wings and brevets, so many of them retained their association with Chadwick's genius by going operational in his Type 683 Lancaster, spawned by the rare failure of a Rolls-Royce engine, the 24-cylinder Vulture. This failure was basically due to lack of development, rather than bad design, but the twin-Vultures of the Type 679 Manchester were replaced on a 12ft (3.7m) longer wing by four Rolls-Royce Merlins, and the Lancaster, truly one of the great warplanes of all time, first flew on 9 January 1941. When production ended four years later, in 1945, a total of 7,374 plus three prototypes had been built.

Chadwick married a square-sectioned fuselage to the Lancaster's mainplanes, power units, undercarriage and tail assembly, to produce the Type 685 York, which saw RAF service in the closing months of World War II and several years beyond. A civil conversion of the Lancaster, first made by Victory Aircraft of Malton, Canada, the Type 691 Lancastrian, was produced to become an early post-war passenger transport and several became engine test-beds for the burgeoning turbojet industry in the late 1940s.

A longer-ranged bomber, designed specifically for the war in the Far East, was a larger variant on the Lancaster theme, Type 694 Lincoln, but two atomic bombs dropped on the Japanese mainland brought a cessation of hostilities and the production run of over 550 aircraft served with the peacetime RAF, plus a few examples being exported to Argentina. Twenty-four were also built in Australia for the RAAF, and again, several British-produced Lincolns operated as engine test-beds.

Avro prepared for the post-war civil aviation market with the Type 688/9 Tudor series of airliners. It was in the crash of the prototype Tudor 2, G-AGSU, on 23 August 1947, due to the incorrect connecting of the aileron controls, that the company lost Roy Chadwick, at the age of fifty-four and one of Britain's most creative aeronautical engineers. However, he left behind his original calculations and drawings for a delta-winged bomber; these were taken over by Stuart Davies, who survived the crash, and developed into the Vulcan.

The company tendered Type 696 to Specification R.5/46 for a long-range maritime reconnaissance aircraft and produced their final multi-piston engine-powered aircraft, the Shackleton.

Affectionately known as the 'Growler', because of the distinctive note of its four Rolls-Royce Griffon 57s driving contra-rotating propellers, the Shackleton remained in service with the RAF for thirty-eight years, the last eighteen of which saw it employed as the United Kingdom's only Airborne Early Warning (AEW) aircraft.

In 1958, the last aircraft design to carry the name of Avro was launched. This was the Type 748, twin-prop-jet powered, medium-range feederliner and many successful variants have developed into the 748 Series. This has included a military freight carrier for the RAF, named the Andover, and the last Type 748 was delivered in February 1989, although by that time it was referred to as the British Aerospace (BAe) 748. This was on account of the rather convoluted history of the company becoming a division of Hawker Siddeley Aviation Ltd on 1 July 1963, which later, on 1 April 1965, was to merge into one conglomerate, the Hawker Siddeley Group (the 748 becoming the Hawker Siddeley 748), and the name Avro ceased to exist. The Group, in turn, was absorbed into BAe on 29 April 1977, although they upheld the name to a certain extent, as Avro International was formed in 1993 to take over production of feederliners, under the title Regional Jets (RJ).

Today, Woodford and Chadderton are still engaged in aviation, Woodford having a production line for the RJ series of variants of the original de Havilland 146 design, while Chadderton is the source of mainplanes for Airbus Industries. The great name of Avro will forever be remembered as a fundamental thread in the tapestry of British aeronautical history.

centre section, with each leading edge being made in a one-piece mould jig, into which the sheet metal was formed.

Like the Valiant, the pressurized section of the crew compartment came from Saunders Roe, arriving at Chadderton as one unit. Entrance was via a door ahead of the nose-wheel bay and the crew operated on two levels, the two pilots being seated in Martin-Baker ejector seats on a higher level than the three rearwards facing observers/electronics operators/visual bomb aimer. A large electronics bay was situated in the sharply tapered nose section ahead of the pressurized compartment, while the rear tailcone housed a braking parachute. Flying controls consisted of two pairs of ailerons and elevators operating on the wing rear spar, plus the rudder hinged to the swept fin.

Construction and assembly of VX770 was given as much priority as possible without jeopardizing other production and the unofficial target was set of getting the aircraft airborne for the 1952 SBAC Display. In June 1952, Avro had received Contract No.6/ACFT/8442/CB.6(a) to produce twenty-five Type 698 bombers, but the elation within the company was tempered by the knowledge that Handley Page had received a similar order for their H.P.80 and their first prototype was already being assembled at Boscombe Down. It was firmly anticipated that both types would be operated by RAF squadrons in order to evaluate which was the better aircraft prior to one type being put into full production.

First Flight

Assembly of the first prototype was completed at Woodford in early August 1952. The aircraft, resplendent in an overall gloss-white finish, broken only by the national markings, an Avro logo on each fin and a black anti-glare panel ahead of

VX770 displays the double underwing airbrakes, changed to a single unit on the Phase 2 wing, and the absence of a visual bomb aimer's blister. Derek N. James

Two days after its maiden flight, the first Type 698 is positioned outside Farnborough's control tower. *Aeroplane*

the windscreen (which was soon discarded as being unnecessary once flying had started), was rolled out for taxiing trials preparatory to its 35-minute maiden flight on 30 August, in the hands of 'Roly' Falk. This was not without incident, as the pilot received an instrument warning that the nose-wheel had not retracted. A Vampire, plus a Type 707A, were scrambled and both pilots confirmed that the leg was fully retracted, the false warning being given due to a defective micro-switch. Further into the sortie, both sections of the undercarriage fairing attached to the main-wheel legs departed from the aircraft, this being attributed to wing flexing that had not been allowed for in Avro's calculations, but after landing Falk reported that he was very happy with the aircraft's performance. He had been able to perform a number of different manoeuvres without any problems – and they had beaten Handley Page into the air!

Showing off at Farnborough

On 1 September, Falk flew VX770 to Boscombe Down, where a further three hours of flying was undertaken, which must have rankled the Handley Page team down there. Then the following day,

'Roly' Falk presented the Avro Type 698 to the assembled guests at Farnborough, flying the great white delta in formation with a vermilion 707A, piloted by Jimmy Nelson, and the blue 707B with Jimmy Orrell at the controls. The weather was rather inclement throughout the week, but the white VX770 shining in the occasional sunlight against dark, foreboding clouds, was a sight to behold. Landing a large delta-wing aircraft was a new attraction, as the low-speed, high-angle of attack, with the throttle closed and the angle maintained without the conventional flare out as it rolled down the runway, produced gasps from the crowds. The undercarriage fairings lost during the maiden flight had not been replaced, but their absence did nothing to mar a beautiful aeroplane, superbly displayed and very few of the spectators were aware that the aircraft was being flown solo. Falk was quoted as saying that flying the Type 698 was easier than flying an Anson.

Engine Problems and a Name

Post-Farnborough, VX770 was grounded to have modifications implemented to the replacement main-wheel fairings, as well as having the second pilot's seat installed; there had not been time before the

display. Falk let it be known that he would like to have a say in the designing of the cockpit, a request that was readily accepted by Stuart Davies. One stipulation he made was that the spectacle-type control column, so reminiscent of the lumbering piston-engined heavy bombers of World War II, should be replaced by a fighter-type stick, which was more in keeping with how the aircraft performed. The cockpit was almost as 'Roly' Falk wanted it, bearing in mind that the specification called for a two-pilot crew. He was of the opinion that the Type 698 only needed one pilot.

Avro had worked hard to get VX770 ready for the SBAC Display, but the fact remained that the installation of four Avons was purely to get the aircraft airborne. They were Canberra powerplants, which had to have their auxiliaries gathered in bunches within the engine bays and certainly were not powerful enough to enable the prototype to be tested to anything like its design potential. Furthermore, the fuel system was incomplete, the Farnborough demonstrations having been flown on the fuselage tanks alone. A special Type 698 wing rig had been built at Woodford and an Olympus installation was tested during 1952, but the engines still required development. In February 1953 Olympus Mk.100s were fitted in the rig and, with a static thrust of 9,750lb (4,423kg), they were more representative of the power for which the aircraft had been designed. But the engine was still being flight-tested in the Canberra and, furthermore, it was in a derated form so, when VX770 was again grounded, after thirty-two hours of flying, four 7,500lb (3,400kg) thrust Armstrong Siddeley Sapphire ASSs.6 engines were fitted. The fuel system was at last completed and tested to ensure the designed constant c.g. was maintained. The pressurization system was made fully operative and by the time that the aircraft resumed flying in July 1953, it had been christened the Vulcan.

Speculation had abounded as to what name would be given to Avro's delta and alliterations such as Avenger, Albion and Apollo had been suggested. Sir John Sesser, the Chief of Air Staff, liked the name Valiant chosen by Vickers-Armstrong's personnel, so decided that both the Avro and Handley Page aircraft would carry names beginning with V. Vulcan was chosen for the Avro Type 698 and the Handley Page H.P.80 would be named Victor, the bombers collectively being known as the V-bomber force. This decision, made at the end of 1952, suggests that the Air Staff

knew then that there would be no competitive fly-off between the two more advanced types, culminating in a full production contract for the winner.

With the more powerful Sapphires, VX770 was able to considerably extend the flight envelope and over sixty hours of test-flying was amassed in fifty-seven sorties, although the advocated operational altitudes for the Vulcan were still not fully attainable.

The Second Prototype Flies

The second prototype was completed at Woodford in August 1953 and for the first time a Vulcan had more representative engines, as VX777 was fitted with four Bristol Olympus Mk.100s. It differed from VX770 in a few details, the most obvious of which was the ventral visual bombing blister under a slightly extended nose, necessary to take a nose-wheel unit that was a little longer than on the first prototype. Working on data supplied by the Type 707B, the leg on VX770 had been made longer than originally designed and a telescoping movement was installed, which activated during the retraction

sequence. The all-white colour scheme of the first prototype was followed, as was the Avro logo proudly displayed on the fin.

Having completed systems checks and taxiing trials, the aircraft was ready for its maiden flight by 3 September. Falk, resplendent in a lounge suit as ever, lifted VX777 off Woodford's operational runway for a successful first flight, in which everything stayed where it should. Two days later, on Monday, 5 September 1953, the annual SBAC Display at Farnborough witnessed one of its historical highlights for the first time. The two Vulcan prototypes were there, together with both 707As, the 707B and 707C, all combining to make a formation fly-by that had hardened aviation buffs cheering – myself included! Incidentally, 1953 was the first SBAC Display where all three V-bombers appeared, although the Valiant contribution was the all-black, one and only Mk.2.

Setbacks

With Farnborough finished, VX770 resumed its test-flight schedule, while VX777 went to the A&AEE at Boscombe Down for high-speed and high-altitude trials, but events did not materialize as

Lined up on Farnborough's main runway on 2 September 1952, VX770 prepares to start its display . . .

Specification – Vulcan

Dimensions:	B.1: span 99ft 0in (30.17m); length 97ft 1in (29.65m); wing area 3,554sq ft (330.16sq m).
	B.2: span 111ft 0in (33.83m); length 100ft 1in (30.5m); wing area 3,964sq ft (368.25sq m).
Powerplant:	Prototypes: four Rolls-Royce Avon RA.3 turbojets each producing 6,500lb (2,950kg) static thrust; or four Armstrong Siddeley Sapphire ASSa.6 turbojets each producing 7,500lb (3,400kg) static thrust; or four Bristol Olympus Mk101 turbojets each producing 9,750lb (4,400kg) static thrust; or four Rolls-Royce Conway RCo.7 turbojets each producing 15,000lb (6,800kg) static thrust.
	B.1: four Bristol Olympus Mk100 turbojets each producing 9,750lb (4,400kg) static thrust; or four Bristol Olympus Mk101 turbojets each producing 11,000lb (5,000kg) static thrust; or four Bristol Olympus Mk102 turbojets each producing 12,000lb (5,500kg) static thrust; or four Bristol Olympus Mk104 turbojets each producing 13,400lb (6,100kg) static thrust.
	B.2: four Bristol Olympus Mk200 turbojets each producing 16,000lb (7,250kg) static thrust; or four Bristol Olympus Mk210 turbojets each producing 17,000lb (7,700kg) static thrust; or four Bristol Olympus Mk301 turbojets each producing 20,000lb (9,000kg) static thrust.
Weights:	From 125,000lb (57,000kg) empty to 200,000lb (90,000kg) maximum loaded.
Performance:	B.1: maximum speed 638mph (1,027km/h) at 40,000ft (12,000m); service ceiling 55,000ft (17,000m); maximum range (B.1) 3,450 miles (5,500km) low level.
	B.2: maximum speed 645mph (1,038km/h) at 36,000ft (11,000m); service ceiling 60,000ft (18,000m); maximum range 4,600 miles (7,400km) high level.
Armament:	B.1: one 10,000lb nuclear weapon or twenty-one 1,000lb iron bombs
	B.2: one Blue Steel stand-off weapon or twenty-one 1,000lb iron bombs.

. . . banks sharply to produce a tip trail . . .

... **touches down at the end of its flying routine** ...

... **and streams its braking parachute.** Author's collection

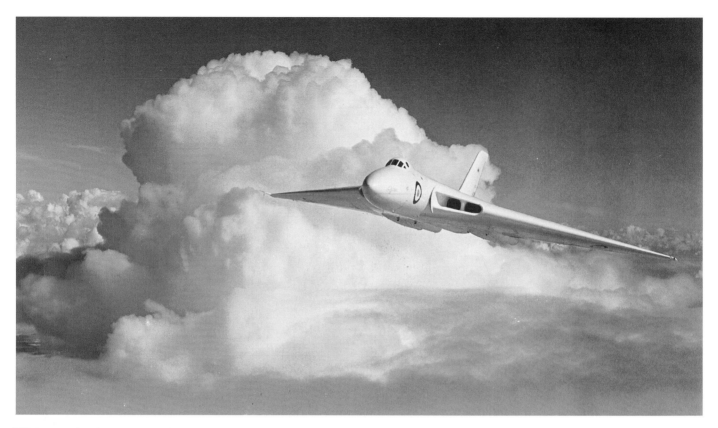

VX770 approaches the camera, dwarfed by a cumulus head of cloud. *Aeroplane*

As the snow flurries behind four Avon RA.3s, VX770 shows the starboard-side hatch for its braking parachute cable. Author's collection

Farnborough 1953. VX771 is followed by VX770, as a Fairey Gannet passes overhead. *Aeroplane*

planned. Urgent modifications to the Olympus engines were put in hand, together with alterations to the fuel and control systems, all of which put back by nearly six months the planned trials at the upper end of the flight envelope. It was the early part of July 1954 before the second prototype was airborne again and trials commenced, based at the RAE. On 27 July they came to a halt, when the aircraft made an exceptionally heavy landing at Farnborough, resulting in considerable damage to the airframe. As VX777 was the only Olympus-powered Vulcan, the entire high-speed and altitude programmes were again disrupted, although, during the aircraft's grounding, the opportunity was taken to replace the existing Olympus Mk.100s with Olympus 101 engines, each rated at 11,000lb (4,990kg) static thrust with a specific fuel consumption of 0.79lb/hr/lb (0.36kg/hr/kg), which were

the chosen engines for the first production batch of Vulcans.

While the second prototype was being repaired, VX770 soldiered on, testing handling with engines out and power controls off. Airbrake trials were conducted, together with general evaluation of manoeuvrability and trimming, as well as test sorties flown with the cockpit canopy removed. The aircraft was also employed on high-altitude and speed trials within the limits of the Sapphires, during which 'buzzing', or buffeting, was encountered at speeds in the Mach 0.80 to 0.85 range and calculations predicted that severe buffeting could affect the fatigue life of the outer wings. A&AEE at Boscombe Down had flown VX777 for 27 hours and they had reported that the Mach number/buffet characteristics were unacceptable for a high-altitude bomber, such that the aircraft was not considered satisfactory for

service use as it stood. As recounted in Chapter 5, various remedies were examined using Type 707A WD280, with the final solution proving to be the recontouring of the outer wing leading edges. The existing 52-degree angle of sweep was reduced by 10 degrees at approximately mid-span, with the 52-degree angle reinstated on the outermost section, the resultant 20 per cent increased wing area having slight negative camber along its length. The new planform was referred to as the Phase 2 wing.

Prototype Swansongs

VX777 flew again in February 1955 following repairs to the damage caused by the heavy landing, but it was grounded yet again at the beginning of July, to have the new wing leading edges fitted. Flying was

The second prototype Type 698 Vulcan at Woodford, after its maiden flight, showing the visual bomb-aimer's blister. Author's collection

Two's company, three's a crowd. Both Vulcan prototypes share an enclosure with the first Victor prototype, WB771, at the 1953 SBAC Display. Author's collection

The two Vulcan prototypes formate with four Avro 707s to make one of Farnborough's greatest highlights . . .

... the display being finished by a slow fly-by, VX777 is followed by three of the 707s. Author's collection

The production Vulcan B.1, VX889, after the revised leading edge had been fitted in February 1956. Derek N. James

Farnborough 1957 and XA889 shares the stage with XA777, now modified to become the prototype B.2. *Aeroplane*

The awful demise of VX770, when it disintegrated over Syerston while being displayed with four Conway RCo.7s. Author's collection

VX777 testing the new wing leading edge in October 1958. Author's collection

resumed on 5 October, which was eight months after the first production Vulcan B.1, XA889, had made its maiden flight on 4 February – with the original wing leading edge. The revised section was retrofitted a year later, in February 1956. The second prototype continued as a trials aircraft for another five years, during which time it was modified to serve as the prototype Vulcan B.2, Avro having received a contract for the production of the new variant in March 1956. It first flew in the new configuration, which featured a wing extended by 12ft (3.7m), on 31 August 1957. Following its final flight on 27 April 1960, VX777 languished at RAE Farnborough for three years before being scrapped in July 1963.

Having finished its useful life so far as Vulcan development was concerned, VX770 was transferred to Rolls-Royce for engine test-bed duties, connected with the company's first bypass engine, the Conway, which had been flown for the first time in a ventral pod on Avro Ashton Mk.2 WD491. This Conway variant was

being tested prior to selection as the powerplant for BOAC's Boeing 707-420 fleet, but a military-rated version, the Conway RCo.11, was to be developed to power the Victor B.2 and this had already flown in a similar pod, on Ashton Mk.3 WE670. Considering the great rivalry that existed between Avro and Handley Page when getting their respective B.35/46 tenders airborne, it was rather ironic that a Vulcan should be flight testing a Victor powerplant.

Four Conway RCo.7s, each producing 15,000lb (6,800kg) static thrust, were installed in VX770 during 1957 and the aircraft was demonstrated by Rolls-Royce at that year's SBAC Display. There followed a year of intensive engine testing before the combination appeared at the 1958 display. One week later, on 14 September, VX770 made a scheduled appearance during the Battle of Britain air display at Syerston, in Northamptonshire. While executing a high-speed, low-level pass down the flight line, the aircraft disintegrated in a most spectacular

fashion and all four crew members were killed. The official cause of the disaster was attributed to fatigue failure of the wing leading edge, but further investigation by Avro concluded that the pilot exceeded the aircraft's flight limitations, by pulling too much 'g' at too high a speed while flying at ground level. Examination of the wreckage revealed that the accelerometer maximum pointers in the cockpit, plus the artificial feel units, had locked when the electricity supply was cut off during the disintegration. They were designed to increase spring-loading on the control column in proportion to dynamic pressure by moving a cam track and the positions of the cams in the wreckage corresponded to a speed of more than 470mph.

Thus did the careers of the two mighty Vulcan prototypes come to an end, one rather ignominiously and the other disastrously. Both were a far cry from the serenity of that majestic formation presented to us at Farnborough in September 1953.

CHAPTER SEVEN

HP's Champion

Unlike Vickers-Armstrongs and Avro, when Handley Page tendered for Specification B.35/46, the company's Chief Designer Reginald Stafford had already been thinking along the lines of a turbojet-powered, high-speed bomber, generated by a confidential memorandum received from his Managing Director, Sir Frederick Handley Page, on 14 June 1945. Stafford's memo, which stated that Sir Frederick considered a Lincoln replacement would be required within six years, was shared with Godfrey Lee, the company's Research Engineer and Frank Radcliffe, Technical Assistant for special investigations. Furthermore, they had experience with unconventional aircraft, having first flown the Manx tailless research aeroplane on 25 June 1943.

The Shape is Set

When the company received the Instruction to Proceed on 1 January 1948, the Ministry of Supply allocated the sum of £50,000 to cover further development work on the H.P.80. Within two weeks, the wing-tip fins had been deleted and the wingspan had been increased by 10ft to 110ft. No one was sorry to see the back of the wing-tip fins, as the consensus of opinion considered that the company had enough new innovations to contend with, but their removal was based on data provided by the RAE at Farnborough, which showed there certainly was not enough fin area in them, plus the stubby pylon on which the tailplane was mounted (*see* page 13) so the whole assembly was disposed of and a conventional fin/rudder unit designed, with the tailplane situated approximately one-third distance up the fin. The new tail unit carried a weight penalty of about 500lb, which had to be accepted, but in common with most design teams, Handley Page was ever optimistic and sure that a weight saving could be made somewhere along the line.

Right from the start, the H.P.80 was to be powered by four Metropolitan-Vickers (Metrovick) F.9 axial-flow engines. With its vast experience in turbines, the company started considering the gas turbine as an aircraft's propulsive source in 1938. Assisted by the design researches made by Dr A.A. Griffith at the RAE, Metrovick never considered centrifugal flow as an option, and its first engine, the F.1, produced 2,150lb (975kg) more thrust than the Whittle/Rover W.2B, which, at 1,450lb (660kg) static thrust, was being used to power the first Gloster Meteors. The succeeding F.2 was their first engine to be test-flown, fitted in a rear-fuselage installation on the Lancaster prototype BT308 and given its maiden flight on 19 June 1943. The F.2/4A variant, giving 3,750lb (1,700kg) thrust, was named Beryl and a pair was installed in each of the three Saunders Roe SR.A/1 flying boat fighter prototypes in 1948. However, by that time Metrovick had decided to discontinue manufacturing turbojet engines, although they had a large axial-flow engine on bench trials. Designated the F.9, the turbojet had been offered to De Havilland Engines, but that company already had its own axial-flow Gyron in development, so Metrovick passed the engine over to Coventry-based Armstrong Siddeley Engines. They amalgamated the design with their own axial-flow ASX engine experience, to produce the Sapphire, which Rolls-Royce went on record as considering to have superior pressure/flow characteristics to its own Avon.

A wind-tunnel model made in February 1948 showed the engines as being in four separate nacelles, although it was always the intention to bury the engines within the wing centre section, and as the final profile showed, this layout was adhered to. In May 1948, Lachmann suggested the tailplane should be moved to the top of the fin, in order to clear it from the turbulence of the engine efflux. Today the T-tail is an accepted layout, but in 1948 this was a bold step and Handley Page did a lot of pioneer work on this configuration, which a later disaster threw in doubt for a while. The MoS gave approval for the company to build a radio-controlled scale model, with a 10ft (3m) wing-span, to flight-test the T-tail principle, but this crashed at Farnborough on its first flight and was completely destroyed, so that avenue of testing came to naught. When the wing-tip fins had been in vogue, the tailplane was to be an all-moving unit, but in the transfer to the fin-top, this was abandoned in favour of a small fixed tailplane, carrying the hinge-points for two enormous elevators. The whole assembly was set at a 15-degree dihedral angle, thereby increasing the clean fin area, which in turn improved the aircraft's directional stability. The tailplane leading edge sweep of 45 degrees reduced considerably at the joint with the elevators, so reiterating to a certain extent the wing layout, and the whole unit carried a large bullet-fairing at its intersection with the fin.

The optimistically hoped-for weight reduction came about with a change to the undercarriage main wheels. A pair of four-wheel bogies replaced the designed two large single wheels and a saving of 300lb came with these units.

The final main alteration was brought about in January 1948, resulting from tests made in RAE Farnborough's high-speed wind tunnel. This showed that drag on the wing increased alarmingly at Mach 0.8, which was a lot sooner than the calculated Mach 0.875. At 8 per cent t/c ratio, the outer wing was just too thick and Godfrey Lee's answer was to reduce the wing-tip ratio to 6 per cent. However, at the other end of the wing, a thicker root was required to house the main-wheel bogies, four Sapphires and two 310-gallon (1,410-litres) centre-section fuel tanks. When tested in Farnborough's wind tunnel, the stall characteristics of such a wing were unacceptable. Lee increased the outer-wing chord by 20 per cent, which repositioned the trailing-edge angle-change

The Aeronautical Patriach

The Regency spa town of Cheltenham in Gloucestershire was home to Frederick Joseph Page and his wife Ann Eliza, when their second son, Frederick, was born on 15 November 1885. His mother's maiden name, Handley, was incorporated into the newborn's name and the world was to know Frederick Handley Page as one of the truly great characters in aviation, who carried the sobriquet 'H.P.' into the logo of the company that he formed in 1909.

While being educated at Cheltenham Grammar School, he appreciated that electrical traction was going to become a growth industry and, on leaving school in 1902, he became a student at the Finsbury Technical College in London, taking a course in electrical engineering. During his three years at the college, an interest in mechanical flight was born and, although he filled the post of Chief Designer at the electrical machinery manufacturers Johnson and Phillips Ltd near Woolwich, his thoughts were turning more to aviation, which he pronounced in his rich Cotswold brogue to the Aeronautical Society of Great Britain, after becoming a member in 1907.

He became attracted to the experiments in wing shapes being conducted by José Weiss and he became a shareholder in the Weiss Aeroplane and Launcher Syndicate which was formed on 10 June 1908. H.P. built his first glider in 1909, which he displayed on a stand shared with Weiss, who exhibited his own monoplane, at the Aero and Motor Boat Show at Olympia in the same year. On 17 June 1909, he founded the first dedicated aeronautical engineering firm in Britain. Titled Handley Page Ltd, the company had an authorized share capital of £10,000 and an initial subscribed capital of £500. Its premises was a large shed at Creekmouth, near the Woolwich Ferry and H.P. built his first powered monoplane, the Type A *Bluebird*, which was displayed at Olympia in 1910.

The company's first really successful design was the Type D monoplane dubbed the *Yellow Peril*, which first flew on 15 July 1911, although unfortunately the plane crashed on landing. Undaunted, a year later the roots of the company's production abilities were laid when Handley Page Ltd moved to Cricklewood near Hendon in North London, and the start of World War I two years later saw the company plunged into the realms of large bomber aircraft. With the land fighting not going too well in Flanders, a naval officer, Charles Romney Samson, made an urgent request to the Admiralty for a 'bloody paralyser' to be sent, which could rain bombs down on the advancing enemy forces. H.P., together with his designer George Rudolf Volgert, were requested to design a large bomber and the resultant Type O, with a 114ft (34.7m) wingspan, was ordered as the H.P.11 O/100, and had its maiden flight from Hendon, on 17 December 1915. The Royal Naval Air Station (RNAS) at Manston, in Kent, started receiving production aircraft in 1916, for crew training.

The first operational sortie by a Handley Page aircraft was a raid on the Metz railway junction carried out on the night 16/17 March 1917; by the signing of the Armistice on 11 November 1918, forty-two H.P.O/100s had been built to serve with four RNAS squadrons. From the O/100 emerged the H.P.12 O/400, which was the company's first large-scale production aircraft, a total of 554 having been built by 1919. They flew with a dozen RAF squadrons, No.216 Squadron operating with O/400s in the Middle East until 1921, and the aircraft is acknowledged to have been the best large bomber of the 1914-18 conflict. The largest bomber of that era was the four-engined H.P.15 V/1500 which,

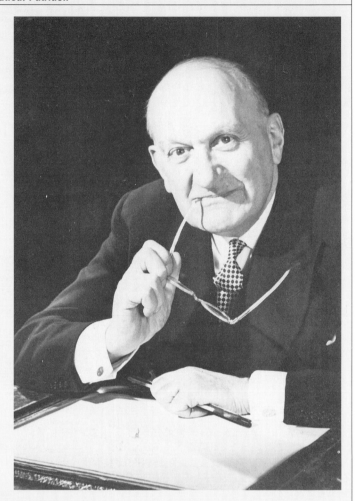

Sir Frederick Handley Page CBE. Handley Page Association

with its 126ft (38.4m) wing-span, carried an internal bomb load of thirty 250lb bombs and had an endurance of seventeen hours. Although 213 aircraft had been ordered early in 1918, the cessation of hostilities brought about cancellations and only forty-one were assembled, with elements of a further twenty-two being delivered for storage as spares.

After the war, appreciating that large aeroplanes could carry passengers in lieu of bombs, H.P. set up Handley Page Air Transport Ltd in August 1919. Using converted H.P.11s, he began services between Cricklewood and various European cities, with Rheims and Brussels being regular destinations. Plans were made to operate internal services in South America, South Africa and India, but political intrigue killed off the ventures before they could, literally, get off the ground. The services from Cricklewood had more success and in the first year of operations, nearly 4,500 passengers were conveyed in a total of 100,000 miles flown, with Handley Page aircraft visiting nearly a dozen different counties.

However, economics became an increasingly worrying factor, as the dual roles of aircraft constructor and airline operator could not be sustained without some form of government subsidy, which was not forthcoming. Consequently, after five years of ever-expanding service, Imperial Airways made H.P. an offer that he could not refuse and in 1924, Handley Page Air Transport disappeared as a name. The Cricklewood shop floor was kept going by a combination of limited overseas orders for aeroplanes and motor car assemblies, while H.P. himself was heavily engaged in developing the slotted wing, in collaboration with Dr Gustav Victor Lachmann, who acted as the company's consultant. H.P. had long been an advocate of safety in aircraft design and the perfecting of an automatically operating slat on a wing leading edge near the tip, to obviate the problems of stalling, resulted in the patenting of the Handley Page Automatic Slat. The slat was recognized within the aircraft industry as an invaluable system, with the resultant royalties paid by various companies throughout the world being instrumental in keeping Handley Page finances more buoyant during the 1920s and early 1930s. The Air Ministry adopted the principle but, in typical governmental fashion, only paid H.P. £100,000 from the Royal Commission of Awards to Inventors for its free use – and charged him £16,000 tax on the award! (With H.P. receiving £100,000 for the slotted wing in 1927, the award of a similar sum to Sir Frank Whittle in May 1948 puts into perspective the miserly manner in which Sir Frank was treated for his contribution to aviation.)

Flying from Cricklewood was becoming increasingly difficult as aircraft became heavier and faster. The Hendon and Hampstead councils brought pressure to bear for the company to look elsewhere for an airfield, in order that the councils could fulfil building development plans. The company received a payment of £100,000 for the airfield, which they vacated on 18 November 1929, moving to Radlett, near St Albans in Hertfordshire, and a modern, purpose-built factory was erected at the Colney Street southern end of the 154-acre site. The airfield was officially opened by Prince George (later King George VI) on 7 July 1930.

Also in 1930, Handley Page introduced the giant four-engined biplane airliner, the H.P.42, with which the company and its operator Imperial Airways will always be associated. Although only eight were built (three *Heracles* Class used on European services, plus five *Hannibal* Class flown on the African and Indian routes), H.P.42s flew a total of over 10 million miles without one peacetime fatality (some aircraft were impressed into RAF service at the beginning of World War II, with consequential attrition).

In November 1933, No.99 (Bomber) Squadron, coincidentally based at Upper Heyford in Oxfordshire, started receiving the last RAF biplane heavy bomber, the H.P.38/50 Heyford. The company built 124 Heyfords, which were unusual in having the upper wing carrying the engines attached to the fuselage, and the lower wing having the bomb-bay fitted in its centre section, between the fixed main wheels, which were encompassed in enormous spats. Four years later, on 12 April 1937, the service received Handley Page's first production monoplane, the H.P.54 Harrow bomber transport, and all ninety-eight that were ordered were built that same year.

The great expansion of the RAF began in 1935 and the company's largest production order to date started in 1937, when construction commenced on the first of 1,451 H.P.52 Hampden medium bombers. This was later eclipsed by the total of 6,135 H.P.56/71 Halifax heavy bombers built during World War II.

In 1942, the year that Hampden production ended, H.P. was knighted Sir Frederick Handley Page, in recognition of his outstanding contribution to aviation. Three years later the war ended and limited civil conversions of Halifax bombers into Halton transports was followed by the H.P.67 Hastings military transport. The civil market was targeted with a version of Hastings, named Hermes, of which various updates in terms of size and tricycle undercarriages enabled BOAC to order twenty-five Hermes IVs, which were later used by a number of charter airlines. Handley Page took over the assets of the Miles Aircraft Co. when it went into liquidation in 1948, to form Handley Page (Reading) Ltd, and attempted to update the Marathon by replacing its four Gipsy Queen piston engines with a pair of Mamba turboprops, but without any commercial success. The Gipsy Queen-powered Marathon saw service with the RAF as a navigational trainer. Handley Page (Reading) made a final entry into the civil aircraft market with the H.P.R.3 Herald of 1955, powered by four Leonides radial engines, which was updated in 1959 by the fitting of two Dart turboprops, and fifty of these H.P.R.7 Heralds were built for operators in many different parts of the world.

Large military aeroplanes were never far from H.P.'s mind and their tender for Specification B.35/46 typified the company's attitude. But politics was rearing its ugly head and the government announced its rationalization policy in 1960, which would see all British aircraft manufacturers amalgamating into two groups. In 1951, in order to secure the independent future of his company, H.P. had £750,000 of reserves converted into paid-up ordinary stock and, for the well-being of his long-service employees, Sir Frederick rejected a merger with either of the two big groups. Although an agreement was reached in principle at the beginning of 1962 that the company would merge with Hawker Siddeley, subject to a military version of the Herald being ordered and the cancelled order for a batch of Victors being restored, ministerial lethargy saw the agreement still not finalized when Sir Frederick died on 21 April of that year.

Several years of uncertainty followed, but, when their small H.P.137 Jetstream twin-turboprop transport design was met with orders, plus options, totalling 182 aircraft, the directors, under the chairmanship of George Russell, considered that the company had turned the corner. But life and commerce are not that simple. The Certificate of Airworthiness for the Jetstream was delayed and the escalating costs of getting the aircraft into production forced the company into seeking a short-term loan. Costs for the Jetstream had got badly out of hand, with the original estimated break-even figure of 400 aircraft now turning out to be 1,000. Such inaccurate finances could not be lived with, and with the Ministry of Defence not agreeing to order the aircraft at that time, Handley Page Ltd was forced to go into liquidation on 8 August 1969.

A temporary shoring-up was made with the Craven Corporation of America in November 1969, but, three months later, that company's bankers withdrew support, and by 1 June 1970 the great name of Handley Page disappeared. Subsequent Victor tanker conversions were engineered by Hawker Siddeley Aviation at Woodford and the Jetstream was manufactured by Scottish Aviation at Prestwick. Naturally, the MoD ordered the Jetstream in its own time, as a navigational trainer, and it is sad to consider that bureaucracy had the last word over one of the genuine giants of British aviation.

Godfrey Lee, Chief Designer, right, with John Allam, CTP after Hedley Hazelden, at a ceremony for No.55 Squadron. Handley Page Association

kink, thereby instantly making the H.P.88 redundant so far as wing research was concerned, as it already had its wings installed, which were scaled-down copies of the original planform. These changes to the H.P.80 required leading-edge flaps to be fitted on the outer half of the wings, which were activated by accumulators energized from a pressure ratio switch in each wing.

Construction and New Techniques

When Handley Page received Contract No.6/ACFT/1875/CB6(a), dated 28 April 1948, for two prototype H.P.80s, serials WB771 and WB775 were allocated to the aircraft and a time lapse of approximately nine months was scheduled between their construction. The company's New Projects Group was headed by Charles Joy, the Assistant Chief Designer, who had worked at both Armstrong Whitworth and Gloster Aircraft prior to joining H.P. He was given the responsibility of getting the H.P.80 from the drawing board to the runway and was ably assisted in this task by Ray Sandifer, the Chief Stressman. A target of getting WB771 airborne in time to participate in the 1952 SBAC Display

was set, which, considering the complexity of the aircraft, was indeed an optimistic goal.

While the aerodynamics of the H.P.80 incorporated several new innovations, the structure was equally different from anything previously handled by Handley Page and new techniques had to be mastered by all concerned with its construction. A considerable amount of energy was expended on perfecting a wing built from honeycomb materials and using adhesive bonding agents, but results did not give the assurance required for a long-service airframe that was going to spend a large portion of its life flying very fast at high altitude. Sandifer perfected a substitute structure devised from contoured inner and outer aluminium panels, spot-welded to a corrugated light alloy lining. The sandwich sheets were fabricated into interchangeable panels by photo-lofted templates and the use of spot welding provided a great weight saving over conventional riveting, plus a superior outer-skin finish.

The Fuselage

The H.P.80 fuselage was designed as three main components. The front section comprised the pressurized crew compartment, with a seating layout similar to the

other two V-bombers but on one level, under which lay the large electronics bay housing the H_2S scanner, with the prone visual bomb-aimer's position ahead of it. When drafting the B.35/46 specification, for the crew compartment official thinking favoured a capsule that could be jettisoned in an emergency, as evacuation by ejector seat was considered too hazardous when operating at 50,000ft (15,000m) with a multi-numbered crew. However, various trials programmes were conducted and, while it was a good idea in principle, the mechanics of such a proposal were too complex for anyone's liking. Handley Page went so far as to design a compartment in which each pilot sat under an individual fighter-type blown canopy, but everyone was pleased when the capsule idea was officially cancelled.

This raised the thorny question, applicable to all three V-bombers, of every crew member being equipped with an ejector seat. Air Ministry reasoning was that the pilots were too far away to reach the exit door in time and therefore needed to be in ejector seats, which was a fair comment. However, it was considered that the rest of the crew could make manual evacuations through the doorway, which, in the case of the Valiant and H.P.80, had a built-in air dam on its forward edge to diminish the airflow at the point of leaving the aircraft. It is significant that when dummies were used to represent rear crew members evacuating the aircraft in an emergency, they struck the engine air intake lips at speeds above 340mph (550 km/h) and live trials were not conducted, as they would have been too dangerous. Economics decreed that the design and structural work required to provide hatches for the rear crew to evacuate by ejector seat was unacceptable, so the whole matter was dropped, and a feasible system devised by Martin-Baker was consequently ignored.

The main fuselage section comprised a vast unobstructed weapons bay that provided space for up to thirty-five 1,000lb iron bombs. Whereas the Valiant and Vulcan bomb-bays had been more or less tailored around the *Blue Danube* atomic weapon, Handley Page considered that, in the event of a limited conflict, conventional bombs were more likely to be deployed and they made sure that the H.P.80 could carry as many as possible. The bomb-bay was enclosed by a pair of double-skinned doors, that vanished

The first publicity photograph of WB771, the first prototype H.P.80, taken at Boscombe Down before its maiden flight. Author's collection

upwards inside the fuselage when opened, actuated by a neat mechanism at each end.

The rear fuselage was joined to the main section by a bulkhead stressed to take tail loads. It contained an equipment bay in the lower portion, a large hydraulically operated airbrake on either side, the base structure for the tail assembly and a rear warning radar scanner enclosed in the tail cone, above which the three or four braking parachutes were housed. The airbrakes had drag-increasing strakes along the top and bottom edges, which eliminated any pitch change when they were extended. They were infinitely adjustable and followed the movement of the airbrake lever, which enabled them to be used to control the approach on a suitable power setting, rather than the throttle, as they gave more precise control. The fin had a dorsal fairing, with an intake for the turbo-alternator, which met the fuselage ahead of the base structure, and the large tailplane atop the fin had a span of 32ft 8in (10m), which was only 12in (30cm) shorter than the Hawker Hunter's wingspan.

The Wing

Fundamentally of multi-spar construction, with load-bearing sandwich panels making multiple torsion boxes, the inner portion of each wing had a three-spar structure along the span, which changed outboard of the undercarriage bay to four-spar construction. Hydraulically operated Fowler flaps situated on the inboard trailing edge had their actuating jacks covered by blister fairings and the two-piece leading-edge flap on each wing of the prototypes was also a hydraulically powered system.

The ailerons were operated by a Hobson control system consisting of electrically actuated hydraulic power units.

The four engines were mounted in the thick inboard sections behind the strong wing boxes, thereby reducing the possibility of fire damage to the most highly stressed part of the entire airframe. This also made the wings more adaptable to larger engines – which materialized later in the production run – and the wing strength was maintained by the absence of any large access doors. The jet pipes of each pair of engines converged on each other, rather than running parallel. The inboard pipes angled slightly away from

the fuselage, while the outboard pipes were angled sharply inwards towards their partners.

The Undercarriage

The two large single wheels of the original H.P.80 design tendered for the specification, that were to retract inwards, were replaced by the Lancashire-based Electro-Hydraulics' design, consisting of a pair of four-wheel bogies, retracting rearwards outboard of the engine bays. Weighing over 300lb lighter than the original proposed units, each neatly designed bogie was attached to an oleo-pneumatic shock absorber and they assumed a trailing position once the aircraft had left the ground, before a retraction sequence that finished with the bogies rotated through 180 degrees to lie completely within the wing inboard section. A twin-wheel assembly was used for the nose undercarriage unit, which had hydraulic steering and retracted rearwards into its bay situated between the under-nose H_2S housing and the bomb-bay.

The Design Becomes an Aeroplane

Construction of both prototypes was split between Cricklewood and Radlett.

Taken on an early photocall, WB771 displays the crescent wing plan, short nose and early cockpit glazing. Derek N. James

WB771 was to be an aerodynamic test air-frame, while WB775 would be a fully equipped prototype. Because of the 10-mile distance between locations, the whole process of building the aircraft had to be carefully planned and the decision to manufacture small components at Cricklewood then transport them to Radlett, was adhered to whereever possible. At Radlett, final assembly was concentrated at the southern Colney Street side of the airfield, and the first H.P.80 started coming into shape during the winter of 1951.

It was during this construction that the myriad of difficulties associated with a complex piece of engineering seemed to come to light on too regular a basis. In particular, the testing of the fuel system operating through twenty-nine individual internal tanks occupied an inordinate amount of time, while powered controls on an aircraft of this size were new territory for everyone. But all were mastered and by the spring of 1952, WB771 was nearing completion. Then the inevitable ministerial intervention took place and a whole new raft of problems had to be overcome. The MoS decreed that Radlett was too small for a maiden flight of such an important prototype.

The Ministry ordered Handley Page to make the H.P.80's first flight from Boscombe Down's 10,000ft runway. It was only 90 miles from Radlett! The aircraft had to be dismantled for transportation by road and a suitable route had to be reconnoitred. In several locations, alterations had to be made to road layouts, with at least two involving quite extensive reconstruction. The fuselage was to be carried on a reinforced bus axle unit, converted into a trailer that would be towed by an articulator tractor, making the assembly 96ft long. For the journey, the fuselage was camouflaged by additional wooden structures, and when wrapped in white sheeting it resembled an upturned boat hull. This encouraged 'Southampton' to be sign-written on the sides as a fictitious destination, above which an anagram of 'Handley Page' was written as the name of the boat. For some reason, the signwriter omitted an 'a' and added an extra 'y', so that the resultant name GELEYPANDHY had a Welsh appearance. Was he from the principality or did he just have an 'off day'? I doubt we shall ever know.

Eight surveys were made to determine the final route and, on the evening of 24 May 1952, the convoy started its journey from Radlett. Following an overnight stop outside London, everyone made an early start and by midday of 25 May, the disguised H.P.80 was safely ensconced at the A&AEE. The journey had not been entirely without problems, one of them including navigation around an abandoned bulldozer that was supposed to make the route easier. (The best-laid plans, etc., etc!)

Handley Page had detailed a sixty-strong team to Boscombe Down, under the leadership of works foreman William MacRostie, to reassemble the prototype, and everyone still considered that an appearance at the SBAC Display remained a good bet. That was until the airframe was once more in one piece and it was found that the centre of gravity was well beyond the aft limit, as the H_2S radar assembly was not installed in the nose, although this was only a contributory factor. Furthermore, as WB771 was basically only to be an aerodynamic trials airframe, the radar would not be forthcoming. The problem was addressed by bolting about half a ton of scrap iron plates to the underside of the flight deck flooring. The eventual remedy on production aircraft was to lengthen the fuselage by 42in (107cm); however, as the second prototype, WB775, was too far advanced for such a major alteration, it also went into the scrap iron business.

Once again, things looked set fair for Farnborough but, while tests were being conducted on the high-pressure hydraulics in the rear fuselage during July, a fire started and three fitters were covered with burning hydraulic fluid. They were rushed to hospital, but sixteen days later one of the trio, Eddie Eyles, died. It took great fortitude on the part of the team to carry on with the same degree of enthusiasm. When resonance checks on the elevators were made, the whole powered flying controls system went into convulsions and everyone acknowledged that they were fated not to make it. It took six weeks to rectify the control system problem and by then, not only had Farnborough started, but Avro had got their Type 698 airborne in time to be there.

The H.P.80 test air-frame was visited by, from left to right, Sqn Ldr Hedley Hazelden DFC, Chief Test Pilot; Sir Frederick Handley Page; AVM Pike, RAF; Charles Joy, Assistant Chief Designer; Reginald Stafford, Technical Director; unknown; William MacRostie, Chief Engineer and Mr Collard, Sales Manager.
Handley Page Association

Hedley Hazelden, Handley Page's Chief Test Pilot at the start of the Victor flight test programme. Handley Page Association

In mid-December, Handley Page's CTP, Sqd Ldr Hazelden DFC and Bar, arrived at Boscombe Down. Hedley George Hazelden ('Hazel') had been a member of No.1 Test Pilot's course at The Test Pilot's School, based at Boscombe Down, in June 1943. The following year the school was renamed The Empire Test Pilot's School. In the early days of World War II, Hazel had flown Hampdens with No.44 Squadron, as well as Manchesters and Lancasters with No.83 Squadron, before being posted, after two operational tours, as senior instructor on Wellingtons with No.11 Operational Training Unit at Westcott. From the OTU he became a student at the Boscombe Down-based school and, after completing the first course, became Commanding Officer of 'B' Flight at the A&AEE prior to joining Handley Page.

On 14 June 1949, the second prototype Hastings, TE583, having completed a temperate climate programme at the Airborne Forces Experimental Establishment at Beaulieu in Hampshire, returned to the Park Street works at Radlett. There the aircraft's two outboard Bristol Hercules 101 radial engines were replaced by a pair of early ASSa.2 Sapphires. The con-

version took nearly eighteen months to complete and it was 13 November 1950 before TE583 flew with its new engines. Not only was the aircraft to act as a Sapphire flying test-bed, but it gave Hazel experience in handling the turbojet engines. This experience was furthered by Canberra B.2 WD933, which had been flying with Sapphires since 14 August 1951, after being re-engined at Bitteswell, and Hazelden was able to get a better feeling for the Armstrong Siddeley engines at higher altitudes. Incidentally, in January 1953, TE583 had an H.P.80 crew door mock-up installed, to assist in the emergency evacuation routine for the three crewmen not equipped with ejector seats.

The week before Christmas, Hazel experienced his first taxiing of WB771, taking it from its hangar to the compass-swinging base; two days later, he commenced fast runs on Boscombe Down's main runway, but heavy rain restricted visibility so no thoughts were given to actually lifting off.

First Flight

On 24 December 1952, while children everywhere were composing their optimistic lists for Father Christmas, the weather at Boscombe Down changed to a crisp, clear winter's day. Godfrey Lee and Charles Joy were at Cricklewood, but the weather prospects galvanized them into scrambling aboard Joy's car, to make a

speedy journey to Hampshire. Both were fearful that they would not arrive in time to witness the flight, but traffic was a little lighter in 1952 than it is today and they booked in at Flying Control in time to see their creation ready to move out from the flight apron. Hazel was accompanied in the cockpit by flight test observer Ian K. Bennett as the checklist was completed and engines started. All the waiting and frustrations were over as WB771 was taxied out to the runway. The CTP locked his radio on to transmit for everyone on the ground to share the occasion and turned on the threshold to face down the vast tarmac expanse that had witnessed so many other maiden flights.

With a fairly low power setting, the H.P.80 started rolling and as speed built up, the nose-wheel lifted off the ground, to be shortly followed by the rest of the aircraft. WB771 weighed in at approximately 95,000lb for its first flight and lifted off in less than 1,500ft, which was about a quarter of the length of Radlett's runway, but no doubt it was better safe than sorry. The flight included a couple of circuits of the A&AEE's large acreage, before Hazel turned the prototype in for a long straight approach and, seventeen minutes after lift-off, WB771 touched down to complete what the CTP described as 'a comfortable flight with no anxieties . . . it is difficult to see why we were so apprehensive.' It was a good Christmas present for the whole company.

The extension of Radlett's runway had taken it over a public footpath on the

TE583, the second prototype Hastings, with ASSa.2 Sapphires in the outer nacelle positions.
Handley Page Association

Cockpit inspection by an American delegation in September 1953. Author's collection

airfield. Then, on 25 February, the Victor and its hard-working detail took leave of Boscombe Down and Hazel brought it down on Radlett's newly extended 6,900ft runway for the first time. The Park Street complex was its new home, from where a concentrated programme of testing was successfully conducted, with the only untoward event occurring in April, when the port bogie skipped on touch-down, jamming in the trail position. Hazel gingerly completed the landing on the four rear port tyres, after which the bogies were fitted with rotation dampers and a temporary ventral camera was rigged up to record the actions of the main wheels on landing. During this time of grounding, WB771 had small Perspex ram deflectors installed on the windscreen, to improve visibility during take-off in the rain.

north side of the airfield, which local by-laws proclaimed must be open for at least 12 hours every year, so Handley Page agreed for it to be available between 18.00hrs on 24 December to 06.00hr on 25 December. It did not get much usage and undoubtedly such a cavalier attitude would receive a very different reaction today. One can well imagine the runway threshold being occupied by a vociferous army of woolly-hatted environmentalists.

Returning Home

Early in February 1953, Hazelden flew WB771 cross-country to Radlett and, without landing, performed a robust demonstration to the workforce that had built it, before returning to the A&AEE's

On Display

In the 1950s, the Royal Aeronautical Society held an annual Garden Party in June at various venues, where cucumber sandwiches and Earl Grey tea were shared with exuberant flying displays by members in their personal aircraft. The 1953 gathering had a brief glimpse of WB771 in the distance, during a test flight. However, the following month, on 15 July, the Queen's

H.P.80 Gets a Name

On 2 January 1953, the H.P.80 was named the Victor, in keeping with the V-bomber naming procedure and so far as Handley Page was concerned this was a fortuitous choice, for it was the second forename of Gustav Lachmann.

Test-flying and handling trials were commenced at Boscombe Down after the Christmas break. On flight number four, several tests were conducted with the undercarriage extended and retracted, in order to record comparative buffeting in the two conditions, after which, on landing, all sixteen of the main-wheel tyres burst. The cause was traced to a malfunction of the system controlling interaction between the parking brake and its use to arrest wheel spin on retraction, so the system was modified to prevent any recurrence.

The paucity of instrumentation in a prototype Victor differs greatly from service aircraft. Handley Page Association

Specifications – Victor

Dimensions:	Prototypes: span 110ft 0in (3.5m); length 98ft 2in (30m); wing area 2,406sq ft (223.5sq m).
	B.1: span 110ft 0in (33.5m); length 114ft 11in (35m); wing area 2,406sq ft (223.5sq m).
	B.2: span 120ft 0in (36.5m); length 114ft 11in (35m); wing area 2,597sq ft (214.2sq m).
Powerplants:	Prototypes: four Armstrong Siddeley Sapphire ASSa.6 turbojets each producing 7,500lb (3,400kg) static thrust.
	B.1: four Armstrong Siddeley Sapphire ASSa.7 turbojets each producing 10,500lb (4,750kg) static thrust or four Armstrong Siddeley Sapphire ASSa.9 turbojets each producing 11,050lb (5,000kg) static thrust.
	B.2: four Rolls-Royce Conway RCo.11 turbojets each producing 17,250lb (7,800kg) static thrust or four Rolls-Royce Conway RCo.17 turbojets each producing 20,600lb (9,350kg) static thrust.
Weights:	Prototypes: from 86,500lb (39,000kg) empty to 104,000lb (47,000kg) maximum loaded.
	B.1 and B.2: from 114,240lb (51,800kg) empty to 223,000lb (101,000kg) maximum loaded.
Performance:	Prototypes: maximum speed 594mph (956km/h) at 36,000ft (11,000m); maximum range 6,000 miles (9,700km).
	B.1: maximum speed 627mph (1,000km/h) at 36,000ft (11,000m); service ceiling 55,000ft (17,000m) ; maximum range 6,000 miles (9,700km).
	B.2: maximum speed 647mph (1,041km/h) at 36,000ft (11,000m); service ceiling 60,000ft (18,000m); maximum range 6,000 miles (9,700km).
Armament:	Thirty-five 1,000lb iron bombs or one 10,000lb Yellow Sun nuclear weapon or one 22,000lb Grand Slam-type bomb or two 12,000lb Tallboy-type bombs or (B.2 only) one Blue Steel stand-off weapon.

WB771, in Sir Frederick's personally conceived colour scheme, en route to the 1953 SBAC Display. Author's collection

WB771 lined up on Farnborough's main runway, prior to filling its flying display slot in September 1953. Author's collection

'Hazel' brings WB771 in to land after its SBAC display, with everything down and airbrakes out.

Author's collection

Coronation Review was held at Odiham in Hampshire, when the enormous formations in the fly-past included the Victor prototype, together with the two other V-bombers, plus just about every other aircraft in the RAF that was not parked on the ground in immaculately drawn-up rows – and there were several hundred of them.

The new Park Street Test House and transonic wind tunnel were officially opened on 21 July, and temporary seating was installed between the two pilots so that Air Chief Marshal Sir John Baker, Chief of the Air Staff, could sample flying in the Victor. His ebullient reaction to the aircraft's manoeuvrability was tempered by his surprise at the limited visibility available to the pilots. Further flights were made during the summer with dignitaries of various social standing, including Lord de l'Isle and Dudley VC, the Air Minister; his Under Secretary of State, the Hon. George Ward, M.P.; and BOAC's Whitney Straight. The aircraft then went into the paint shop to receive a special colour scheme that had been conceived by Sir Frederick for its debut at the 1953 SBAC Display at Farnborough, starting on 5 September. It consisted of a matt black fuselage, broken by a thin red cheat line and all other surfaces painted in silver-grey. The world's aviation press and invited guests were suitably impressed by the aircraft's appearance and performance, the latter meriting greater acclaim had it been known that WB771's display was made on three engines, as one igniter plug failed just prior to take-off.

Into Production

Production Specification B.128P had been raised in June 1952 and Handley Page received Contract No.6/ACFT/8441/CB6(a) dated the same month, for twenty-five Victor B.1s, with serials XA917 to XA941, at an agreed price of £450,000 each, excluding items from outside manufacturers. The first production aircraft was scheduled to fly in March 1955. In order to meet this target, the company requested monetary assistance for the expansion of floor space at the Colney Street end of Radlett and to be placed on the super-priority list for raw materials. They had already received a contract for the building of 150 Canberra B.2s under licence from English Elec-

XA917 and XA919 are shown in the publicity line-up of the first five production Victor B.1s at Radlett.
Author's collection

tric and the production order for Victors placed them in a position where something would have to go. They therefore asked for a reduction in the Canberra order, which was acceded to and only seventy-five Canberras came out of Radlett. A design conference on 22 August discussed the Victor being used in a photo-reconnaissance role, for which the structure would be strengthened, and updated variants of the Sapphire, or Rolls-Royce Conway, would be installed. Internal fuel capacity would remain at 4,840 gallons (22,000 litres) and underwing tanks would provide additional fuel. Talk of a remote-control, radar-sighted tail-defence armament was dismissed, although production aircraft were to have the rear fuselage strengthened, just in case the proposal was resurrected. Actually, this structural strengthening did have its rewards when later variants had electronic countermeasures installed. The photo-reconnaissance conversion kit proposal, with ten cameras and the ability to fit within the bomb-bay, was carried forward. It will feature later in this book.

Flight Trials Continue

On 15 October 1953, Hazel took WB771 up to 50,000ft (15,240m) for the first time

and a day later he reached Mach 0.83 in level flight at 47,000ft (14,325m), without any buffeting. Gradually speed was increased, with Mach 0.88 being achieved on 3 November and Mach 0.91 at 47,000ft, later in the same month. The only irritation was a noise encountered at Mach 0.75 above 35,000ft (10,670m). Finding the source proved difficult, but when it was eventually traced to the air-conditioning ducting under the crew compartment flooring, curing it took even longer. A flush NACA-type intake was situated on either side of the visual bomb-aiming glazing in the nose and changes to their dimensions were tried, as well as replacing them with raised intakes, but this only altered the pitch of the noise. The fitting of small vortex generators ahead of the NACA intakes proved to be the answer. On the last day of 1953, WB771 lost its port inner flap, due to excessive engine vibration, although such was the stability of the aircraft that Hazelden and the rest of the crew were totally unaware of the mishap until they had landed.

Hazel's assistant K. Dalton-Golding had become more involved in the Victor trials, together with Johnny Allam, who used to race Vauxhall saloon cars, and together the pilots increased the flight envelope, with Mach 0.925 being attained at

The second prototype, WB775, was also finished in Sir Frederick's chosen colour scheme when rolled out, with a larger than usual serial. *Aeroplane*

45,000ft (13,700m) in February 1954, without any compressibility problems. Sadly, Dalton-Golding was killed on 25 February during a pre-delivery test flight of the Radlett-built Canberra B.2 WJ622. The aircraft's controls jammed and it crashed into the GWR embankment adjacent to the company's airfield. His place on the Victor team was taken by Ronald Ecclestone, a former RAE test pilot.

Tail Troubles and Tragedy

Having amassed over 60 hours of flying time by the end of February, WB771 was due for an overhaul inspection and the installation of new operational equipment that would bring it more in line with forthcoming production aircraft, as it had ceased to be just the aerodynamic test vehicle that it was during its early flights. Modifications were also to be incorporated, including revision of the throttle controls, plus an increase to the aileron rate, so that it could increase its flight test range and performance. Shortly before it was scheduled to be grounded, Johnny Allam unintentionally flew at Mach 0.98, which put a strain on the tailplane, buckling the skin to a point where it could not easily be rectified. WB771 went into the shops and, as the second prototype, WB775, was nearing completion, with all

its assemblies complete, the tailplane due for this aircraft was installed on the first prototype, in order to get it airborne again as soon as possible. Its damaged unit was stripped and rebuilt, before being installed on WB775.

By the end of May 1954, WB771 was back in the air and on 14 June Hazel flew it for over an hour at its heaviest weight

to date, just under 100,000lb (45,350kg). Another 24 hours of flying had been logged by 14 July 1954, when Hazel had a Handley Page (Reading) Marathon sales demonstration to perform at Woodley, which could not be undertaken by any other pilot. This could interrupt a series of airspeed calibration flights being flown at the College of Aeronautics, Cranfield, Bedfordshire, where more sophisticated ground speed measuring equipment was available than Handley Page had at Radlett.

Hazel delegated the Cranfield flying for 14 July to Ronald Ecclestone, who had Ian Bennett (the test observer on WB771's maiden flight), Albert Cook and Bruce Heithersay as his crew for the day. The tests required several accurate low-level flight paths to be maintained, past a camera sited on top of a hangar. Observers measured the aircraft's height above the camera position in order to calibrate the barometric pressure differential between the aircraft and the camera site. Having these observers present enabled a precise chronology of the events that occurred to be recorded. Ecclestone, increased the aircraft's speed with each succeeding fly-past. Suddenly, the tailplane was seen to become detached from the top of the fin and flutter down to earth. The rest of WB771 continued forward, with a continuous nose-down attitude, until it hit the runway with such velocity that it dis-

WB775's fin shows the one-piece skin, supplied courtesy of Vickers-Armstrongs. Author's collection integrated into thousands of little pieces, enshrouded in a cloud of black smoke. The crew stood no chance of survival and all four perished in the disaster. The staff of the New Design section collaborated with all at the Park Street Test House, in a concentrated analysis of all the possibilities, and by 3 August Sir Frederick was informed that tail flutter had induced fatigue cracks around the three bolt holes in the fin, which in turn had allowed the bolts to shear in rapid succession. He was also apprised of the fact that having four bolts at the attachment point, in place of the three on WB771, would reduce the stress concentration in that area, which, in conjunction with a corrugated sandwich construction for the fins of production aircraft, would increase torsional stiffness. Assessing the right amount of stiffness in the fin had to be conducted on a trial-and-error basis. Later, Handley Page test pilot Jock Still, flying in WB775 with a crew of experienced flight observers, performed the difficult task of gradually building up performance to within 25mph of the critical flutter speed, with great courage and competence, in order to confirm wind-tunnel data findings.

The Second Prototype Flies

Like Vickers-Armstrongs two years earlier, Handley Page had lost its first prototype before the second had finished being constructed. Whereas at Weybridge it was three months before the second Valiant got airborne, at Park Street the assembly of WB775 was further advanced and on the morning of 11 September 1954, its maiden flight of 57 minutes was made from Radlett's extended runway, even though the main undercarriage doors had yet to be fitted. But Farnborough was again the catalyst and the aircraft qualified for a flying-past appearance in the afternoon, which was the penultimate day of that year's event. It, too, was bedecked in Sir Frederick's colour scheme that had been applied to WB771 a year earlier.

Being the only Victor now flying, all further evaluation had to be made with WB775 and the question of flutter characteristics was high on the agenda. The decision to construct production fins with the corrugated sandwich was assessed as being correct, but the fin's height did not help and the conclusion was reached that

For the 1955 SBAC Display, WB775 was repainted in overall glossy cerulean blue.
Author's collection

a reduction of 15in should be made. Giving the tailplane dihedral was its Achilles' heel and the strength of the attachment point to the fin had been miscalculated in the early days by not making allowance for the dihedral. However, the structural stiffening incorporated in the second prototype, together with the sandwich construction and this proposed reduction in the fin's height, provided a rigidity that lasted the Victor throughout its career. On production Victor B.1s, the dorsal fillet from the fin was deleted and a small ram air inlet at the base of the fin leading edge fed cold air to the pump, providing anti-icing for the tail assembly.

WB775's fin could not be modified to production standard, so it was decided to fit a new one-piece skin on either side of the unit and, as these were larger than any sheets held at Park Street, Vickers-Armstrongs supplied them from their Valiant production stock. The second prototype was grounded just before Christmas 1954 for these tail alterations and it resumed flight trials on 1 February 1955, when the bomb doors were opened in flight for the first time. The resultant buffeting was within the calculated limits, but when the flash-bomb compartment doors, further aft, were first opened on 2 March, these limits were exceeded by a consider-

WB775 lands at the 1955 Farnborough show, as Valiant B.1 WZ365 follows the flight line. Author's collection

able margin. It was fortuitous that the Air Staff had already decided to cancel the flash-bomb requirement on the V-bombers and the compartment's doors were deleted from production aircraft. On WB775, the doors were permanently locked and sealed.

First Trials by the A&AEE

The prototype had completed the majority of its manufacturer's trials by 14 March, when it was flown to the A&AEE at Boscombe Down for preliminary assessment by the Establishment's pilots, three of them putting in 8 hours of flying with the aircraft in the first week. The report on night flying gave the aircraft a satisfactory rating, and when it went to the Orfordness bombing range for evaluation in June, it was rated as a good bomber aircraft with auto-stabilization; without this facility, it was rather tiring on long flights.

The Establishment considered that WB775 was easy to fly and twice it reached Mach 0.95. All controls were found to be pleasant, with the airbrakes considered as very effective at all altitudes and speeds, which, together with the low level of buffeting they produced when the bomb doors were open, singled the units out as being very good. It was thought that the aircraft would be even better with more powerful engines, although it was not rated as underpowered with its existing Sapphires. It was considered possible that a Victor powered by four Olympus engines would be a better aircraft than the Vulcan fitted with the same engines.

The original installation of three or four braking parachutes had not been an overall success, as they had been prone to failure on far too many occasions. Therefore, a single G.Q. ring-slot parachute, with a 32ft diameter was chosen as a replacement. The aircraft also had vortex generators fitted to the top surface of the outer-wing section, to create the rotating vortices that were required to assist the boundary layer.

1955 was a year of demonstrations for the Victor. In July WB775 appeared at the RAE's Golden Jubilee Open Day, and later in the same month it made its first visit to the Paris Air Show, which in those days was an annual event like Farnborough. Then on 5 September, it was time for Farnborough itself and WB775 flew to the SBAC Display once again, having logged 120 hours of flying time and resplendent in an overall cerulean blue gloss finish. Good as its flying was, however, Avro's Roly Falk stole the honours by rolling XA890, a production Vulcan B.1, in the climb from take-off.

The second prototype Victor continued development trials, but its use was becoming limited. Talks were already well in hand for installing new engines in later production Victors, increasing the wingspan, installing the capability for carrying 'stand-off' weapons and generally upgrading the abilities of an airframe which, in the words of the RAE as well as the A&AEE, 'obviously had great potential'. WB775 gave good service until the late 1950s, when it was grounded and finally dismantled before going to the Proof and Experimental Establishment at Foulness in 1961. At Radlett, the first production Victor B.1, XA917, made a maiden flight on 1 February 1956 that lasted 15 minutes, in the hands of Johnny Allam. Handley Page had received a follow-up order in May 1955 for thirty-three more B.1s, which was later amended to twenty-five, with the remaining eight being the first of the B.2s. The Victor had proved itself and would serve alongside, rather than be evaluated against, Avro's delta. Sir Frederick was a happy man.

CHAPTER EIGHT

Debut of the B.1s
in Service

When Valiant B.1 WP199 made its maiden flight on 21 December 1953 in the hands of Jock Bryce and Brian Trubshaw, it established several firsts. It was the first production Valiant, given the Vickers-Armstrongs designation Type 674, and was the first of the type to be assembled at the company's Weybridge plant, the three prototypes having been constructed at Fox Warren and Wisley. It was also the first Valiant to fly out from Weybridge. With a single runway measuring only 3,600ft, set within the old Brooklands motor racing circuit, it was a far cry from the substantial tarmac track at Woodford or the extended facility at Radlett, but they were fully operational airfields from where test-flying could be undertaken, whereas Brooklands, in those days, was a means of getting aeroplanes from their site of construction to the test-flying airfield at Wisley.

At one end of the runway, an embankment carried the former Southern Railway track to Bournemouth and at the other, part of the motor-racing track banking had to be removed as a safety factor. Engine running and system checks had been carried out over the previous days, before WP199 was towed from the tarmac outside the production buildings, carrying only a light fuel load, along the roadway that crossed the River Wey, to the runway, where engines were started before it taxied under the power of its four Avon RA.14s. Turning at the end of the runway, with its tail tucked under the shadow of the railway embankment, it accelerated down the tarmac strip under the impetus of 36,000lb (16,330kg) thrust to clear the gap in the track banking and, with its undercarriage still down, turned on a heading for Wisley, where it landed a few minutes later. This procedure was to be followed by another 103 Valiants over the next three and three-quarter years, with few variations.

Like WP199, the next four production aircraft were also Type 674s, with the serials WP200 to WP204, and all five, powered by Rolls-Royce Avon RA.14s, were used for type testing with Vickers-Armstrongs, the A&AEE and RAE Farnborough. Although referred to as production aircraft, it would be more accurate to describe them as pre-production, as all five were practically hand-built. They were fitted out with operational radar and Type Clearance was given by Boscombe Down. The only incident of real import encountered during the whole programme was when test pilot Bill Aston was making high-Mach number dives in WP199 and the aileron rods fractured due to aileron vibration. Aston displayed great airmanship in getting the aircraft safely back to Boscombe Down without any aileron control. The modification of fitting steel rods was subsequently incorporated in the Valiant production line.

While I was with Vickers-Armstrongs, there was a bit of excitement that had several of us from Technical Publications hurrying over to Wisley. The taxiway from the runway to the apron outside the hangars was on a slight decline. One of the test pilots, Colin Allen, was taxiing down to the apron when he had a complete brake failure and his descent had a lot more velocity than he would have wished, considering there were several aircraft parked on the apron. The company's Guided Weapons Division was using a couple of B-29 Washingtons at the time and both received alterations to their profiles as the Valiant rolled round the outside of the apron, before terminating its journey in the rear end of another pre-production aircraft. It was quite a sight to behold.

Valiant production averaged about three aircraft a month for the whole of its run, with an aircraft a week being flown out from Brooklands during one period in 1954. Not one aircraft was ever late in delivery against any order, which was a great source of pride to GRE, as well as to all of us engaged on the project in some way or other. The first true production aircraft for allocation to the RAF was B.1 WP204, which was categorized as a Type 706 by the company, as were twenty-nine further B.1s. The second, WP205, was the first of the day- or night-time bomber/photographic reconnaissance variant, the Type 710 Valiant B(PR).1, of which a total of eleven were built, their serials being WP205, WP217, WP219, WP221, WP223, WZ377 to WZ379, WZ381, WZ383 and WZ384. Five were included in the first order and Vickers-Armstrongs received their second order, for twenty-four aircraft, with Contract No.6/Air/7375/CB6(c), which included six Type 710s. The PR role will come up again later in this chapter, when the production of inflight-refuelling tankers and receivers is covered.

The dual high-altitude, long-range bomber/photo-recce role for the Valiant had been planned almost from the beginning. A purpose-built carrier, which could carry up to four F49 and eight F96 cameras, was designed for installation within the bomb-bay. The conversion could be accomplished in a short time under operational conditions and sliding panels within the bomb doors cleared glazed windows for ten cameras, while there were two more cameras mounted obliquely in the rear fuselage. In its PR role, the Valiant had the ability to give full horizon-to-horizon coverage throughout its altitude range. One year at Farnborough, I remember seeing a giant enlargement of a photograph taken by a Valiant from over 40,000ft (12,200m), showing a section of London containing people rowing boats on the Serpentine in Hyde Park, where the individual oars were clearly visible.

With the Valiant being the RAF's first

Production Mark 1s all. The thirteenth Valiant, WZ373, formates with the fourth Vulcan, XA892, and the third Victor, XA919. Handley Page Association

four-turbojet bomber, there was no rule book or procedure to follow and operating techniques had to be worked out 'on the job'. To this end, No.138 Squadron, a Lincoln B.2 operator until disbanding at Wyton on 1 September 1950, was reformed on 1 January 1955. This reformation was made at Gaydon, which in July was officially designated No.232 Operational Conversion Unit (OCU) and was the base tasked to form the Service's first V-bomber crews.

No.232 Operational Conversion Unit

The OCU was a constituent of No.3 Group, Bomber Command, under the leadership of Gp Capt B.P. Young, while No.138 Squadron was commanded by Wg Cdr Rupert G.W. Oakley, who was well versed in all matters concerning the Valiant, having been Bomber Command's liaison officer with Vickers-Armstrongs for the previous three years. These included

all stages of the aircraft's manufacturers' and A&AEE acceptance trials, and he had flown, as a Sqn Ldr in the co-pilot's seat, alongside Brian Trubshaw, for a large number of WB215's flying hours.

An entirely new approach was made when it came to selecting Valiant crews, which followed through to both the Vulcan and Victor. Gone were the days of the Canberra's introduction into service, when students got their wings and then progressed to No.231 OCU, which had

Valiants were built on a twin production line at Weybridge. Author's collection

Valiant B(PR).1s WP221 and WP223, in formation with WZ382, the second B(PR)K.1. Author's collection

been formed on 1 December 1951 at Bassingbourne in Cambridgeshire with an assortment of Mosquito T.3s, Meteor T.7s and, two months later, Canberra B.2s. V-bombers were expensive aeroplanes and their role of strategic bombing with nuclear weapons carried a responsibility which Bomber Command considered could only be borne by experienced officers.

Consequently, aircraft captains were selected from officers who were 'above average' in assessments, had a minimum of 1,750 hours as captains and had at least one complete tour on Canberras, plus, if possible, experience on four-piston-engined aircraft, such as the Lancastrian, Lincoln or Hastings. Second pilots had to have flown at least 700 hours as captains and completed a Canberra tour, while rear

crew-members had to be recommended by their Commanding Officers, with navigator/bomb-aimers selected from those who had passed the course at the Commands' training school at Lindholme in Yorkshire. Signallers were recommended from those who had flown at least one tour with Bomber, Coastal or Transport Command. Selected aircrews were to be posted to a V-bomber squadron for a five-year period, compared with the usual two-and-a half to three years currently being operated in the Service. New flying clothing had to be designed, as was a new range of ancillary ground equipment and vehicles. Aircrews were to have specially prepared pre-sortie meals and, what must sound like Utopia to a World War II fitter/airframes, or engines, V-bombers would be maintained in heated hangars. Ground crews would be formed in groups, to handle one particular aircraft throughout its life and each group would have a Chief Technician in charge. A Valiant servicing school at Gaydon was staffed by instructors who had been on extensive courses at Vickers-Armstrongs servicing school at Weybridge, plus similar establishments at Boulton Paul for systems and Rolls-Royce for engines. Thus were the parameters formed for a V-bomber squadron and No.138 Squadron's part in this formulation cannot be overemphasized, for they

WP209, the fifth production Valiant B.1, shows there was no change compared with WP215, the second prototype, apart from the dielectric nose cover.
Author's collection

82

From Wellingtons to Rovers

In the early days of World War II, airfields sprung up like mushrooms in the Midlands and when I lived in Banbury, Oxfordshire, no fewer than twenty-four were within reasonable cycling distance. One of them was Gaydon, in Warwickshire, which, like so many more, was built by John Laing & Son Ltd, and when I first visited it, I was surprised to find that the A41 Banbury to Warwick road intercepted a taxiway from a 'T2', outside which a solitary Oxford was parked.

Gaydon was finished in the spring of 1942, with the standard three-runway pattern, and on 13 June it officially became a satellite for No.12 OTU, based nine miles away at Chipping Warden, just over the Northamptonshire border. The Unit was operating with a mixture of Wellington Ics, plus a few of the new IIIs, but by the end of August Gaydon's satellite status was transferred to Edgehill, so that on 1 September the base came under the jurisdiction of No.22 OTU, No.91 Group, which had been at Wellesbourne Mountford in Warwickshire since 14 April 1941. Two Flights of Wellington Ics moved to Gaydon in September while Wellesbourne's runways were being repaired and later in the same month, the base operated its first bombing raids.

Leaflet dropping sorties over enemy-occupied Europe, codenamed Operation *Nickel*, were flown on many occasions during 1943, as well as various bombing missions, and in September feint raids were carried out against Pas de Calais targets, under Operation *Starkey*. The base operated Air Sea Rescue sorties over the North Sea in daylight on numerous occasions and, with the concentrated bombing campaign being waged against Germany in 1944, it was inevitable that diversions had to be made due to weather conditions at home bases or operational damage to aircraft, to which ends Gaydon was often brought into use.

On 1 July 1945, No.22 OTU was disbanded and twenty-four days later Gaydon became an element of No.23 Group Flying Training Command. No.3 Glider Training School arrived from Exeter with a miscellany of Hotspur gliders, plus Miles Master II glider tugs. This was followed by the transfer of the Glider Instructor's Flight from Croughton in Oxfordshire, but on 15 August 1946 Gaydon was closed as a glider base. On 28 August it was placed on Care and Maintenance, but did become No.21 (Pilot) Advanced Flying Unit's satellite a year later without actually being used for flying.

By 1952, it had been decided to make Gaydon an OCU for the forthcoming V-bomber force, and so rebuilding, to bring it up to the necessary requirements, was put in hand in 1953. One runway was extended to 3,200yds and dedicated electronics buildings were constructed, together with new hangars. 1 January 1955 saw No.138 Squadron re-formed to operate with Valiants and within six months, when it was declared operational, the squadron moved to Wittering in Northamptonshire. No.543 Squadron was reformed at Gaydon on 1 April 1955, to become the second V-bomber squadron, which moved to Wyton on 18 November, when it too was declared fully operational with its Valiant B(PR).1s. The base was given the designation No.232 OCU in July 1955 with its own aircraft, a few Valiants for ground handling and maintenance courses, while some Canberra T4s were employed for runway approach and training.

On 11 November 1957, the first Victors arrived and, although no squadrons were formed there, all Victor crews received their training at Gaydon, simultaneously with later Valiant crews. This routine continued, with a secondary segment of No.232 OCU operating at Wittering on Victor 2s until June 1965, when the last Victor course passed out and the OCU was disbanded. Three months later, on 1 September, No.2 Air Navigation School arrived with its Vickers Varsity T.1s and Gaydon was host to the School until May 1970, when it departed to Finningley in Yorkshire and that was virtually the end of regular flying at the Warwickshire base.

The headquarters of the Central Flying School took over command of Gaydon on 10 June 1970 and the Strike Command Special Avionics Servicing Unit of No.1 Group was stationed there until being disbanded on 1 December 1971. No.71 Maintenance Unit at Bicester in Oxfordshire became the controller of Gaydon on 1 April 1972 and once again it was on Care and Maintenance. It stayed in that state until finally being closed on 31 October 1974, whereupon the site was bought by the British Leyland car conglomerate. Ownership changed again in 1994, when the Rover division of BMW took over, but since BMW's sell-off of Rover many hundreds of technical engineering staff working in the purpose-built research facilities at Gaydon are as unsure about their personal prospects as is the future of the former airbase.

---

started at Gaydon six months before it was officially an OCU.

First Valiant Squadrons

Following the move on 6 July 1955 to Wittering, where the RAF already held a stockpile of nuclear weapons, the squadron started proving trials with the six aircraft, WP206, WP207, WP211, WP212, WP213 and WP215, that it had brought from Gaydon and two more arrived later to bring the unit up to full complement. On the last day of July, a trials Valiant B.1, WP209, flew from the RAE at Farn-

borough, to the Weapons Research Establishment range at Woomera in South Australia, establishing en route two official records: London to Baghdad at 523.5mph (842.3km/h); and Singapore to Darwin at 518.4mph (834.1km/h). The aircraft remained at Woomera throughout the rest of 1955 engaged on weapons trials, during which it dropped a variety of dummy bombs of various shapes and sizes.

In September, a mixed Vickers-Armstrongs and MoS crew flew to Tripoli for preliminary tropical trials, while No.138 Squadron joined with the second V-bomber unit, No.543 Squadron, to put up a twelve-Valiant formation to fly over

the 1955 SBAC Display at Farnborough. On 5 September, No.138 Squadron sent two of its aircraft, under the command of Sqn Ldr R.G. Wilson, on a proving flight to Singapore under the codename Operation *Too Right*, staging through Habbaniya, Karachi and Negombo, before arriving at Changi on the eastern tip of Singapore Island. The two Valiants then went on to Australia and New Zealand on a goodwill visit.

As mentioned earlier, No.543 Squadron, a Spitfire PR.XI operator when disbanded at Benson on 18 October 1943, was the second Valiant unit to be formed and it picked up the photographic-recon-

No.232 OCU receives its first Valiants and draws them up for a photocall on 19 March 1956. From front to rear, the aircraft are B.1s WZ364, WZ372, WZ377, WP216, WZ365, WZ374, WZ362 and WZ361. It can be seen that WZ364 and WZ365 have blunter tail-cones than the rest. Author's collection

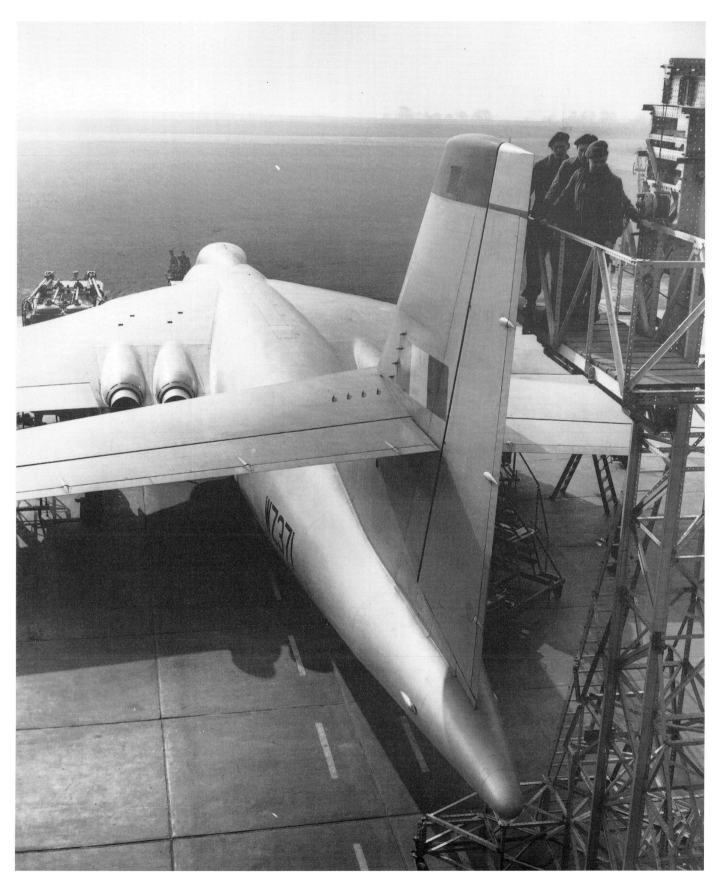

Ground crews at Gaydon got their Meccano sets out to service the Valiant's tail assembly! Author's collection

Valiant B.1 WP209 at RAE Farnborough, before flying to Woomera for weapons trials. Author's collection

WP209's crew for the Woomera flight was made up of RAF officers attached to RAE Farnborough. From left to right: Wg Cdr J. Finch, captain; Sqn Ldr J. Tanner, co-pilot; Flt Lt A. Sacks, navigator; Flt Lt D. Dish, navigator; Flt Lt C. la Belle MBE, signals, plus Mr B. Maries who accompanied them as a technical engineer. Author's collection

naissance traces again by being equipped with Valiant B(PR).1s. WP205, the first of the PR variants, arrived at Gaydon at the end of May 1955 to be attached to No.138 Squadron, although No.543 Squadron had been administratively reformed on 1 April. By early winter, the bomber/reconnaissance squadron had four operationally cleared B(PR).1s and left Gaydon on 18 November for its permanent home at Wittering, where it remained until being disbanded on 24 May 1974, by which time it was flying Victors.

First Production Vulcans

Avro's Contract No.6/ACFT/8442/CB6.(a) for twenty-five Vulcan B.1s, with serials XA889 to XA913, arrived in June 1952, which was a year before the wing high-frequency buzzing problem arose on the Avro 707A WD280. Therefore several production aircraft had been completed before the phenomenon had been finally cured and full-size Phase 2 wings had been built for introduction to the assembly lines.

The first production aircraft, XA889, came out from Woodford during January 1955 and had its maiden flight on 4 February. This was the first Vulcan to be finished in the overall silver finish, with black dielectric radar housing in the lower nose section and powered by four 11,000lb (4,990kg) static thrust Bristol Olympus 101 turbojets. Almost immediately, the aircraft was engaged in an extensive manufacturer's trials and, as Avro had received its second order for Vulcans in the previous September, certification trials with XA889 were given high priority.

A&AEE Reports

The aircraft was delivered to the A&AEE at Boscombe Down in March 1956 for service acceptance trials, which were compared with trials conducted previously

Vulcan B.1s XA902 and XA904 formate with Valiant B(K).1s XD822 and XD868. *Aeroplane*

involving the second prototype, involving twenty-seven flying hours.

With VX777, it had been found that above Mach 0.89, the aircraft was difficult to keep on a steady course, due to a decrease in pitch damping, which Avro said would be rectified by the installation of a pitch damper in subsequent aircraft. The Establishment found an unacceptable nose-down attitude started at Mach 0.6 and this increased as the aircraft approached its maximum permitted Mach 0.95, to a point where it was difficult to restrain from exceeding this limit. Again, Avro had this problem in hand and an artificial stability Mach trimmer was being proposed for production aircraft.

VX777 was powered by 9,750lb (4,420kg) thrust Olympus 100 engines and the A&AEE estimated that, with Olympus 100 engines, there would still be a lack of high-altitude performance with a 10,000lb bomb load. All in all, Establishment pilots were none too enamoured of the Vulcan as an operational bomber.

Prior to going to Boscombe Down for assessment during the period 26 March to 17 April, XA889 had been retrofitted with the Phase 2 wing. Compared to VX777, the Vulcan B.1 was a different aeroplane and in 48hrs 15min of flying, XA889 was tested over its full operational envelope, including a take-off at a maximum weight of 165,229lb (74,948kg). The modifica-

tions incorporated to rectify the criticisms of the second prototype were adjudged as having produced the desired results and the revised wing had converted the Vulcan B.1 into an aircraft that was fully able to meet its role as a high-altitude medium bomber for the RAF. The type was given its initial CA Release which, in the official jargon of the time, was Release by the Controller, Aircraft for operational use, to which the second production aircraft, XA890, had contributed radio and radar trials. The third, XA891, was used for engine and fuel system assessment, while XA892, the fourth production aircraft, undertook weapons trials.

XA890, the second production Vulcan B.1, before receiving the revised wing leading edge, takes off smartly at the 1955 SBAC Display. For the spotters, the aircraft in the background include Sperrin VX158, Ashton WB491, Ambassador G-ALFR, Heron G-ANCJ, Pembroke WV750, Provost 382 for the Iraqi AF and Canberra WD952. Author's collection

XA890 touches down after its 1955 Farnborough flying display, with the four underwing airbrakes of the straight leading edge wing. Author's collection

Vulcan B.1 XA892 flares out over a wet Farnborough runway. Author's collection

XA893, with the old wing, paid a visit to Gloster's Moreton Valence facility and parked alongside examples of the RAF's other delta, the Javelin. Derek N. James

Waddington

The Vulcan had a separate OCU from the Valiant and Victor, this being No.230 OCU at Waddington. Formed on 31 May 1956, the Unit received its first aircraft, the eighth production Vulcan B.1, XA897, on 20 July 1956. However, its stay at Waddington was short-lived, as it returned to Woodford for modifications required prior to starting a goodwill flight to New Zealand on 9 September. XA895 touched down at Waddington for the first time on 16 August but again this was a fleeting visit, as the aircraft soon departed to the newly formed Vulcan Operational Reliability Trials Unit at Boscombe Down. It was not until 3 January 1957 that No.230 OCU took delivery of the first aircraft designated for its own use, XA898, followed on 19 January by XA895, back from Boscombe Down; the Unit was in a position to commence crew training on 21 February.

The goodwill flight to New Zealand by XA897 was a diplomatic exercise, codenamed *Tasman Flight*, but it was also a good proving flight for the Vulcan B.1 as a type and it must be rated as a successful

XA907 leads two more No.83 Squadron B.1s, as they are seen en route to Embakasi Airport, Nairobi, on 18 September 1957. Author's collection

mission, despite a disastrous conclusion. Although it was raining and visibility was minimal, a gathering of dignitaries stood on the roof of Heathrow's Central Terminal Building awaiting the aircraft's return. Captained by Sqn Ldr Donald Howard, DFC, AFC and with Air Marshal Sir Harry Broadhurst, C-in-C Bomber Command as co-pilot, XA897 hit a field of Brussels sprouts on the approach, some 2,000ft short of the runway threshold. The impact on the main wheel assembly fractured the undercarriage drag strut and the legs swung back into the wing under-surface, damaging the aileron control rods. The first sight that the awaiting VIPs had was XA897 climbing steeply about 500ft over the runway, with the pilot and co-pilot ejecting as the aircraft turned over to starboard and crashed at the intersection of two runways with a violent explosion. At the subsequent RAF Court of Inquiry, the fact that the aircraft was being guided down by a Ground Controlled Approach (GCA) controller, who had earlier advised the captain that

Two silver and a white B.1s lined up at Waddington in June 1957. Aeroplane

Seen after landing at Khormaksar in 1963, B.1 XA895 was still in silver finish and as it taxied to the main pan, the crew opened the access hatch to let some of the African heat out. Ray Deacon

B.1, XA905, taken at Khormaksar during a stopover from Finningley in 1963. Ray Deacon

The first production Vulcan B.1, XA889, went to No.2 School of Technical Training (SoTT) at Cosford in 1965, where it became Instructional Airframe 7812M. Ray Deacon

Eighty Years of Service

Situated five miles south of the county city of Lincoln, Waddington started life as a flying training unit in November 1916 and remained as such until closing in 1919. During those three years, a substantial aerodrome had been established and the station remained in that state until October 1926, when a minor resurgence of RAF strength brought it back into service so that No.503 (Bombing) Squadron was formed there, heralding nearly sixty years of the base being synonymous with bombers.

A renaming to No.503 (County of Lincoln) Squadron in the early 1930s saw a change to the night-bombing role with Handley Page Hyderabads, but a reversion to day bombing with Westland Wallaces came in 1935. New hangars and administrative buildings were constructed and No.50 Squadron was reformed at the station on 3 May 1937, followed by another, No.110 Squadron, being reformed on 18 May, both operating with Hawker Hinds. The next month No.44 Squadron arrived and No.88 Squadron was posted to Waddington in July. During 1937 No.44 Squadron re-equipped with Bristol Blenheim Is, as did No.110 Squadron in January 1938, before moving to Wattisham in Suffolk, as Waddington was becoming a little crowded.

The outbreak of World War II on 3 September 1939 saw Nos 44 and 50 Squadrons operating Handley Page Hampdens and the former flew its first sortie of the conflict later in the same day. In June 1940, No.142 Squadron brought its Fairey Battles back from France, before moving to Binbrook the next month, with No.50 Squadron also leaving Waddington the same month. This left the coast clear for the RAF's last twin-engined night bomber design, the Manchester, to arrive and form the striking capacity of the reformed No.207 Squadron. Their arrival initiated an association between Avro aircraft and Waddington that was to last over forty years. The squadron had an unpleasant period with the Manchester and its Vulture engines, as did No.97 Squadron, which had reformed at Waddington on 25 February 1941. Both squadrons had departed by 24 December 1941, when No.44 Squadron received a lovely Christmas present, in the shape of its first Lancaster, and the station's great wartime achievements started.

The low-level daylight raid on the MAN diesel engine factory at Augsburg on 17 April 1942 earned Sqn Ldr Nettleton, of No.44 Squadron, the Victoria Cross, but proved to the Service that a night-bombing offensive would have a more favourable survival percentage – the Augsburg raid losses being nearly 60 per cent. No.9 Squadron arrived at Waddington in August 1942 and the Bomber Command assault on enemy-occupied Europe intensified. Three concrete runways were laid down in the summer of 1943, following which No.467 Squadron of the Royal Australian Air Force (RAAF) arrived and remained there until the end of World War II.

Three Vulcan B.1s and Canberras, at Waddington, display the City of Lincoln Coat of Arms on their fins.
Author's collection

An additional RAAF unit, No.463 Squadron, was formed at Waddington on 23 November 1943 and, like its fellow antipodean neighbour, operated with a mixture of Lancaster Is and IIIs. On the night of 25/26 April 1945, the two squadrons flew their last mission of the war and departed for home in the summer. One of the great names of the 1939–45 conflict, No.617 Squadron, took their place for six months, after which, on 25 January 1946, No.61 Squadron brought their Lancaster IIs to the station. The squadron re-equipped with Lincoln B.2s in May and remained at Waddington until 6 August 1953, when it moved to Wittering.

Several units, Nos 12, 49, 57 and 100 Squadrons re-equipped with Lincoln B.2s at Waddington in the early 1950s, each staying for a few months before returning to their respective parent bases, after which, in the first week of August 1953, Waddington was put on Care and Maintenance, pending upgrading to the status of being a V-bomber base. The extending of the main runway to 3,000yd necessitated a diversion of the A15 trunk road, and new buildings, including, as at Gaydon, a specialized electronics complex, were nearly completed when Nos 21 and 27 Squadrons started flying from the base with their Canberra B.2s on 1 June 1955.

On 31 May 1956, Waddington officially became No.230 OCU for Vulcan crew training and No.83 Squadron re-formed there on 21 May 1957, to commence a three-year stay. No.44 Squadron re-formed at the base on 10 August 1960, then No.50 Squadron did likewise on 1 August 1961, and by the time that No.9 Squadron arrived in January 1975, the Waddington Wing was an all-Vulcan B.2 unit. No.44 Squadron disbanded as the last Vulcan operator on 21 December 1982 and, for the first time since 1926, Waddington ceased to be associated with bombers.

In 1991 Waddington became host to No.8 Squadron and American-built aircraft operated from the station on a regular basis for the first time in its history. Flying E-3D Sentry conversions of the basic Boeing 707 airframe, the squadron is the RAF's sole AEW-dedicated unit and with this in mind, Waddington looks set to remain an operational airbase for the foreseeable future.

he was 80ft above the glide path but failed to inform him when he got below it, was given as one main cause of the crash. However, it was also recorded that there had been a degree of pilot error and full blame could not be attached to either party.

The first qualified Vulcan course at Waddington produced 'A' Flight of No.83 Squadron, a Lincoln B.2 operator when disbanded at Hemswell on 1 January 1956 and reformed at Waddington as the first Vulcan squadron on 21 May 1957. It borrowed OCU aircraft for seven weeks until 11 July, when it took delivery of XA905 as the first Vulcan B.1 to put on its own inventory. The second OCU course produced the balance of No.83 Squadron crews and by 30 September the squadron had ten aircraft, all of them resplendent in the new overall 'anti-flash' gloss white finish, which was introduced on the Valiants engaged on Operation *Grapple* in the autumn of 1956.

Finningley

The second Vulcan B.1 operator was No.101 Squadron, whose roots went back to 12 July 1917, when it was formed at Farnborough and flew FE.2Bs in France during the 1914–18 war. It was disbanded in December 1919 to be re-formed again in March 1928 and was operational throughout World War II, after which it was the first RAF squadron to enter the turbojet age, when Canberra 2s started arriving in June 1951. Another disbanding at Binbrook in February 1957 enabled the unit to re-form as a Vulcan squadron at Finningley, in Yorkshire, on 15 October of the same year. The squadron took delivery of its first Vulcan B.1, XA909, two weeks before the official re-forming and by the end of 1957 three additional B.1s, XA910, XA912 and XA913, had joined the squadron, XA913 being the last aircraft from Avro's first contract. The crews were compiled from the third course at No.230 OCU.

Three more Vulcan B.1s arrived at Finningley during 1958, XH476, XH479 and XH481, which meant that when XH506 touched down at the Yorkshire airfield on 17 April 1959, the squadron was up to full complement. Its tenure of Finningley lasted until June 1961, when it moved to Waddington, to be replaced by No.232 OCU from Gaydon, but a

lot had happened at the Warwickshire station prior to this move, not the least being the arrival of Sir Frederick's crescent-winged bombers at the end of 1957.

First Production Victors

Like Vickers-Armstrongs and Avro, the first few aircraft from Handley Page's Victor assembly lines were employed on acceptance and operational trials. The first production Victor B.1, XA917, had its maiden flight on 1 February 1956 in the hands of John Allam and, like early variants of its two contemporaries, was finished overall matt silver. Power was supplied by four Armstrong Siddeley ASSa.7 Sapphire turbojets, each delivering 10,500lb (4,762kg) static thrust. Handley Page retained the aircraft for trials, and on 1 June 1957 Allam had the distinction of being at the controls when XA917 became the largest aircraft of that era to fly at supersonic speed. Being in a shallow dive at 40,000ft (12,200m), the aerodynamic qualities enabled the aircraft to attain Mach 1.1 in a perfectly stable condition, before the Machmeter was observed and speed reduced. The fact that the crew was unaware of the incident was not matched by inhabitants of the south Midlands, who heard the double sonic boom from as far apart as north Oxfordshire and Hertfordshire. XA917 went to the A&AEE for some of the 500 hours that it spent during its trials life, which ended in January 1964 when it crash-landed at Radlett.

Production Victor B.1s differed from the two prototypes in several aspects, not the least being the 15in (38cm) reduction in fin height, plus the removal of the dorsal fillet and the 40in (102cm) lengthening of the front fuselage, ahead of the wing root, both modifications resulting from events referred to in Chapter 7. The lengthened front fuselage brought the crew entrance/emergency exit hatch further forward from the port engine intakes, which was viewed as being beneficial by the three rearward-facing crew members, or at least the best that they were likely to get, as they did not have ejector seats. A row of vortex generators was added to the top surface of the outer wing, the bullet fairing at the fin/tailplane joint had a subtle change in contour and two additional glazed panels were added

above the windscreen to improve the view from the flight deck.

XA918 first flew on 26 March 1956 and went straight to Boscombe Down, with ownership being transferred to the Controller, Aircraft (CA) on 23 June. The third production aircraft, XA919, was held back for twelve months as a 'conference airframe', before its maiden flight on 25 March 1957. XA920, which first flew in June 1956, became the first Victor to be flown inverted, during trials to test the camera installation for a proposed photo-reconnaissance variant. One aspect of the Victor's flying controls, expressed during preliminary trials for the Service, was that they were too light. The aircraft differed from the Vulcan in having a conventional 'spectacle' control column, as compared to the Avro's fighter-type stick. This variation reflected the difference between the two company CTPs, Falk believing that the Vulcan had a manoeuvrability similar to a fighter, which more naturally accepted the joystick control column. Hazelden, on the other hand, considered that an aircraft's control column should always indicate the type of aircraft that the pilot was flying. Irrespective of the personal opinions of the two CTPs, the RAF, as the customer, wanted the Victor controls to be heavier, so they were modified. The customer is always right!

Gaydon Gets Victors

The fifth production aircraft, XA921, was the first Victor to be finished in the overall white anti-flash colour scheme that all three V-bombers carried for seven years. After its maiden flight on 12 June 1957, the aircraft went to Marham in Norfolk the following month, as a static display for the Queen's Review of Bomber Command that took place on 23 July. In the fly-past, the V-bomber force was represented by eighteen Valiants, three Vulcans and a trio of Victors. When a No.232 OCU crew collected the unit's first Victor B.1 from Radlett, on 28 November 1957, it was the all-white XA931 and its landing at Gaydon that formed the nucleus of 'A' Squadron, which was charged with type conversion for incoming crews. The small number of Valiants that remained at the Warwickshire base were formed into 'B' Squadron.

The arrival of four further B.1s, XA926, XA932, XA933 and XA934, early in 1958

Victor B.1 final assembly at Colney Street, circa **1957.** Author's collection

B.1 XA900 carries the Finningley shield on its fin, as it takes off from RAF Muharraq in 1963. Ray Deacon

On 26 March 1956, the Minister of Supply, Reginald Maudling, opened Handley Page's new erection hall at Radlett, where B.1 XA918 was demonstrated, minus main wheel undercarriage doors. Author's collection

enabled the first course to be completed by April and nearly all of them were posted to Cottesmore in Rutland, to join the newly re-formed No.10 Squadron. This unit had been formed at Farnborough on 1 January 1915, had disbanded in 1919 and re-formed again in 1928. After World War II, it once again disbanded, this time in India at the end of 1947. Re-formed on 15 January 1953 as a Canberra B.2 unit, it finished as such exactly four years later. The squadron officially became the RAF's first operational Victor B.1 unit on 15 April 1958, although it only had XA927

and XA935 on its inventory at the time. However, XA936 arrived on 25 May and five more aircraft were delivered during the year.

In order to ascertain the Victor's abilities under operational conditions, the type was flown at Gaydon for a concentrated 1,000-hour schedule spread over June to August 1958. Following these trials, a detailed examination of the aircraft involved was carried out, with, in view of its past history, emphasis being placed on the tail assemblies. One tailplane was found to have a fatigue crack at its attachment point to the fin, which further examination revealed to be caused by over-enthusiasm with a power tool during assembly at Radlett. On the basis of it being better to be safe than sorry, the Victor as a type was grounded for all tailplanes to be replaced and amendments were introduced into assembly procedures by the manufacturer as well as the Service.

The OCU took delivery of a trio of early B.1s, XA923, XA924 and XA925, during the first three months of 1958. These had been fitted with *Yellow Aster*, a Royal Radar Establishment (RRE) developed reconnaissance radar, envisaged for use by No.543 Squadron at Wyton. With their Valiant B(PR).1s, Gaydon was to provide training for the prospective crews due to go to Wyton. On 21 March, XA924 moved to Wyton and the following month the other two *Yellow Aster*-equipped Victors joined it, to establish the Radar

Production Victors' instrumentation was greatly increased, compared to the prototypes. Handley Page Association

By September 1958, No.10 Squadron at Cottesmore had its full complement of eight B.1s. The fifth aircraft in the line-up, XA937, was later converted into the first K.1 tanker. Author's collection

Victor B.1A XH615 of No.15 Squadron taxies in to
Khormaksar's arrivals apron in 1963. Ray Deacon

A No.44 Squadron Vulcan
K.2 lifts off from Waddington
on 17 December 1983, during
the activities to mark the
Vulcan's retirement from the
RAF. Gordon G Bartley LRPS

Camouflaged Valiant
XD818 as a gate guardian
at Marham in 1971.
Ian Mactaggart

Looking rather weather-worn, Vulcan B.2 XM573 is seen at Offutt AFB, Nebraska, in 1991. Ian Mactaggart

Vulcan B.2 XM569 seen at the 1982 Mildenhall Air Fête. George Pennick

On 17 December 1983 at Waddington, a Vulcan B.2 with air sampling pods on the Skybolt hardpoints was kept well away from the cameras, but not too far away! Gordon G. Bartley LRPS

Victor K.2 XM717 Lucky Lou, **wearing No.55 Squadron's seventy-fifth anniversary zap, plus forty-four Gulf War refuelling symbols, at the 1991 Mildenhall Air Fête.**
George Pennick

Victor K.2 XL160 of No.55 Squadron arrives at the 1986 Mildenhall Air Fête.
Author's collection

Vulcan B.2 XL425 of No.617 Squadron shares a Mildenhall apron with B-17 Sally B **and Don Bullock's A-26 Invader in 1980.** George Pennick

With the 707C on its port side, Vulcan B.2 XH478 of the Waddington Wing attends
Coltishall's Open Day on 19 September 1964. George Pennick

Until recently, K.2 XM715 Teasing Tina had
Meldrew nose-art on the starboard side. Dave
Jackson

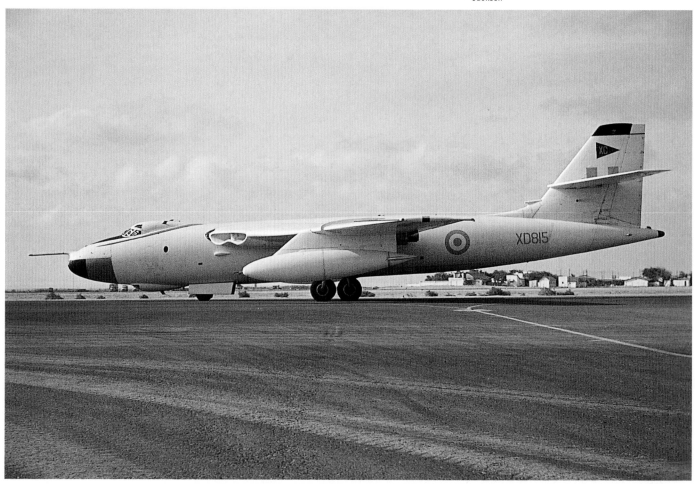

Valiant B(K).1 XD815 of No.90 Squadron basks in the sun at Khormaksar in 1964. Ray Deacon

Vulcan B.2 XM605 photographed at Castle AFB in California. Ian Mactaggart

No.543 Squadron's crest was carried on the fin of XL165, the prototype Victor SR.2, when it was on display at Coltishall's 1973 Battle of Britain Air Show. George Pennick

Coltishall's air display programme on 15 September 1973 included Vulcan B.2 XL427 of No.230 OCU.
George Pennick

No.55 Squadron's Victor B.1A XH650 taxies in at Khormaksar in 1963. Ray Deacon

Victor K.2 XH671 at the Wattisham photocall in 1990.
Author's collection

Barksdale AFB in Louisiana is host to Vulcan B.2 XM606, photographed in 1986.
Ian Mactaggart

Portent for things to come? Vulcan B.2 XH558 catches the sun at the 1988 Mildenhall Air Fête and, although at present under the guardianship of the British Aviation Heritage Collection at Bruntingthorpe, there are hopes for it flying again in the future. Author's collection

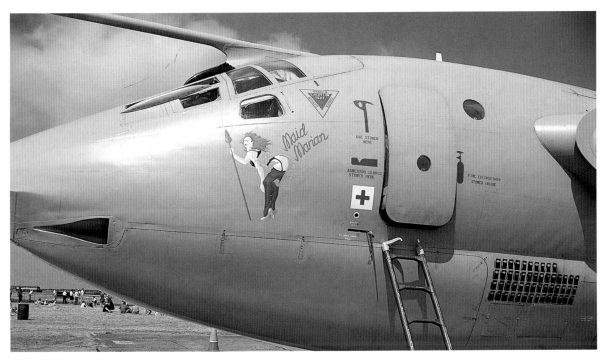

Gulf War veteran Victor K.2 XH672 shows off its Maid Marian nose-art and symbols recording fifty-two refuelling hook-ups during the conflict, when it was in the static display area at Alconbury on 3 August 1991. George Pennick

Victors with Blue Steel rounds did not appear at air displays too often, but XH669 was fully equipped when it attended Mildenhall's 1988 Air Fête. George Pennick

Valiant B(K).1 XD870 of No.214 Squadron bids farewell to Khormaksar as it heads back to Marham in 1964. Ray Deacon

No.55 Squadron's Victor K.2 XH672, resplendent in its hemp finish at Alconbury in August 1991.
George Pennick

XH651, a No.15 Squadron Victor B.1A, lifts off Khormaksar's operational runway in 1963.
Ray Deacon

A No.10 Squadron Victor has work being done on its radar compartment, with the H$_2$S scanner visible between the two fitters. Author's collection

Victor B.1 XA941 adds to the collection of skid marks on Cottesmore's runway, as it touches down on 16 September 1958. Author's collection

XA923/A spent the majority of its life at No.232 OCU, apart from a spell at the Radar Reconnaissance Flight, where it was fitted with Yellow Aster. In 1965, it is seen at No.2 SoTT, Cosford. Ray Deacon

A Wyton trio of Victor B.1, Valiant B(PR).1 and Canberra PR.7. Author's collection

Reconnaissance Flight (RRF). A fourth Victor B.1, XA935, was added to the RRF on 11 May 1959. These Victors were never classified as B(PR).1s, as they were fitted out purely as training aircraft for the squadron's Valiants.

More Squadrons

No.15 Squadron, another graduate from Farnborough in 1915, was re-formed at Cottesmore on 1 September 1958, to become the second Victor B.1 squadron. It too had been disbanded in 1919, when flying RE 8s, to be re-formed on 20 March 1924 with de Havilland DH 9As. It operated non-stop throughout World War II, progressing from Fairey Battles to Bristol Blenheims, Short Stirling IIIs, Lancaster Is and IIIs, then saw post-war service with Avro Lincolns and Boeing B-29 Washingtons. It entered the turbojet era with Canberra B.2s, flying them for four years before disbanding on 15 April 1957. Their first Victor B.1, XA941, which was the last aircraft from Handley Page's first order, arrived on 17 September 1958.

The company had received Contract No.6/ACFT/11303/CB.6(a) in May 1955,

for the construction of a further thirty-three Victor B.1s, but this was amended in February 1956, whereby the twenty-fifth airframe would be the last B.1 and the remaining eight in the order would become the first Victor B.2s. Of the B.1s, the first eight would have Sapphire ASSa.7s as in the first contract, but the remainder would be powered by Sapphire

ASSa.9s, developing 11,050lb (5,012kg) static thrust and referred to as Phase 2 aircraft.

No.15 Squadron received its second aircraft, XH587, on 17 October 1958 and three more before the end of the year. By 2 February 1959, when both XH592 and XH593 were delivered, the squadron had ten Victor B.1s and it was nearly eighteen months before XH613 arrived, on 18 July 1960. This was the squadron's first Victor B.1A and subsequently all their aircraft, except XA941, were returned to the manufacturer for upgrading to this standard, each aircraft being away from Cottesmore for an average of five months.

The conversion from B.1 to B.1A included the strengthening of the pressure cabin, provision for a flight refuelling probe above the windscreen, new electronic-countermeasure (ECM) equipment in the nose and rear fuselage along with tail-warning radar, while the wings had drooped leading edges. Twenty-four of the twenty-five B.1s in the second order became B.1As by conversion after initial RAF squadron service. The one exception was XH617, which crashed on 19 July 1960 while serving with No.57 Squadron, before its scheduled return to Handley Page for upgrading.

The Honington Wing

Honington in Suffolk first opened on 3 May 1937 with No.77 Squadron flying Hawker Audaxes and Vickers-Armstrongs

Victor B.1, XA918, deploys a quartet of small braking parachutes, which were not used extensively, the single large one being found to be superior. Author's collection

A fine landing shot, as the sixth production Victor B.1 XA922 comes in to land at Radlett. Author's collection

Victor B.1 XH594 stands on a No.15 Squadron pan at Cottesmore. *Aeroplane*

Victor B.1 XA918 was displayed at Farnborough in 1957, with one of the several revisions made to the intakes in the extreme nose, in an attempt to eliminate a noise in the cockpit. The second Vulcan prototype, converted into the prototype B.2, awaits its flying display slot, to be started once XA918 had cleared the runway. *Aeroplane*

Before serving with the Honington Wing, B.1 XA930 was converted to flight refuelling standard and its probe is seen with a bracing strut, which was later deleted when the rooftop probe housing was redesigned. *Author's collection*

Victor B.1A, XH590, of No.55 Squadron, was on a 'lone-ranger' training flight from Honington when photographed taxiing in at Embakasi Airport, Nairobi, in October 1963. Ray Deacon

Victor B.1A, XH649, at high altitude without a flight refuelling probe, test-flying an early ventral aerodynamic trials HDU housing. *Aeroplane*

Wellesleys. It was host to RAF Bomber Command, as well as the US Eighth AF during World War II, then Canberras, together with Valiants, came during the 1950s, before the station was chosen as the base for the third Victor squadron. This was No.57 Squadron, which re-formed at the base on January 1959 and received its first aircraft, B.1 XH614, on 23 March. Another six aircraft arrived during 1959 and when XH651 was received on 1 April 1960, it was their last Victor B.1, subsequent arrivals being B.1As. The squadron had its first loss on 19 July 1960, when XH617 crashed at Oakley in Norfolk, but the rest of their aircraft were converted to B.1A standard during 1960/61.

No.57 Squadron was joined by No.55 Squadron at Honington on 1 September 1960. Formed at Castle Bromwich on 6 June 1916, the squadron was disbanded on 22 January 1920, to be re-formed a month later at Suez as the renumbered No.142 Squadron. It remained in the Mediterranean theatre for twenty-six years, until being disbanded on 1 December 1946, having flown twin-engined aircraft throughout World War II. The Victor was therefore not only its first turbojet experience, but also, when B.1A XH646 was delivered on 24 October 1960, this was the first four-engined type in the unit's history. Other Victor B.1As arrived over the months and together the two squadrons operated as the Honington Wing, which had detachments deployed to Singapore during the Indonesian Confrontation in the 1960s. On 3 March 1961, the Wing accepted a factory-fresh B.1A, which was the last aircraft from Handley Page's second order and the last of fifty Mark 1 variants that had progressed down the production line over the past five years.

Honington-based No.55 Squadron's B.1As XH619 and XH649 are both seen taxiing in at Khormaksar. Ray Deacon

B.1 powerplants

Valiant
Rolls-Royce Avon RA. 14 or 28 turbojets.
Overall length: 113in (287cm); overall diameter: 41.5in (105.5cm).
Dry weight: 2,890lb (1,311kg).
Maximum thrust: 9,500lb (4,300kg) or 10,000lb (4,500kg).
Specific fuel consumption: 0.86lb/hr/lb (0.39kg/hr/kg).

Vulcan
Bristol Olympus 100, 101, 102 or 104 turbojets.
Overall length: 124in (315cm); overall diameter: 40in (101.5cm).
Dry weight: 3,650lb (1,656kg).
Maximum thrust: 9,750lb (4,400kg) to 13,400lb (6,100kg).
Specific fuel consumption: 0.79lb/hr/lb (0.36kg/hr/kg).

Victor
Armstrong Siddeley Sapphire ASSa.7 202 or ASSa.9 207 turbojets.
Overall length: 132in (335cm); overall diameter 37.4in (95cm).
Dry weight: 3,075lb (1,395kg).
Maximum thrust: 10,500lb (4,763kg) or 11,050lb (5,012kg).
Specific fuel consumption: 0.88lb/hr/lb (0.40kg/hr/kg).

CHAPTER NINE

A Short Life, but a Full One

The tempo of Valiant production at Weybridge enabled five squadrons to be formed during 1956 and the year witnessed the first dropping of a nuclear weapon by the RAF, as well as the introduction of the V-bomber to war. Both events featured GRE's 'unfunny' bomber.

Marham

Marham in Norfolk epitomizes the RAF's world of bombers. Initially, however, when opened in August 1915 (then named Narborough as this was the more substantial village adjacent to the aerodrome at that time), the base was principally a training station for fighters, until it was closed after the 1914–18 war. When re-opened on 1 April 1937, the RAF's first monoplane heavy bomber, the Fairey Hendon, which equipped No.38 Squadron, established the renamed Marham as a bomber station and a bomber station it has remained. The squadron became only the second unit to convert to the Wellington, in November 1938, and the type was operated by a miscellany of other squadrons until 1 June 1943, when Marham started receiving the de Havilland Mosquito B.IVs to replace the legendary Vickers-Armstrongs bombers. Boeing B-29s of the USAAF (which became the USAF on 18 September 1947) arrived in June 1947 and the base became a virtual Boeing monopoly when the RAF accepted the B-29 in April 1950, calling it the Washington. Canberra B.2s resided at Marham with four squadrons for a couple of years before No.214 Squadron was re-formed at the station on 21 January 1956 and took delivery of its first Valiant B.1, to become the third V-bomber unit.

With its full complement of eight aircraft, No.214 Squadron was joined on 1 April by No.207 Squadron, which was already in residence at Marham, having

been operating with Canberra B.2s until 27 March, when it disbanded and re-formed five days later as the RAF's fourth Valiant squadron. On 1 July, No.148 Squadron, which until a year earlier had been flying Lincoln B.2s, also started receiving its Valiants at the Norfolk base.

Over at Wittering, the first Valiant operator, No.138 Squadron, watched as No.49 Squadron re-formed there on 1 May 1956 to receive the first of its eight B.1s. Then, on 1 November, the fifth unit to be re-formed in 1956 and armed with the Valiant was No.7 Squadron, the ceremony taking place at Honington, where it received the first of its four-jet bombers on the same day. All five squadrons had roots going back to the 1914–18 conflict, with subsequent disbanding, and all were re-formed prior to World War II, in which they served as bomber units, with Nos 7,

49, 207 and 214 Squadrons flying Lancasters, while No.148 had Wellington Ics, then Liberators, in the Middle East.

A Year of Action

The 22 January 1956 saw the start of a big change in bomber procedure, brought about by the appointment of Sir Harry Broadhurst as the Commander-in-Chief (C-in-C) of Bomber Command. His background was fighters, having been a member of the pre-war Hendon Air Display team, and he won the DSO and Bar plus a DFC and Bar with Fighter Command during the 1939–45 hostilities. The quick-reaction philosophy inbred in him from those days was shaken to the core when he first encountered bombers that could fly faster than his wartime fighters,

A Marham line-up of two Valiant B(K).1s, XD812 and XD813, in the foreground, with two B.1s, WP212 and WZ377, plus B(PR)K.1 WZ405, keeping company with twenty assorted Canberras. Author's collection

A&AEE-owned Valiant B.1 Type 706 WP210 at Prestwick when used for 'Dectra' trials. These consisted of many comparative trial fights of Decca and VOR/DME navigation systems over the North Atlantic. The first trial was flown from Prestwick to Gander on 17 April 1957 and the crew for this sortie was made up by, from left to right, Gp Cpt H.A. Purvis, CTP Civil Air Test Squadron, MoS; Sqn Ldr E.H. Hare, Experimental Navigation Division, Air Ministry; Wg Cdr A.H. Gibb, Senior Experimental Navigation Officer; Mr W. Poulter, Decca Navigation Co. Ltd; Mr J. Mills, Radio Officer; and Lt Cdr W. Stuart DSC, co-pilot. Author's collection

defences in the Mediterranean theatre and southern Europe, conducted under the codename Exercise *Thunderhead*. Four months later, Valiant B.1s were back in the area, but this time it was no exercise.

Operation *Musketeer*

The importance of maintaining stability in the Middle East with its natural minerals, of which oil was the pre-eminent commodity, brought about the signing of the Baghdad Pact in February 1955. Iraq and Turkey were the co-signatories and in April Britain signed a treaty with Iraq, to which Iran was added later in the year. It was agreed that all countries would honour the Baghdad Pact, which, while being an economic agreement, was also viewed as security against the growth of Communism within the oil states.

Prior to the Baghdad Pact, Colonel Gamely Adbel Nasser had become President of Egypt under a rising tide of nationalism, which was advocating the rescindment of the 1936 Anglo/Egyptian Treaty, which granted Britain the use of military bases within the country. The British government, under the premiership of the newly elected Anthony Eden, was prepared to evacuate the bases, but this had to be conducted as a phased withdrawal, in order to ensure the security of that most important aquatic thoroughfare, the Suez Canal, so indispensable for the transportation of oil and trade to the Far East. The Anglo/Egyptian Agreement of 1954 was signed in the October and by June 1956, as the Canal's status quo seemed assured, the British withdrawal from Egypt was completed.

However, relations between neighbouring countries had deteriorated and Iraq rejected the Baghdad Pact. An amended agreement was drawn up under the title Central Treaty Organization (CENTO), in which Pakistan was included, but it became patently obvious that some form of armed assurance would have to be provided in order for CENTO to work. The onus for such an assurance would have to fall on Britain, with the RAF being the spearhead of any action. It was decided to withdraw the Venom FB.1s of Nos 32 and 73 Squadrons, as well as the Venom FB.4s of Nos 6 and 249 Squadrons. In their place, a medium-range strike wing made up by four Canberra B.2 squadrons would be established on the island of Cyprus.

yet took anything up to six hours from briefing to lifting off and setting course for the target. He brought in new men, with like minds, such as Air Vice Marshal (AVM) Kenneth Cross and AVM Augustus Walker, to back up his approach, as well as Gp Capt 'Johnny' Johnson, the RAF's top scoring fighter pilot in World War II's European theatre of operations.

In June 1956, the Valiant went to the Middle East for the first time, when an aircraft from each of Nos 214 and 543 Squadrons flew to Idris, 15 miles south of Tripoli in Libya. From there, they participated in the testing of NATO air

However, on 26 July 1956 events overtook CENTO's intentions, when Nasser declared his government's decision to nationalize the Universal Suez Canal Co. and his agents were undertaking the action even as the President was addressing his vociferous admirers in Alexandria. The Central Treaty Organization's aspirations were declared null and void. The British and French governments had already drawn up an outline plan for the Middle East Air Force (MEAF), should events materialize as they did, under the codename Operation *Musketeer*, which involved a joint operation between the two countries, plus possibly Israel, against Egypt. It was optimistically considered that military action against the country, in order to return the Canal to some measure of international control, would bring about the fall of the Nasser government, but such optimism proved groundless. On 11 August 1956, Gen Sir Charles Keithly was appointed C-in-C of all proposed *Musketeer* operations, with Air Marshal D.H.F. Barnett commander of the Air Task Force.

The first phase of the Operation was the proposed annihilation of the Egyptian Air Force (EAF) and to this end the three airfields on Cyprus were put on alert to accept a lot more aeroplanes than they were used to handling. In the event of there being more metal than tarmac, Luqa and Hal Far, on Malta, were on standby to accept the overspill. These plans were quickly amended when Nos 138, 148, 207 and 214 Squadrons were assigned to the Operation, deploying a total of twenty-four Valiants to Luqa. Because of their range, they had no trouble operating from Malta, thereby leaving the airfields on Cyprus free to accommodate the shorter-ranged RAF and French Air Force (FAF) aircraft. The FAF supplied 137 aircraft out of the 548 involved in the whole Operation.

The threat that the EAF posed was not taken lightly. In 1955, it had obtained a considerable number of modern aircraft from Czechoslovakia, which were purported to include over 100 MiG-15s and about fifty Il-28s. Added to the fifty or more Vampire FB.52s, plus a large proportion of the twenty-five Meteors that it had received over the past few years, the EAF was potentially capable of providing strong opposition to any Anglo-French offensive against its country.

Air operations commenced on 31 October 1956, when, apart from the four Valiant squadrons, the RAF's strike force had four additional squadrons based on Malta, plus eight more on Cyprus, all flying Canberras and on standby to attack EAF airfields. The four Venom squadrons were still available in the area for a strike role, together with several Hunter and Meteor units that could be deployed in either an offensive or defensive role. The first sorties were made by four Canberra PR.7s, together with seven Republic RF-84Fs of the FAF, which undertook photographic-reconnaissance missions over the principal EAF airfields, to ascertain the strength and disposition of the various types of aircraft. From the photographic evidence that the missions provided, targets at Abu Suier, Cairo West, Inchas, plus Kabit, were selected for the Valiant and Canberra missions launched that night. En route, the Cairo West-bound aircraft are reported to have been sent an urgent signal, changing the target to Almaza, as Americans were reported to be awaiting flights from Cairo West, but the whole incident has become the subject of considerable confusion, as no American civilians were in Cairo West at that time and the primary target, as well as Almaza, was attacked.

Despite the combined assaults by nearly fifty aircraft, results were far from outstanding, as only fourteen EAF aircraft were confirmed as having been destroyed on the ground and no airfield was put out of commission. Debriefing revealed that the attackers were spread too thinly over too many targets for a successful night operation, so the following daylight period saw twenty-one raids made and Valiants were flown against a more condensed list of targets. Reconnaissance showed 158 EAF aircraft to have been destroyed. The raids were also a good enough invitation for many surviving EAF aircraft to take refuge in neighbouring Arab countries.

The deployment of Valiant squadrons to Operation *Musketeer* provided mixed results and identified some shortcomings. The night sorties were initially flown because it had been understood that the Egyptian early-warning radar was unserviceable and the chances of interception were therefore minimized. However, many of the Valiants were still without their full complement of navigational and radar-operated bombing equipment, which meant that the World War II system of target marking had to be employed, while

ex-Lincoln sighting heads were fixed in temporary fittings. Of the navigation and bombing systems (NBS) that were installed, a depressingly high unserviceability rate was encountered. The NBS had been evolved by the RRE, who initially had the second pre-production Valiant, WP200, for final development. This aircraft was damaged beyond repair in a take-off accident at Pershore on 14 March 1961. It was replaced by B.1 WZ370, with WZ375, a similar variant, as a back-up to the programme. A centrimetric pulse system was packaged so that it could be attached to any Valiant, in support of the ongoing work in one of the Establishment's Canberras. To this end, Pershore re-engineered the front of an underwing fuel tank on WZ375, but the aircraft could not continue with the programme once the spar metal fatigue problem materialized, as covered later in this chapter. This provided additional problems when the aircraft returned to Luqa, as each aircraft had to arrive overhead in order to confirm its position prior to landing.

Further attacks on Egyptian targets over the next couple of days and nights proved that the RAF was quickly coming to terms with operating multi-engined turbojet aircraft under battle conditions. Opposition was slight as targets including the Cairo radio station, communication centres, barracks and transport complexes were attacked on 2 November. Further heavy damage was inflicted on the strategically important Nfisha railway marshalling yards outside Port Said where a Venom was hit by anti-aircraft fire during one low-level sortie, killing the pilot. These attacks heralded the landing of British and French paratroops on 5 November, together with Israeli land forces crossing the border under an umbrella of combined air support.

While military action in the Canal Zone was increasing, so was diplomatic activity in New York. The United Nations called an emergency Security Council meeting, to order a ceasefire with effect from midnight on 6 November, which was adhered to by the services involved. A United Nations Emergency Force took over from the ground forces, following which the British and French troops gradually withdrew, the evacuation being completed on 22 December. An assessment of the RAF's contribution to *Musketeer* showed the loss of two Canberras – a PR.7 shot down by a Syrian Air Force MiG-15 and a B.6(BS) crashing on take-off following battle damage repair – plus the Venom already mentioned, which represented just over one per cent of the aircraft involved. The four Valiant squadrons had a trouble-free conflict, apart from the electronic malfunctions, although one Valiant crew reported seeing an EAF Meteor NF.13 during a night sortie. Royal Navy attrition was higher. The two Wyverns, two Sea Hawks and two Whirlwinds lost amounted to over 5 per cent of the Navy's total contribution.

Possibly the most important outcome from the whole operation, so far as Britain was concerned, was the realization that the United States' non-cooperative stance confirmed the necessity to have an independent nuclear weapons capability and that capability, together with the means of delivering it, should be increased without delay.

Operation *Buffalo*

While Marham and Wittering were deploying the two dozen Valiants to the build-up for Operation *Musketeer*, No.49 Squadron, also at Wittering, was preparing a pair of B.1s to embark on the first mission for which the V-bombers were primarily designed, the dropping of thermonuclear weapons. WZ366 and WZ367, from Vickers-Armstrongs' second order, were selected for Britain's first dropping of a live atomic bomb, to be made on the Maralinga range, deep in South Australia, under the codename Operation *Buffalo*.

Commanded by Gp Capt Menaul, the Air Task Group carried out training from Wittering during July and early August 1956, but the vagarious British weather, together with the late clearance of some of the aircraft's equipment, contributed to the programme falling behind schedule. The modified T.4 bombsight that was installed in each aircraft was only tested in a Valiant for the first time at the beginning of June, and clearance for its restricted use in Operation *Buffalo* was given after the dropping of 10,000lb practice bombs had proved that the system did work, although the results were only marginally above the pass standard. Nevertheless, both aircraft left for Australia during August, to be based at the RAAF station of Edinburgh Field, outside Adelaide in South Australia.

The whole test drop programme, involving some 1,400 scientists, technicians, observers and assorted ground staff, was led by Dr William Penny, Chief Superintendent of Armament Research at the MoS. He was only too aware of the necessity to restrict the area of radioactivity to a minimum and the tests were postponed more or less on a day-to-day basis, until ideal weather conditions presented themselves. These occurred on 11 October 1956, when Sqn Ldr Edward J.G. Flavell took off in Valiant B.1 WZ366, with a *Blue Danube* round tucked in its bomb-bay. The weapon's explosive yield had been reduced from the set standard 40 kilotons, down to 3 kilotons, to meet Dr Penny's stipulated minimum radioactivity area requirements.

Sqn Ldr Flavell had Gp Capt Menaul as his co-pilot and WZ366 climbed to 38,000ft (11,580m) before being levelled off for radio contact with the ground observers to be confirmed. The programme called for the aircraft to make a series of passes at 30,000ft (9,140m) above the aiming point, to establish that all airborne and ground equipment was functioning correctly. The weapon-release was scheduled for the fourth pass and at 15.27 hours, after a radar-controlled run-up, Flt Lt Eric Stacey activated the electronic circuitry that established Britain as a credible atomic power, with the ability to convey a nuclear weapon to a target. As the *Blue Danube* left the aircraft, the pilot made a tight 1.9g starboard turn, so that WZ366 was in the correct position for its thermal measuring equipment to record the airburst, set at 500ft (150m). For the resultant explosion being within 300ft (90m) of the aiming point, the pilot and bomb-aimer were both awarded the Air Force Cross (AFC).

Operation *Grapple*

While Operation *Buffalo* was a good and necessary mission, which proved the elements involved as well detecting some of the shortcomings, it was really only a curtain-raiser for the proposed ultimate air-dropped nuclear weapon, the hydrogen bomb (H-bomb). Codenamed Operation *Grapple*, which encompassed many individual units that were collectively referred to as Task Force 308, it had a 'pencilled-in' target date of May 1957.

The United States' first H-bomb test had taken place in November 1952, at Eniwetok Atoll, one of the many Marshall Islands collectively grouped as Micronesia, in the Pacific Ocean. The enormous destructive power unleashed in that test, followed by an even bigger H-bomb test at Bikini Atoll on 1 March 1954, convinced the Australian government that, while they had been prepared to assist with Operation *Buffalo*, on no account would they allow an H-bomb test drop to be made on their territory and furthermore, they wanted Britain to look for a test site well away from their shores.

Avro Shackletons of No.240 Squadron, on detachment from Ballykelly, set on the edge of Lough Foyle in Northern Ireland, made extensive reconnaissance flights over various sectors of the Pacific and from these explorations, Christmas Island, known locally as Kiritimati, was selected as the operational base, with the island of Malden, 400 miles to the south-east, being designated as the target zone. At some 4,000 miles from the Australian mainland, this was met with full approval in Canberra!

Christmas Island, a small coral tract which is 25ft above sea level at its highest point, in 1956 had a population consisting solely of thousands of land and hermit crabs. Nowhere did it feature as a tourist attraction. The C-in-C of the Task Force was to be AVM W.E. Oulton, with W.R.J. Cook as the scientific director. The preparation of the island for its forthcoming role was quickly got under way, so that by April 1957 two runways and hardstandings had been constructed, plus provision for 1,300 people, the majority living in tents. A detachment of English Electric Canberras from No.100 Squadron, designated as No.1323 Flight, carried out high-level meteorological and photographic flights in a large radius around the base, together with Malden Island, during which time the Flight was redesignated No.542 Squadron. Four additional Canberra B.6s arrived in Australia during the summer of 1956, two being stationed at Darwin/Nightcliffe in the north of the territory, while the other two were accommodated at Laverton, the RAAF base outside Melbourne. These Canberras had been modified at Weston Zoyland in Somerset for their *Grapple* role, with monitoring and photographic equipment installed within the fuselage, while each wing-tip fuel tank had been converted to operate as a collecting tank for samples

No.49 Squadron's detachment of XD818, XD822 and XD824, with just the fin of
XD823 showing above it, amid the coral of Christmas Island for Operation
Grapple. Author's collection

taken as the aircraft flew through the cloud produced by the actual explosion.

No.49 Squadron at Wittering was selected as the unit to perform the H-bomb test and training for the mission began on 1 September 1956, using the Squadron's B.1s, pending the arrival of the specially modified aircraft from Weybridge, XD818. This was a product of Vickers-Armstrongs' fourth order, Contract No. 6/ACFT/9446/CB.6(c) for fifty-six Type 758 aircraft designated B(K).1s, the 'K' referring to the tanker role, which started with the forty-first aircraft, WZ376 and having no bearing on the modifications for Operation Grapple. The fifty-six aircraft covered by the contract had serials XD812 to XD830 and XD857 to XD893 allocated, but production ceased with the thirty-eighth aircraft, XD857, and the eighteen serials XD876 to XD893 were not reallocated. A further order for six aircraft, XE294 to XE299, as an extension of the same contract, was issued to the company, but cancelled before any elements were constructed.

When XD818 arrived at Wittering in the third week of November, it was resplendent in the overall anti-flash gloss white finish that had been tested to withstand over seventy calories of energy per square centimetre and would become the standard finish for the V-bombers for many years. Additional cameras and sensors had been installed, removable metal anti-flash screens were fitted to all the windows in the pressure cabin, including the visual bomb-aiming position, while all control surfaces had been strengthened to bear up against the pressure of the weapon's shock wave.

Following a period of training at Wittering, XD818 left for the south-west Pacific area on 2 March 1957, via Aldergrove in Northern Ireland, RCAF Goose Bay and Namao in Canada, Travis AFB in California, then to Hickman AFB, which shared Honolulu International Airport alongside Pearl Harbor, before arriving at Christmas Island on 12 March. The number of staging posts was dictated by the Valiant, as a type, not being cleared for underwing fuel tanks at that time. The pilot for the flight was Wg Cdr Ken G. Hubbard, No.49 Squadron's Commanding Officer.

XD818's arrival was followed on 13 March by XD822, with XD823 and XD824 being delivered a couple of days later. It took several days for both aircrews and ground crews to get acclimatized to their new environment, but training sorties were started within a week for the Valiant crews to work out the required routines for the weapon release manoeuvres. New telemetry equipment had to be installed in all the aircraft, after which it was checked following each flight and the crew had to become fully conversant with its operation. Exact weapon release altitude and speed had to be adhered to, as there would be no 'go round again' about this operation. Mach 0.82 at 45,000ft (13,700m) were set as the point-of-release performance figures, after which a steep 60-degree turn to clear the Malden Island target area would be made. The H-bomb's barometrically activated fuse was calibrated to detonate at 10,000ft (13,700m), which gave the Valiant approximately 40 seconds to get clear, placing it close to its stress limitation factor.

At 09.00hrs on 15 May 1957, XD818 took off, captained by Wg Cdr Hubbard, followed by XD824 carrying a crew of observers to experience the detonation of a thermonuclear bomb. Called Grapple 1, it had a sub-codename Green Granite Small for the actual 0.3 Megaton nuclear device contained within the aerodynamically proven Blue Danube casing. The shock wave from the blast was felt by XD818's crew 2.5 minutes after the bomb-aimer, Flt Lt Alan Washbrook, had released the weapon at 10.36hrs. Shutters were re-

Air samples were taken by No.76 Squadron Canberras, fitted with modified wing-tip tanks. The Canberras flew through the nuclear bomb's cloud at various altitudes to collect the samples, which were flown back to the UK for analysis. A Canberra is here having the port tank cleared out, prior to another sortie. Author's collection

One of No.49 Squadron's aircraft returns to Wittering on 26 June 1956, after being engaged in Operation Grapple. Author's collection

Sir Alan Cobham, whose vision made in-flight refuelling possible. Author's collection

moved from all the windows after another 3.5 minutes and Wg Cdr Hubbard made one circuit of the vast mushroom-shaped cloud before setting course for Christmas Island, where he touched down 2hrs 20 min after take-off. For the skilful and professional airmanship displayed during the mission, Wg Cdr Hubbard and his crew were each awarded an AFC.

On 31 May, Sqn Ldr Roberts captained XD822 for *Grapple 2*, carrying a *Blue Danube* containing an *Orange Herald* high-yield bomb rated at 0.72 Megatons. The test was scheduled for a weapon drop from 45,000ft (13,700m) and, following a run over the target area to check the weather conditions, XD822 released its *Blue Danube* at 10.49hrs while flying at Mach 0.75. The escape manoeuvre of a 60-degree bank to port enabled the aircraft to be 2min 55sec flying time from the point of release before two shock-wave blasts were experienced. After two more minutes, the screen shields were removed and the sight of the bomb's peach-coloured cloud towering some 10,000ft (3,050m) above them was an awe-inspiring spectacle that was still vivid in the crew's minds as XD822 was brought back to base 3hrs 40min after lift-off.

XD823 was used for *Grapple 3*, when a *Purple Granite* bomb within a *Blue Danube* casing was dropped on 19 June. This was the final sortie of the series and it was not until November 1957 that Operation *Grapple* X was initiated. No.49 Squadron was again the unit involved, with Valiant B.1s XD822, XD824, XD825 and XD827.

With the experience of the previous test drops behind them, the scientists decided that it was not necessary to haul the weapons across 400 miles of Pacific Ocean before releasing them. Consequently, a new drop zone was set 20 miles from Christmas Island and XD825, with Sqn Ldr B. Millet in command, made the test drop on 8 November. The weapon was a modified *Green Granite Small*, which surprised the boffins by delivering a 1.8 megaton yield, thereby being the first genuine megaton detonation, and the results of the first *Grapple X* test precluded any further drops until 28 April 1958. This was *Grapple Y*, involving XD824, the follow-up aircraft in *Grapple 1*, nearly a year previously. Sqn Ldr R.M. Bates was XD824's captain for *Grapple Y* and the resultant explosion, yielding 3.0 megatons, was by far the largest experienced in any previous British test.

The story of No.49 Squadron and Operation *Grapple* ended in September 1958, when two further test drops were made. On 2 September, XD822, this time captained by Sqn Ldr G.M. Bailey, was again used, for the penultimate action over the target point off Christmas Island, and nine days later, Flt Lt S. O'Connor was at the helm of XD827 as it made the final sortie over the same target point. Both flights were grouped with two balloon-suspended test firings, as *Grapple Z*. It was then a case of packing the flight bags and setting course for Wittering, where the Valiants were restored to pre-*Grapple* condition.

Flight Refuelling

By the end of 1951, Sir Alan Cobham's Flight Refuelling Ltd (FRL) was in discussions with Vickers-Armstrongs, Avro and Handley Page regarding the installation of in-flight refuelling systems in their respective turbojet bombers, using the probe and drogue system. FRL received Canberra B.2 WH734 at their Tarrant Rushton base in Dorset in May 1953 and the aircraft was fitted with the prototype Mk.16 Hose Drum Unit (HDU) being developed for the Valiant. Air Marshal Sir George Mills, Air Officer Commander-in-Chief, Bomber Command, had decreed that the unit would be installed in eighty Valiants by mid-1956, which was a bit fanciful, to say the least.

Two tanker variants of the Valiant were scheduled at Weybridge, the Type 758 Valiant B(K).1, a bomber with flight-refuelling receiver capabilities, and the Type 733 Valiant B(PR)K.1, a bomber/photographic reconnaissance aircraft with flight-refuelling receiver/tanker capabilities, both variants being conversions of the standard B.1 and B(PR).1 respectively. Two Valiant B(PR)1s, WZ376 and WZ390, were taken off the production line, to go to Tarrant Rushton for trials of the FRL system. Both aircraft were con-

The Mk.16 HDU prototype, ready for installing in Valiant B(PR).1 WZ376. Author's collection

Flight Refuelling Ltd's Mk.9 drogue, as used by Valiant tankers. Brooklands Museum

verted by FRL, with a neatly faired probe housing fitted in the nose, just above the centre line, into which the probe itself could be screwed within a few minutes when required, with the housing being plugged when not in use. The fitting of the fuel lines was not quite so neat, as they had to be routed on the outer skin around the flight deck blister on the port side, in order not to penetrate the pressurized crew compartment, and a long faired duct encased them. The HDU was housed in the rear of the bomb-bay, with its doors removed, and an additional fuel tank took up the remainder of the space for the tanker variant, which was tested by both Vickers-Armstrongs and FRL.

Brian Trubshaw flew Meteors and Canberras at Tarrant Rushton to gain some familiarization with the air-to-air refuelling procedure, before trying a Valiant, with FRL's Pat Hornidge as co-pilot, in a hook-up with one of the Canberras. When approaching the Canberra's drogue, it drifted sideways before any contact could be established. Numerous attempts were made but all were unsuccessful and the pilots came to the conclusion that the Valiant was larger than any previous aircraft used in FRL test flights and it produced a stronger bow wave of air, therefore requiring a longer probe. The length was actually doubled and with trials the revised probe were commenced using one of the other Valiants as a tanker. This was made possible by a decision taken earlier, whereby, in order that the trials were not interrupted should either WZ376 or WZ390

be grounded, B.1s WP218 and XD866 were detached to Tarrant Rushton for short periods.

Dry contacts, where no fuel was transferred, were first flown in order to master the procedure with Valiant-to-Valiant contacts. Trubshaw has recorded that the closing speed had to be the quite precisely held 1 knot per second for a successful contact. Slower than that, the fuel cou-

pling did not mate, resulting in fuel being spilled, while too fast an approach usually had the drogue whipping around and removing the end of the probe. Once the probe was in the drogue, the receiver continued to close on the tanker, with the surplus hose being wound back onto the hose drum. Turbulence over the receiver from the tanker's open bomb-bay was severe, until a bomb-bay fairing was

The triple flight refuelling pipes on a Valiant, which were covered by a long fairing. Brooklands Museum

designed and installed. The shape of the drogue was also very critical and many modifications, including cones of various angles, were tried before the optimum shape, known as the Mk.9 drogue, was achieved, with longitudinal slots cut around the whole cone circumference.

Valiant-to-Valiant in-flight refuelling was cleared for service, in a joint operation between Vickers-Armstrongs and the A&AEE. WZ376 was used as the tanker, with WZ390, piloted by Brian Trubshaw, as the receiver. He had Wg Cdr Clive Saxelby of the A&AEE's 'B' Squadron as his co-pilot. The clearance schedule called for WZ390 to take off at maximum load and fly about ten hours before making a night link-up with the tanker, for a 28-minute fuel transfer to bring WZ390 back up to take-off weight. On release from the tanker, another eight hours of flying was to be made before returning to Boscombe Down. The trial went well and the transfer from the tanker was executed in the stipulated time, but weather conditions at the Establishment deteriorated and the second leg was curtailed. On landing, Trubshaw said that twelve hours strapped in a hard ejector seat was a very uncomfortable experience and he found that he was extremely stiff once he stepped onto terra firma.

Valiant tankers were cleared for RAF service and No.214 Squadron at Marham re-equipped with the new variant in April 1956, flying them alongside the B.1s and B(PR).1s received earlier in the year. On 1 January 1957, No.90 Squadron was reformed at Honington, having been flying Canberras when disbanded at Marham on 1 May 1956. The squadron received its first Valiant B(K).1s in March 1957 and B(PR)K.1s two months later.

Flight crews from No.214 Squadron went on detachments to Tarrant Rushton and Boscombe Down, for training on the flight-refuelling Valiants. They were formed into 'A' Flight, which was the tanker-role conversion unit, flying B(K).1s XD869 and XD870, with 'B' Flight having a pair of Valiants fitted with two 1,650-gallon (7,500-litre) underwing tanks for the receiver-role conversions. On being type-cleared, the first crews returned to Marham, taking XD869 and XD870 with them as the squadron's first tanker aircraft. The squadron gave the first public demonstration of Valiant-to-Valiant hook-up, at the 1958 SBAC Display, but the unit's first actual fuel transfer was not accom-

A dramatic view of WZ390, nearest the camera, being refuelled by WZ376. Author's collection

plished until January 1959. From then on, there was no holding the squadron, with no less than a dozen non-stop long-distance flights being made during 1959 and 1960, which proved not only the flight-refuelling system, but the adaptability of the Valiant. In 1961, a joint-Service refuelling exercise, Operation *Floodtide*, saw Valiants being refuelled by USAF KB-50 tankers fitted with single-point HDUs.

WZ376 was retained at Tarrant Rushton for clearing flight-refuelling on several other types of that era. Trubshaw

found both the Vulcan and Victor initially shared the Valiant's experience of the probe being too short. The Javelin's acceptance trials were conducted with WZ376, as was the Lightning, which lost its probe on the first attempted hook-up.

Competition with Uncle Sam

In October 1957, RAF Bomber Command was invited for the first time to take part in the USAF Strategic Air Command

B(K).1 XD812 of No.214 Squadron, based at Marham, taxies in at Khormaksar.
Ray Deacon

Three No.90 Squadron Valiant B(K).1s stopped over at Khormaksar in 1963, while escorting a Javelin squadron to Singapore. Ray Deacon

Wyton-based No.543 Squadron's Valiant B(PR)K.1 WZ391 shares the Embakasi pan with a Britannia C.1, in July 1963. Ray Deacon

(SAC) Bombing Competition at Pinecastle AFB in Florida. A Valiant B.1 from each of Nos 138 and 214 Squadrons formed the Valiant Wing, accompanied by a pair of Vulcan B.1s from No.230 OCU. This first venture in the SAC competition was not too auspicious an occasion, for Bomber Command was up against Boeing B-47 crews with over four years of type experience. The Valiant Wing was placed twenty-seventh out of the forty-five Wings participating, with No.214 Squadron's Sqn Ldr R.W. Payne and his crew coming eleventh out of the ninety crews competing.

One year later, the competition was held at March AFB in California, where the Valiant Wing came seventh out of the forty-one Wings taking part in the combined bombing and navigation section, with Sqn Ldr R.W. Richardson of No.148 Squadron earning ninth place out of the 164 crews taking part.

Nos 199 and 543 Squadrons

Operating from Hemswell in Lincolnshire, with Lincoln B.2s and Canberra B.2s, No.199 Squadron established a specialized ECM section known as 'C' Flight in May 1957, which was moved to Honington on 1 October, leaving the Lincoln B.2s behind as No.1321 Flight. Prior to the move on 10 July, the squadron took delivery of its first Valiant B.1, fitted out with additional ALT-7, APT-16A, Airborne Cigar and Carpet-4 jamming electronics, plus APR-4/9 search receivers ECM equipment, together with a plentiful supply of chaff. The Flight eventually operated six of these modified Valiant B.1s, which, for a limited period, along with a small number of modified Canberra B.2s, became the only dedicated ECM unit for all the V-bomber force. The limited number of specialized aircraft operated by the Flight ruled out their use for the defence of the whole United Kingdom. Therefore the ECM capacity was principally operated as a demonstration facility to indicate to Britain's air defence radar units the type and volume of electronic interference that could be expected under wartime conditions. However, it was a start, showing the way for later Marks of Vulcans and Victors to have ECM equipment installed in each individual aircraft, which was to become a bit of a nightmare for Avro, as will be shown in a later chapter. In the ECM

Global Valiants			
Flight	Distance miles / km	Time hr.min	Average speed mph / km/h
Marham – around UK	8,500 / 13,677	18.05	470 / 756
Marham – Johannesburg	5,845 / 9,405	11.03	529 / 851
Marham – Nairobi	4,350 / 7,000	07.40	562 / 904
Marham – Salisbury	5,320 / 8,560	11.03	529 / 851
Marham – Changi	8,110 / 13,050	15.35	523 / 842
Butterworth – Marham	7,770 / 12,500	16.16.5	476 / 766
Marham – Offutt	4,336 / 6,977	09.30	461 / 742
Offutt – St Mawgan	4,400 / 7,080	09.03	488 / 785
Marham – Vancouver	5,007 / 8,056	10.28	481 / 774
Vancouver – Marham	5,007 / 8,056	09.35	523 / 842
Heathrow (o/h) – Cape Town	6,060 / 9,750	11.28	530 / 853
Cape Town – Heathrow (o/h)	6,060 / 9,750	12.20	492 / 792

Agadir region of Morocco, together with another disaster area in the island of Tristan da Cunha, following a volcanic eruption. The effects of Hurricane *Hattie* on British Honduras in 1961 were covered in a ten-day period by a pair of squadron Valiants deployed to Montego Bay, on the northern tip of the island of Jamaica. Three Valiants were detached by the squadron to Townsville, on the north-west coast of Queensland, Australia, during May 1962. Their task was to make a complete survey of the Santa Cruz and Solomon group of islands in the south-west Pacific, which took them the best part of nine weeks to complete.

Valiants, the bomb-aimer was dispensed with, as he had nothing to operate. The standard Navigation and Bombing System had to go to make room for the ECM jamming equipment, which was powered by its own specially incorporated alternator.

Having moved to Honington and had time to settle down, in typical administrative fashion No.199 Squadron was disbanded on 17 December 1958. The ECM 'C' Flight, however, lived on, although it again had to move, this time to Finningley, where it became the re-formed No.18 Squadron on the same date. The schedule was the same as in the 'C' Flight days, but with the build-up of Vulcans and Victors in service, operations were gradually wound down, until on 31 March 1963 No.18 Squadron was disbanded for the sixth time in its forty-eight years' history.

As recalled in Chapter 8, No.543 Squadron was re-formed to become a Valiant B(PR).1 operator, under Wg Cdr R.E. Havercroft, AFC, at Gaydon in 1955, which moved to Wyton on 18 November of the same year. In 1956 the squadron became the official Valiant display unit, which led a special fly-past display put on at Marham on 23 April, for the benefit of the visiting Soviet dignitaries Messrs Bulganin and Khrushchev. The following month, the squadron showed its aircraft and prowess at the Zurich International Air Display.

An increasing number of air survey commitments began in 1956, the first being the coverage of the 112,000 square miles that constituted the Aden Protectorate. Numerous photographic reconnaissance sorties flown throughout the late 1950s and early 1960s included the survey of earthquake damage in the

No.214 Squadron made many flights from Marham to Khormaksar in the 1960s. Here B(K).1s WZ390 and XD859 bask in the midday sun. Ray Deacon

111

B(K).1 XD820 of No.90 Squadron taxies in at Embakasi Airport, in October 1963, while B(K).1 XD815, from the same squadron, visits Khormaksar. Ray Deacon

In June 1964, three aircraft went on detachment to Salisbury in Southern Rhodesia (now Harare in Zimbabwe), to carry out a vertical photographic survey of Northern Rhodesia (now Zambia), Southern Rhodesia and Bechuanaland (now Botswana). The whole operation occupied about eleven weeks, but the results enabled the most accurate maps of the region to be produced and they still form the basis of the modern cartography of the three countries.

Super Sprite

As mentioned in Chapter 4, Vickers-Armstrongs' Assistant Chief Test Pilot at that time, Brian Trubshaw, had an unhappy experience with the first trials of the de Havilland Engines Super-Sprite rocket motors on the one and only Valiant B.2, WJ954. The idea of rocket-assisted take-offs (RATOG) at high all-up weights and from high-altitude tropical bases had been mooted as early as 1951, with the idea of having fourteen small solid-fuel rockets grouped externally, seven either side, being an initial conception. The name *Scarab* was given to the installation, which was tested on a section of Valetta fuselage.

Wittering-based No.138 Squadron's Valiant B(K).1 XD859 joins B-47s and crowds of Americans, on the pan at Pinecastle AFB in 1957.
Author's collection

Solid-fuel rockets were not held in very high esteem, however, and the Super Sprite liquid-fuel rocket motor was favoured. WB215, the Type 667 second prototype, was chosen for more realistic trials than were attempted on WJ954. In January 1956, the aircraft was fitted out with the electrical circuitry necessary for operating and jettisoning the rocket units, so that in February it could fly to De Havilland Engines, who shared the airfield at Hatfield with the aircraft manufacturing side of the Group. A Super Sprite, mounted inside its own pod, which had fore-planes to control its flight after being jettisoned, was suspended from between each pair of Avon engines.

Ground running tests started during February and these were followed by successful jettisoning tests carried out on the ground later in the month. On 27 March 1956, the first measured take-off using RATOG motors started a long series of trials that occupied the rest of the year, with a week being taken out at the beginning of September for the Valiant/Super Sprite combination to be effectively demonstrated at the SBAC Display. At the beginning of 1957, WB215 went to Boscombe Down for the A&AEE to make clearance trials of the system.

The aircraft took off on 29 April with the RATOG operating, piloted by Flt Lt R. Bray, an RAF pilot seconded to the A&AEE after graduating from the ETPS. An RAAF test pilot together with A&AEE scientists were also aboard when, having got airborne, a loud bang shook the aircraft. Boscombe Down dispatched a Meteor, for its pilot to give a close external inspection, and he reported that a section of wing skin had come loose, adding that one wing appeared to have slightly more dihedral than the other. As the flying controls felt normal to Flt Lt Bray, he opted to jettison fuel in order to bring the aircraft's weight down prior to making a trouble-free landing back at Boscombe Down.

Close examination after landing revealed that the rear wing spar on one side had cracked, adjacent to the wheel well. Several factors had contributed to the situation. The aircraft had been flying since 11 April 1952 and in those five years it had been a test airframe, suffering all the buffeting that intensive handling trials entail. Also, the wings of the two prototypes were not as stiff as those on production aircraft and maybe the Super Sprite

The second prototype Valiant, WB215, with a pair of Super Sprite RATOG pods attached, with the control vanes used when the units are jettisoned clearly visible. Author's collection

A No.543 Squadron Valiant displays the unit's crest on an underwing fuel tank, as a V-bomber trio overflys the Chivenor flight line. Author's collection

trials had been the last straw.

Useful – and successful – as the trials had been, the introduction onto the production line of Avon RA.28 205 engines, fitted with methanol injection to give increased take-off power in tropical climates, negated the use of additional rocket power. Therefore, the provisional production order given to De Havilland Engines was cancelled and their rocket motor disappeared from V-bomber history.

Blue Steel

Early in B.35/46 thinking, the Vickers-Armstrongs Guided Weapons Division's *Blue Boar* guided bomb had been considered as a possible weapon. It was designed to carry a 5,000lb nuclear warhead, giving an equivalent yield to 1,000 tons of TNT and it looked a good prospect. However, Air Staff interest waned, in favour of an Avro Weapons Research Division's project, and OR.1132 was issued to that company.

The resultant stand-off bomb, code-named Blue Steel, designed with a megaton warhead, was capable of being

WB215 gets airborne with Avons smoking and Super Sprites flaming. Author's collection

gramme and was delivered to Marshall of Cambridge, who had modified WP204 for its model dropping, for conversion to carry a full-size weapon. Parallel with WZ373's conversion, Air Service Training at Hamble, outside Southampton, were tasked to produce six light-alloy free-fall missiles, in order to evaluate the aerodynamics at full size. These were dropped by WP204 during 1958. The full-size models were followed, in 1959, by versions powered by a de Havilland Double Spectre rocket motor, capable of delivering 16,000lb (7,258kg) full-throttle thrust. These were launched from WZ373 in a series of tests after the Marshall conversion had been finished and the aircraft flown out to Woomera. The programme in Australia was managed by No.4 Joint Services Trials Unit (JSTU) based at Edinburgh Field, outside Adelaide in South Australia, less than 300 miles from the range. Although the two Valiants were instrumental in clearing Blue Steel for service, it was never intended to be a part of the Valiant's armoury and when the weapon was cleared in December 1962 that was the end of the Vickers-Armstrongs' bomber's involvement.

Down, and Out

On 1 May 1960, Francis Gary Powers, an American Central Intelligence Agency (CIA) pilot, was flying his Lockheed U-2 high-altitude reconnaissance aircraft at 65,000ft on a set course from Peshawa in north Pakistan, to Bode in Norway. With the aircraft's assortment of cameras fully activated, he received an unexpected

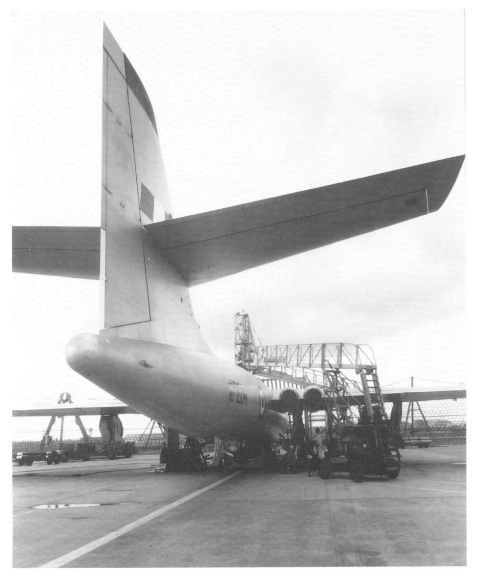

WP204, the sixth pre-production Valiant, with a Blue Steel test round in position.
Avro Heritage

carried by Vulcan B.2 and Victor B.2 aircraft. Powered by a Bristol Siddeley Stentor rocket motor delivering 20,000lb (9,070kg) thrust, it was to be launched at 40,000ft (12,200m), 100 miles (160km) from the target. An order for fifty-seven Blue Steel rounds was placed with Avro in March 1956, the guidance system being the responsibility of Elliott Brothers at Newbury and one-eighth scale models were built to be dropped from the bomb-bay of one of the pre-production Valiants, WP204. These flights were undertaken at RAE Aberporth in 1959, to determine the aerodynamics, as well as the telemetry, before a larger version could be built.

The thirty-fourth production Valiant B.1, WZ373, was introduced into the pro-

WP204 on the Blue Steel ramp at Woodford, with three Vulcans and a Victor.
Avro Heritage

A one-eighth Blue Steel scale model, installed in WP204's bomb-bay. Avro Heritage

interruption to his flight in the shape of a Soviet surface-to-air missile (SAM), which encouraged him to make a hasty evacuation of his U-2, irrespective of the prospect of facing the USSR judiciary.

This single act had repercussions throughout the then-titled 'Western world', not the least being RAF Bomber Command. They had their glistening white Valiants, Vulcans and Victors serenely operating around the globe at 50,000ft and above, happy in the knowledge that they were theoretically above possible interception, with only the need to get a refill from a Valiant tanker to interfere with their exercise or mission.

During 1960 and 1961, Nos 49, 148 and 207 Squadrons were assigned to NATO in a tactical-bomber role, which came under the authority of the Supreme Allied Commander, Europe (SACEUR), although Bomber Command still had the last word on any action under wartime conditions. The squadron's assorted types of Valiants were to replace the Canberras that had previously operated in that role. The thinking behind this move was the desire to keep some of the Valiants operational in their bomber capacity, although the growing number of Vulcans and Victors coming into service meant that their use in the originally designed role of a high-altitude bomber was no longer

required. Forward Air Staff plans were for a maximum of 144 aircraft being required to keep the RAF's medium bomber force at full strength, so the advent of Mk.2s coming off the assembly lines at Woodford and Radlett placed the B.1 variants of all three types on the redundancy list, although the two squadrons operating Valiant tankers were a vital ingredient in these plans.

For the SACEUR role, the Valiants were armed with up to twenty-one 1,000lb

conventional bombs. Alternatively, the American Mk.5 or Mk.28 tactical nuclear weapons could be carried. In 1963, the aircraft of the three squadrons involved were introduced to the spray guns, to have their overall white replaced by grey/green camouflage on the upper surfaces and light aircraft grey underside, for their new low-level task.

The Valiant was designed for high-altitude, long-range missions, which is far removed from the stresses encountered in a low-level environment. The Air Staff considered that GRE's bomber was good for another five years' service, which was possibly true at high altitude. But the new employment really does not say too much about their knowledge of flying underneath the opposition's radar.

1964 was the year of finality, so far as the Valiant was concerned. On 23 May, B(PR)K.1 WZ396 took part in a display at Bentwaters in Suffolk. En route to their home base at Wyton, the crew heard a loud bang, after which they observed that the starboard main undercarriage door was missing. Arriving over Wyton, it was found that the main landing gear would not come down, so it was decided to use the foam landing strip, available for emergencies, at Manston. A good landing was made on the nose-wheels, plus the two underwing fuel tanks, but although the aircraft sustained very little damage, it was considered uneconomic to repair and WZ396 was struck off charge.

Two months later, Wyton was in the saga again. It had to dispatch three

B(K).1 XD825, in the low-level camouflage finish. Brooklands Museum

116

27 August 1957, and B(K).1 XD875, the last production Valiant, comes out of the Weybridge assembly hall.
Author's collection

Valiants on a long-range exercise to Salisbury in Southern Rhodesia, where it was noticed that B(PR)K.1 WZ394 had a crack in the rear wing spar. The aircraft promptly flew back to Wyton for repair, although it has not been recorded how the crew felt about this return flight with the aircraft in that state. Then, on 6 August, a No.232 OCU Valiant, WP217, the second Type 710 B(PR)K.1 to come off the assembly line, was engaged on a training exercise when its crew heard a loud bang, followed by a severe tremble throughout the airframe. On the approach back at Gaydon, the starboard flaps would not extend but the pilot brought WP217 in for a successful flapless land-ing and examination showed the rear wing spar to be cracked, together with the starboard flap drive being completely sheared.

This prompted a signal to be sent to all Valiant squadrons, whereupon it was found that nearly every aircraft had cracks of varying severity in the rear wing spars. Valiant flying was immediately restricted to important sorties only, pending repairs being implemented. Further inspections made over the next couple of months uncovered even larger cracks in many front spars and a signal was dispatched to Bomber Command on 9 December, grounding all Valiants, except in a national emergency (how crews would have felt

should such a predicament have arisen, is interesting to consider!). Only one aircraft was found to have a clear bill of health.

On 26 January 1965, by which time several aircraft had been repaired at their bases, the Ministry of Defence issued a Press Release, stating that the replace-ment of spars in every aircraft was too long and costly a process to undertake. GRE's magnificent 'unfunny' bomber had reached the end of the line and the con-sequential slaughter of those fine aircraft was a sight not to behold, but always remembered. Today, Type 758 Valiant B(K).1 XD818, the aircraft that made the

first Operation *Grapple* drop on 15 May 1957, is the only whole aircraft extant. It resides in the Bomber Command Museum at Hendon, silently representing all the type's many pioneering achievements.

A question has to be asked. For two years before the demise of the Valiant, Handley Page at Radlett had 100 Hastings go through their shops. They were com-pletely dismantled and rebuilt, having DTD683 components removed and replaced by new alloy sections. What was so special about the Hastings and why was the Valiant not treated similarly? Perhaps we will know one day – but I doubt it!

XD875 undergoes its pre-delivery inspection at Wisley, before joining its squadron. Author's collection

CHAPTER TEN

Enter the Mark 2s

The build-up of Vulcan B.1 squadrons continued during 1958, when one of the Service's most famous units from World War II, No.617 Squadron, was re-formed at Scampton on 1 May and accepted its first four-turbojet bomber, XH482, five days later. This was the eighth aircraft from Avro's second order, placed as Contract No.6/ACFT/11301/CB.6(a) for twenty Vulcan B.1s. XH483 was delivered on 20 May and XH497 ten days later. By 11 November, when XH502 arrived at Scampton, the squadron had its full complement of eight aircraft and it stayed that way until its first Vulcan B.2, XL318, was received on 1 September 1961.

The first Vulcan B.1 unit, No.83 Squadron, re-formed at Waddington on 21 May 1957, was reduced to a cadre on 10 August 1960, to form the nucleus of a re-formed No.44 Squadron, which took over several ex-No.83 Squadron B.1s and operated with them until September 1966, when B.2 variants started to arrive.

On 1 August 1961, No.50 Squadron was re-formed at Waddington from a nucleus of No.617 Squadron, to become the fifth and final unit to receive Vulcan

Twenty-Eight Vulcan B.1 Aircraft Confirmed as Being Converted to B.1A Standard
From original Contract No.6/ACFT/8442/CB.6(a) XA904, XA906, XA907, XA909, XA910, XA911, XA912, XA913. Eight aircraft. *From original Contract No.6/ACFT/11301/CB.6(a)* XH475, XH476, XH477, XH478, XH479, XH480, XH481, XH482, XH483, XH497, XH498, XH499, XH500, XH501, XH502, XH503, XH504, XH505, XH506, XH532. Twenty aircraft.

B.1s. XH482, XH497, XH498, XH499 and XH502 were all ex-No.617 Squadron aircraft, which were soon converted to Vulcan B.1A standard, while XH483 was delivered straight from Woodford after conversion.

The Vulcan B.1A

The conversion of twenty-eight B.1s into B.1As was an interim measure, as it was considered uneconomic to convert all B.1s up to B.2 standard. It was estimated that such a programme would have each conversion costing over 50 per cent of the total cost of building a new B.2, which was

ridiculous, and so to speed the operation along, Armstrong Whitworth at Baginton became involved in the conversion exercise.

The conversion involved the fitting of a redesigned, extended and fatter tail-cone, containing *Red Steer* tail warning radar developed by the RRE at Defford. The aerodynamics of this tail-cone had first been tested on XA895 at Boscombe Down in 1958. Additional advanced ECM equipment consisting of a battery of large drums stuffed with electronics was shoe-horned into the rear fuselage, while a further ECM component, the *Red Shrimp* flat-plate aerial, was installed underneath and between the starboard jet-pipes. The aircraft also got rid of their full strength national markings and introduced the pale anti-flash roundels and fin flash. The conversions commenced with No.230 OCU's XH505 on 17 July 1959, the aircraft being delivered as a B.1A to No.617 Squadron at Scampton, in August 1960 and were completed when XH503 was returned to Waddington on 6 March 1963. By this time, Nos 44, 50 and 101 Squadrons were collectively called the Waddington Wing and the last production Vulcan B.1, XH532, was an element of the Wing as a B.1A.

The Victor B.1A

By September 1960, the fourth Victor B.1 unit, No.55 Squadron, had reformed at Honington and the last of the Mark, XH667, had come off Handley Page's

Vulcan B.1A XA912, of the Waddington Wing, in company with two Shackletons and a Valiant in 1961. *Aeroplane*

The Red Shrimp flat-plate aerial, mounted between the starboard jet-pipes, was installed during the B.1A conversion programme. Later, a few B.2s carried a unit on the port side as well. *Aeroplane*

the ECM conversion. Like the Vulcan, the converted Victors were designated B.1As and all the second order aircraft, XH587 to XH594, XH613 to XH621, XH645 to XH651, plus XH667, were involved, except XH617, which crashed on 19 July 1960. XH651 was the final aircraft to depart from Radlett as a B.1A.

Naturally, the Mark 2 variants of both the Vulcan and Victor showed considerable changes compared with their predecessors and had greatly improved capabilities. Avro received Contract No.6/ACFT/11301/CB.6(a) in September 1954 for seventeen Vulcan B.2 aircraft, while, as stated earlier, Handley Page's first Victor B.2 order was an amendment to Contract No.6/ACFT/11303 made in February 1956. This contract when received in May 1955, originally covered the building of thirty-three Victor B.1s, but the last eight became B.2s by the amendment. The first Vulcan B.2 order carried the serials XH533 to XH539 and XH554 to XH563, while the first Victor B.2s were XH668 to XH675.

assembly line, which was quickly following up with Victor B.2s. As with the Vulcan, Bomber Command wanted *Red Steer* ECM installed in the Victor B.2, so it was suggested that as an interim measure a number of B.1s should return to Radlett to be converted to incorporate the new electronics, together with modifications made to their cockpit layout. The installation of the *Red Steer* tail warning radar in the Victor was a much easier exercise than on the Vulcan, due to its standard rear fuselage being much deeper and the rear tail-cone only needed to be slightly shorter and rounder than the *Orange Putter* originally fitted. Jammers were installed in the rear hatch, as well as a passive radar warning receiver and transmitters fitted under the nose floor. A Freon glycol cooling system was installed in the defunct flash-bomb bay and provision was made for fitting a flight-refuelling probe in a 'unicorn-like' housing above the windscreen. XH587, the first of twenty-five aircraft off Contract No.6/ACFT/11303/CB6(a), Handley Page's second order, left No.15 Squadron at Cottesmore in April 1960, to return to Radlett and become the test aircraft for

Victor B.1A XH615, of No.232 OCU, follows the North Wales coastline. Author's collection

Victor B.1A XH621 displays the redesigned flight refuelling probe attachment to the cabin roof-line. Author's collection

Vulcan B.1 XA902 climbs out of Farnborough 1957, under the smoky power of four Conway R.Co.11s.
Aeroplane

More Power

During Vulcan B.1 production, the power of its Bristol Olympus engines had gradually been increased. First production aircraft were powered by four Olympus 101s, producing 11,000lb (4,990kg) static thrust; later, Olympus 102s were fitted, giving 12,000lb (5,440kg) thrust. By the time that the last B.1s were going down the line, Olympus 104s, rated at 13,500lb (6,120kg), were installed. Two Vulcans were used as flying test-beds for B.2 variants of both the Vulcan and the Victor. XA891 was fitted with four Olympus 200 series engines, each giving 16,000lb (7,260kg) static thrust, which were the intended powerplants for Vulcan B.2 production aircraft. As things turned out, only XH533, the first production B.2, was fitted with these engines, as Bristol Engines had developed the Olympus 201, with a 17,000lb (7,710kg) output and these became the B.2 engines, from XH534 onwards. Vulcan B.1 XA902 was used as a test-bed for the Rolls-Royce Conway R.Co.11, the 17,500lb (7,940kg) thrust engine proposed for the Victor B.2.

XH533, the first production Vulcan B.2, before having the ECM rear fuselage installed. Author's collection

Mark 2 Vulcan Prototype

Because of the potential that the newer Olympus engines were offering, Avro's design team went to work on the Phase 2 wing fitted on Vulcan B.1s, which, while curing the buffeting experienced with the original straight leading edge wings, was really only a modification to the wing forward of the main spar. The new design, classified as the Phase 2C wing, had 519 sq ft (48.2sq m) greater wing area and the Phase 2 span of 99ft (30m) was increased to 111ft (33m). This provided the same wing loading as the Phase 2 wing, although the aircraft's all-up weight increased from 170,000lb (77,100kg) to 200,000lb (90,700kg). The 12ft (3.7m) increase in span was made by lengthening the middle wing section, which had decreased sweep, and designing a new wing-tip contour, while the trailing edge sweep-back was increased from 2.5 degrees to 5 degrees. Flying controls on the Phase 2C wing also differed from those on its predecessor in having two large inboard elevons, plus two smaller outboard ones, compared with the inboard elevators and outboard ailerons previously employed, the new system giving a much-improved aileron control during the landing sequence. The new wing also had larger engine air intakes for the increased per-

formance of its Olympus 201s and in anticipation of the requirements of the later Olympus 301s that Bristol Engines were perfecting.

Avro received a contract in March 1956 to convert the second prototype

Type 698, VX777, into the prototype Vulcan B.2, although it did not have the revised ECM rear fuselage, as production B.2s were coming down the line before the decision was made to fit the ECM jammers and *Red Steer* tail warning radar. This would consist of a battery of four jammers in dustbin-like containers, set in a recontoured fuselage rear end, cooled by air drawn in via a protruding intake on the starboard side, together with the tail warning radar. A *Red Shrimp* flat plate aerial was also installed between and below the starboard jet-pipes. The prototype completed the phase of Vulcan development on which it was engaged by August 1956 and was then taken into the Woodford plant for the considerable engineering work required for the conversion. The company was ever aware of the public relations value of the annual SBAC Display and they got the revised VX777 back into the air on 31 August 1957, so that on 2 September it was filling a flying slot in the Farnborough programme, together with its stablemate at Woodford back in 1952, VX770, which was being flown as a Conway R.Co.7 test-bed.

Post-Farnborough, VX777 commenced trials to evaluate the Phase 2C wing, which was proved to be capable of extending Bomber Command's target range by up to 25 per cent and enable the Vulcan B.2's

A Victor B.1A of No.55 Squadron stands on the Embakasi Airport pan, alongside a No.12 Squadron Shackleton Mk.3, in July 1963. Ray Deacon

Victor B.1A XH590 of No.55 Squadron formates with a pair of F-111s of No.55 Tactical Fighter Wing USAF, based at Upper Heyford. Author's collection

crashed outside Detroit on 24 October 1958, while on a *Lone Ranger* training exercise, when there was a short circuit on the main busbar and the reserve batteries were completely drained within three minutes. Three years later, on 1 March 1961, XA904 crash-landed at Waddington because the electrics had failed due to the aircraft running out of fuel during a long stacking wait and again the emergency batteries were not able to supply power for the controls.

Mark 2 Victor Prototype

The transition from the Victor B.1 and B.1A to the Victor B.2 entailed much decision-making by Handley Page. Due to the increase in Soviet SAM installations, the Air Staff wanted the Victor's power to be increased, to enable it to operate at a higher altitude and have the 'poke' to enable it to get away from a target area more quickly. The aerodynamics were there, but the engines could not let it operate to its full potential. Armstrong Siddeley were developing the Sapphire ASSa.9 with an output of 14,000lb (6,350kg) thrust and a better high-altitude performance. Rolls-Royce had been extolling their new Conway bypass engine, but Sir Frederick was sceptical about the figures that were coming out from Derby, as the engine was not a high-bypass, its cold air bypass flow being only three-tenths of the mass passing through the core.

Handley Page's Chief Designer Reginald Stafford knew that a new wing centre section would have to be designed, therefore he felt that six ASSa.9s would meet the Air Staff demands quicker and would be a better proposition than four Conways. The Sapphire installation was referred to as the Phase 3 development, with the Conway fitment being Phase 2 and the Phase 3 proposal met with approval all round. However, the MoS were anxious for the Conway to be developed, so Stafford suggested a Phase 2A development, to appease them, with a wing slightly increased to 120ft (36.6m) span. The Ministry was happy and design of the new centre section was well advanced when an MoS decision fouled everything.

The Sapphire ASSa.9 was principally being developed for a 'thin-wing' Gloster Javelin variant for a photo-reconnaissance

Aircrew Manual, under the subheading 'Airframe Limitations', to state that 'there is no height restriction on the aircraft because of airframe limitations.' Another big difference from the B.1 was the electrical power changeover from a dc generating system to a constant-frequency main ac system. This had four alternators, divided into two pairs, so that if the pair on one side failed, the remaining two were capable of supplying full power. A Plessey ram air turbine (RAT), installed below the port intake, flush with the outer skin,

could be lowered into the airstream should all four alternators fail at high altitude, in order to provide power for the flying controls to bring the aircraft down to an altitude where the Rover Airborne Auxiliary Power Plant, sited outboard of the starboard outer Olympus, could handle the essential services.

With the Vulcan being an electrical-dependent aircraft, the change to an ac system was considered very desirable, as two Vulcan B.1s had been lost due to electrical failure. XA908 of No.83 Squadron

(Left and below) When XH668, the Victor B.2 prototype, was rolled out on 13 March 1959, it showed the ram air turbine intakes that had become retractable units ahead of the tail assembly. Trials to eliminate the noise in the cabin were still underway. *Author's collection*

The larger engine air intakes are shown to advantage here. XH668 was lost over St George's Channel on 20 August 1959. *Author's collection*

role to Specification PR.118D. The Ministry decided to drop the Gloster project, together with the development of its engine, so the Sapphire 9 was dead. This placed Handley Page in a dilemma, with the result that they had little option but to do away with Phase 2 and proceed with Phase 2A, trusting in Rolls-Royce's predictions for the Conway.

The amended contract covering the last eight Victor B.1s being built as B.2s started at the fifty-first airframe, XH668, and this aircraft was brought forward on the Radlett production line to become the prototype for the new Mark. The Conways, the 17,500lb (7,940kg) thrust R.Co.11 versions, were 5in (12.7cm) fatter than the Sapphires and required a 100lb/sec (45.4kg/sec) increase in airflow, which necessitated much deeper intake ducts. During ground running trials, considerable surging with the engines was experienced and vertical plates had to be incorporated within the intakes, to lessen the air swirl before it arrived at the Conway's compressor.

The wing area was increased by 194 sq ft (18 sq m) over the B.1's 2,406 sq ft (223.5sq m) and the span from 110ft (33.5m) to 120ft (36.6m), which was achieved by an increase of 1ft 6in (0.46m) at each root and 3ft 6in (1.07m) at each tip, thereby retaining the aerodynamic centre in the same relative position as on the B.1.

Like the Vulcan, Handley Page changed the Victor's electrical system to a constant frequency 115/200V ac system, which was greatly assisted by a new Constant Speed Drive Unit (CSDU) developed by the Sundstrand Corporation of America and built under licence by English Electric at their Bradford works. By installing the CSDU between the engines and the four alternators, a constant frequency of 400Hz was obtained, irrespective of the throttle settings. Two Rotax alternators were fitted in the top of the rear fuselage for emergency power. Placed one each side of the proposed dorsal fin (XH668 did not have a dorsal fin), they were driven by turbines fed by ram air taken in by two retractable intakes on top of the rear fuselage. A Blackburn-built Turbomeca Artouste auxiliary power unit (APU) delivering 400hp was housed in the starboard centre section between the inboard Conway and the fuselage, fed by a separate retractable intake duct that extended from the underside of the wing

when the APU was required. While principally intended as an emergency engine starter, it could also supply emergency power and was cleared in this role for use up to 10,000ft (3,050m).

Further Adversity

Johnny Allam took XH668 into the air for its maiden flight on 20 August 1959. Following successful manufacturer's proving trials, the aircraft went to the A&AEE at Boscombe Down on 3 June, to acquaint the Establishment with its handling. In the six months between 20 February and 20 August, XH668 had put in just over 100 of test flying, when it was taken on the latter date for a series of high-speed turns at 52,000ft (15,850m), over St George's Channel between the south-west tip of Wales and County Wexford in Eire. An A&AEE crew of Sqn Ldrs Ray Morgan and Jerry Stockman were at the controls, backed up by Flt Lt R.J. Hannaford, with Flt Lt L.N. Williams completing the Boscombe Down crew. Handley Page's Chief Flight Test Observer, Bob Williams, was also on board to monitor the engines and Mach 0.87 was set as the test point.

At 11.30hr, 46sec after the aircraft had made two or three turns, it disappeared from the ground radar trace being kept at RAF Wartling and set in motion a sea search, salvage operation and numerous inquiries that occupied the best part of a year. The exact sequence of events is open to conjecture. Fragments of conversation were found on XH668's wire recorder, including Jerry Stockman calling out 'Mach 1.1' during the descent, which, from 52,000ft, was judged to have taken approximately 60 to 75sec. The aircraft hit the water wings level at about 760mph and it is believed that Ray Morgan was still trying to get it back to level flight when it was as low as 20,000ft. Stockman's ejector seat had only moved about 18in up the rails, when the aircraft hit the water, so there must have been hopes of righting the situation before pieces started coming off from 8,000ft.

The inquiries came to the conclusion that, because the starboard pitot head was not on the salvaged wing-tip, whereas the port one was, albeit crumpled by the impact with St Bride's Bay, off the Pembrokeshire coast, then this must have come adrift during the high-speed turn

trials. This would have allowed the Mach trimmer to run fully in, which would have forced the elevators to put the aircraft into a nose-down attitude and the resultant buffeting would have been impossible to control, although the closed throttles showed that an attempt had been made to slow down the descent, which would by that time have been close on supersonic. While the senior pilot of the A&AEE's 'B' Squadron, which was equivalent to a Flight Commander on an RAF squadron, had reservations about the two pilots' experience being enough to handle XH668's programme on that day, it is doubtful if anyone would have been able to cope with the situation that arose any better than they did.

The aircraft had maintained radio silence throughout the trials, but the crew of a small vessel in St Bride's Bay heard bangs in the air (presumably sonic booms) and later a splash several miles south of their location. RAE Farnborough's Accident Investigation Branch hired the salvage vessel *Twyford*, plus four trawlers, to organize a search pattern in the Bay, but it was six months before the main wreckage was recovered from a depth of 400ft. The salvage fleet was increased to more than a dozen vessels and by 19 November, over 590,000 separate pieces, amounting to over 70 per cent of the aircraft, had been dredged up. They were all taken to Farnborough, to be located on a wooden frame of the aircraft that the Branch had built, for Dr Percy Walker's team to analyse. To assist them, WB775 was taken apart at Radlett and transported to the RAE, so that various elements could be identified and compared with the salvaged items.

The Squadrons take Delivery

The first seven Vulcan B.2s off the Woodford line, XH533 to XH539, spent several years with the A&AEE at Boscombe Down on a range of trials, before at least three, XH534, XH537 and XH538, went to No.230 OCU. The first to go direct to a squadron was the seventeenth aircraft, XH563, which went to No.83 Squadron at Scampton as a nice Christmas present on 23 December 1960. The squadron had been flying Vulcan B.1s at Waddington for three years, before being reduced to a cadre on 10 August 1960 and re-established as a squadron, at

Three views of XH669, the first production Victor B.2, was devoid of a serial number, except for one on the crew entrance wind shield. It shows the new fin root intakes for cooling the ECM bay and, by the revised NACA intakes beside the visual bombing window, that the cabin noise had not been cured. Author's collection and Derek N. James

The third production Vulcan B.2, XH535, was used by the A&AEE, before it crashed near Andover, on 11 May 1964. Derek N. James

Scampton, exactly two months later. Their second B.2, XJ780, was delivered on 13 January 1961. This was the first aircraft from Contract No.6/ACFT/11830/CB6 (a), issued on 31 March 1955, for eight B.2s. It was Avro's fourth Vulcan order and XJ780 was the eighteenth B.2 to come off the assembly line.

Vulcan B.2 XH538, having been involved in Blue Steel and Skybolt trials, was on the strength of No.27 Squadron at Scampton, as it awaits No.617 Squadron's XL392 to land, on 10 April 1974. Dave Thomas

No.27 Squadron had been operating with the Canberra B.2, first at Scampton, then Waddington, between 15 June 1953 and 31 December 1957, when it was disbanded. On 1 April 1961, it was re-formed back at Scampton and their earliest Vulcan B.2 is believed to have been XH555, which was delivered on 14 July. No.617 Squadron had been flying Vulcan B.1s and B.1As at Scampton since May 1958 before they started to re-equip with the B.2 on 4 September 1961 when XL318 arrived. Grouped together, the three squadrons became the Scampton Wing. XL318, the twenty-seventh B.2 to be built, was the second aircraft off Avro's fifth Vulcan order, Contract No.6/ACFT/13145/CB6(a) issued on 25 February 1956, for twenty-four aircraft.

1962 was a busy year for the Service, for Avro and for Handley Page. On 1 February, No.139 Squadron was reformed at Wittering, having been a Canberra B.6 squadron when disbanded at Binbrook on 31 December 1959. It took delivery of its first Victor B.2, XL231, on the same day, followed by XL232 a month later. Both aircraft came from Handley Page's second

No.230 OCU's B.2 XH559 lands at Finningley, where it operated for twenty years. Dave Thomas

XH534, a No.230 OCU B.2, was photographed at Upper Heyford on 14 June 1969.
George Pennick

Vulcan B.2 XH560 of No.12 Squadron, still retained the all-white finish when it visited Khormaksar in 1963, with Nos. 8 and 43 Squadron Hunters lined up in the background, ready for another sortie during the Yemen troubles. Ray Deacon

No.12 Squadron's B.2 XJ781 arrives at Khormaksar in 1963.
Ray Deacon

By 1965, Vulcan B.2s were camouflaged, as shown by XH559 of No.230 OCU, photographed at a Coltishall Open Day, and XH479, seen at the RNAS Air Show at Brawdy, one year later.
George Pennick and Ray Deacon

Victor B.2 Xl164 was an A&AEE-based aircraft when it visited Khormaksar.
Ray Deacon

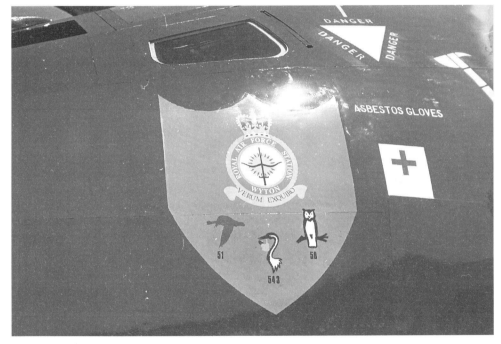

Victor XL230 was an SR.2 when carrying the Wyton crests of Nos 51, 58 and 543 Squadrons in July 1969, although the latter unit was the only one to use V-Bombers.
George Pennick

Vulcan B.2 XL320, belonging to No.83 Squadron, visited Wildenrath on 15 June 1969. George Pennick

Vulcan B.2s of the Akrotiri Wing of the Near East Air Force in 1973.
Author's collection

No.617 Squadron's markings on Vulcan B.2 XL361 look very appropriate for the weather at Farnborough on 4 September 1962. George Pennick

B.2 order, Contract No.6/ACFT/12399/CB6(a) dated January 1956, for eighteen aircraft, which was amended on 27 February 1956 by the addition of a further three aircraft. No.100 Squadron was also reformed at Wittering three months later, on 1 May, after having been disbanded at the same location on 1 September 1959, when flying Canberra B(I).8s. Grouped with No.139 Squadron as the Wittering Wing, the unit received XL192 in

September, followed by XL193 a month later.

Two months before No.100 Squadron, on 1 March, No.9 Squadron had been re-formed at Coningsby, where it had been a Canberra B.6 operator when disbanded on 13 July 1961. The squadron took delivery of its first Vulcan B.2, XL385, on 17 April and its second, XL386, arrived three weeks later. Coningsby's units were further increased on 1 July. This was the day that

No.12 Squadron was re-formed, it too having flown Canberras (the B.2 variant) until disbanding on 13 July 1961, but its first Vulcan B.2 did not arrive until 26 September, when XH560 arrived after being flown for ten months by the manufacturer. The aircraft had previously been operated by No.230 OCU and No.12 Squadron's second B.2, XJ782, was also 'second-hand', as it had previously served with No.83 Squadron at Scampton. On 1 December, Coningsby's Vulcan B.2 force was completed as the Coningsby Wing, when No.35 Squadron re-formed and its first aircraft, XJ823, arrived on 2 January 1963. One month later, its second aircraft, XJ825, was delivered.

The whole Wing moved to Cottesmore between 2 and 17 November 1964, so its identity was obviously changed to the Cottesmore Wing and remained thus, although No.12 Squadron was disbanded on 31 December 1967. The Wing disappeared in 1969 when No.9 Squadron moved to the island of Cyprus on 1 January and No.35 Squadron followed suit the next month. On Cyprus the squadrons became the Akrotiri Wing, forming the Near East Air Force (NEAF) Bomber Wing as Britain's contribution to CENTO.

In-flight Refuelling

It may seem rather strange, but from Vulcan B.1 XA904 all the aircraft that were converted to B.1A standard had the internal equipment for in-flight refuelling installed, but no probe was fitted on the assembly line. The twenty-ninth Vulcan B.1, XH478, was assigned as a Ministry of Aviation aircraft from its maiden flight on 31 March 1958. Later modified to B.1A standard, the aircraft had a probe installed and was used for flight-refuelling trials in conjunction with WZ376, the Valiant that Flight Refuelling Ltd held as the tanker. As with the earlier Valiant trials, the first probe fitted to XH478 was found to be too short, but a lengthened unit proved the system and the Vulcan, as a type, was cleared for squadron in-flight refuelling operations.

To a certain extent, selected crews of both Nos 617 and 101 Squadrons had already proved the Vulcan's flight-refuelling capabilities. Over 20/21 June 1961, No.101 Squadron's Sqn Ldr Mike Beavis captained the crew of B.1A XH481

No.27 Squadron's elephant crest was carried on the fin of B.2 XM570 when it arrived at Khormaksar in 1964. Ray Deacon

Vulcan B.1 XH478 engaged in flight refuelling trials with FRL's Valiant B.1 WZ376. Author's collection

No.44 Squadron's B.2 lifts off from Waddington, on the squadron's sixtieth Anniversary celebrations, 22 July 1977. Patrick Little

Waddington Wing B.2 XM655 of No.50 Squadron shows the nose radar housing oversprayed when camouflage was applied. Ian Mactaggart

for the longest non-stop flight made by the RAF at that time, which, in fact, is still recognized as a record. Leaving the United Kingdom at 11.36hr on 20 June, the Vulcan took on fuel from Valiant tankers in the vicinity of Nicosia, Karachi, Singapore, plus a final top-up about 600 miles (965km) down the final leg from Singapore to RAAF Richmond, Australia, where it arrived overhead at 16.39hr on 21 June. The flight had taken 20hr 3min 17sec, at an average speed of 588.23mph (946.46km/h) over the 10,000 miles (16,090km). For each refuelling, taking approximately 12 minutes, XH481 had reduced speed to 410mph (660km/h) and received approximately 5,000 gallons (22,730 litres) of fuel.

Following the clearance of all Vulcans for in-flight refuelling, Nos 101 and 617 Squadrons flew intensive training programmes to acquaint all crews with the requirements of the operation. Between 8 and 10 July 1963, the Waddington Wing took part in a large-scale air-to-air refuelling exercise. This involved Vulcan B.1As XH503 of No.44 Squadron, XH482 of No.50 Squadron and XH481, once again, from No.101 Squadron. They flew non-stop the 8,600 miles (13,840km) from Waddington to Perth, Australia, at approximately 40,000ft except to rendezvous with Valiant tankers over Libya, Aden and the Maldive island group at 25,000ft. Over the following nine years, Vulcan B.1As and B.2s became regular visitors to the Australian continent and took part in at least a dozen air defence exercises with the RAAF, to test the

defences of the majority of main cities. While on these deployments, the opportunity was usually taken whenever possible to include a Vulcan at an air display, which was always much appreciated by the Australian spotting fraternity.

The operation of in-flight refuelling with the Victor started in 1958 at Boscombe Down. Aircraft came off the assembly line fitted with the necessary internal plumbing and the fifth production B.1, XA921, was originally allocated for the air-to-air refuelling trials. Bombing trials being deemed more important than flight

refuelling at the time, the aircraft was transferred to a conventional bombing test programme and its place was taken by XA930. A probe and under-wing tanks were fitted on the aircraft and it made its first flight with this installation on 27 August 1958.

After showing off its new accoutrements at the year's SBAC Display, XA930 went through the same routine as the Valiant and Vulcan, in so far as finding the optimum probe length, followed by over six months of receiver trials with WZ376, Flight Refuelling's ubiquitous Valiant tanker. With the Victor's probe, it was found that an intermediate length was better than the full-length versions used on its two V-bomber companions, possibly because it was sited higher on the airframe. The trials terminated in November 1960 and the Victor was cleared, as a type, for air-to-air refuelling up to the fully-laden Valiant tanker's maximum altitude of 34,000ft (10,360m).

No.15 Squadron at Cottesmore was the first unit to fit a Victor B.1A with a probe, when they modified XH620 in March 1962. It was followed soon after by both Nos 55 and 57 Squadrons of the Honington Wing.

After the sudden demise of the Valiant as the RAF's air-to-air refuelling tanker, the Victor was its only logical successor, as will be recalled in a later chapter.

Victor B.1 XA930, the flight-refuelling trials aircraft, comes in to land, after its flying slot at the 1955 SBAC Display. Author's collection

CHAPTER ELEVEN

The Armament Saga

While Operation *Grapple* had been a successful test programme and the Valiant as an operational aircraft was capable of delivering a *Blue Danube* atomic bomb to a target, the *Grapple Y* test drop of a thermonuclear (hydrogen) device in a *Blue Danube* shell on 28 April 1958 showed the way for future production weapons.

Yellow Sun

OR1136 had been issued on 6 June 1955 to develop a thermonuclear bomb, codenamed *Yellow Sun*. The parameters were set at a maximum weight of 7,000lb (3,175kg) and a diameter no greater than 50in (127cm). Its length was left open, but it had to be able to fit within a standard V-bomber, with its bomb doors closed around it, which set its limit to about 25ft (7.6m). During March 1956, members of the Operational Requirement committee presented a mock-up to RAE Farnborough for their comments. Keeping within the OR's given limits, *Yellow Sun*'s diameter was set at 4ft (1.2m), the length worked out at approximately 20ft (6m) and an all-up weight of 6,500lb (3,000kg) included a 3,500lb (1,600kg) warhead. With a small cruciform fin assembly at its rear, the weapon was unusual in having a blunt nose. This was designed as such, because it was felt that in free fall, with a pointed nose-cone, the weapon's velocity would make it less stable. This would mean that the barometric detonation equipment installed would have to be that much more sophisticated, in turn requiring a degree of testing and evaluation that might prejudice the whole weapon's development schedule.

As was to be expected, the development of *Yellow Sun* did take time, despite its simplified detonation system. The *Grapple Y* test drop was still a year away when the RAE stated, in April 1957, that the choice of warhead for it was still in the balance. The weapon was being designed around a warhead under devel-

opment by the Atomic Weapons Research Establishment (AWRE) at Aldermarston, known as *Green Bamboo* (they had such colourful names for these elements of mass destruction!). Later in the same year, doubts were expressed about *Green Bamboo* and it could be gathered from various statements issued that hopes were being pinned on the *Granite* series of warheads that were going to be used in the Operation *Grapple* tests to be made in the forthcoming year.

Such was the uncertainty, it was suggested that an interim nuclear weapon should be considered, pending the delivery of *Yellow Sun* rounds to the RAF, which OR1136 had laid down as being in 1959. The original intention was that *Yellow Sun* would be carried by all three V-bombers, but an amendment was made to the Operational Requirement late in 1957, when the Valiant was cancelled as an operational *Yellow Sun* aircraft, leaving the Vulcan and Victor as the weapon's delivery system. This was rather ironic, as the Valiant was the only aircraft available for a large proportion of *Yellow Sun* trials in the early days of the weapon's evaluation, but the Variant's role as an in-flight refuelling tanker had emerged as a vital one, that should not be jeopardized.

Violet Club

The interim megaton weapon went under the equally flamboyant but cryptic title *Violet Club*. It was accepted that the weapon's development, testing and clearing for operational use would take time, but it could still be available for issue to the RAF earlier than *Yellow Sun*, although possibly a smaller number of rounds would be required. It was also understood that *Violet Club* would have considerable limitations compared to *Yellow Sun*, but to say that the Air Staff were anxious to have a megaton capacity weapon available to the two V-bombers was putting it mildly. The Deputy Chief went on record as saying

that as few as five *Violet Club* rounds in service before the arrival of *Yellow Sun* would be acceptable, which in retrospect seems an amazing statement, incurring a large expenditure of finances and resources for which there would be so small a return. However, over forty years ago the international climate between the Western powers and the Soviet Union was very different from today – and even now, it is far from perfect!

Such was the experimental nature of *Violet Club*, that early in 1958 it was entirely under the control and jurisdiction of the AWRE in so far as handling, conveyance and storing were concerned, which just about covered everything to do with *Violet Club* as a weapon. However, it was a prudent decision, for squadron usage of any weapon was different from the handling and attention given by scientific engineers – but the RAF would learn.

Bomber Command was informed at the end of February 1958 that five *Violet Club* rounds would be available for assembly on nominated stations by July and Wittering was selected as the first recipient, despite the fact that it had Valiants, which were not going to carry either the weapon or its successor, *Yellow Sun*. Such is official logic, enhanced by the fact that Victor B.2s were to be based at the station later, but the type was never cleared to carry *Violet Club*.

The weapon had a similar profile to *Blue Danube* and shared its barometric triggering equipment, which could be recalibrated to the desired burst height. On 1 March 1958, the elements of twelve *Violet Club* rounds arrived at Wittering and AWRE engineers were deployed to the base as instructors, to train base personnel on assembling procedures. During the year, four weapons were retained at Wittering following assembly, with the elements of another three going to Finningley and the remaining five being forwarded to Scampton for assembling. Due to the weapon's sensitivity, it had to be assembled on the site of the operating unit, with the distance between its storage

Impression of the Avro 730, as a complete aircraft, based on company general arrangement drawings. Author's artwork

and the aircraft that was to carry it on a particular mission being kept to a minimum.

Yellow Sun production enabled a number of rounds to be released for service towards the end of 1958, which certainly pleased the Air Staff, for, while early in 1957 they had wanted a megaton weapon as soon as possible, they did not in fact like *Violet Club*. During the spring of 1959, sufficient *Yellow Suns* were available for warheads to be removed from *Violet Club* rounds and transferred to the larger weapons. By the end of the year, the warhead relocations had been completed and *Violet Club* was demobilized without a single tear.

Blue Steel

As recalled in Chapter 9, Valiants WP204 and WZ373 were engaged in the clear-for-service programme for Blue Steel, in conjunction with No.4 JSTU at Edinburgh Field, South Australia. In the overall picture, *circa* 1955, the Air Staff saw the Blue Steel stand-off weapon as a stop-gap, pending the arrival of the Hawker Siddeley *Blue Streak* intermediate-range ballistic missile (IRBM) and the Avro 730 supersonic bomber.

OR330/Specification R.156T was issued in 1954, for a reconnaissance aircraft with a three-man crew, capable of cruising at Mach 2.5 or above at an altitude of 60,000ft (18,290m) and a range of at least 5,000 miles (8,045km). Avro, English

Electric, Handley Page and Vickers-Armstrongs all submitted designs, which resulted in Avro receiving a contract for ten prototypes in May 1955, the first of which was to fly before the end of 1959. The company considered that their canard design could, in modified form, be built as a bomber, with the same performance capabilities. The Air Staff concurred with Avro's suggestion and a revised Specification RB.156D was issued by the MoS.

The stainless-steel bomber was to have a wingspan of 65ft 6in (20m), a length of 159ft (48.5m) and fuselage diameter of 9ft 4in (2.8m). Eight Armstrong Siddeley P.176 turbojets, four in each of two nacelles centrally mounted on the wings, was the propulsive force for this very advanced aircraft and it would be capable of carrying a free-fall thermonuclear weapon or stand-off bomb. Metal was cut in 1956 and the first fuselage was in an advanced state on 2 April 1957 when Duncan Sandys delivered his knock-out blow to the British Aircraft Industry and cancelled almost every aircraft project in sight. The Avro 730 had cost an estimated £2.05 million and the round fuselage was cut up into sections to be used as scrap-metal dump bins around Avro's Chadderton plant.

Following the cancellation of the Avro 730, the available resources were channelled into the *Blue Streak* IRBM, which was a fixed-site liquid-fuelled rocket, as was the Douglas Thor. Sixty of the latter had been obtained from the United States on a temporary basis, following Sandys' White Paper on Defence, with sites being established at Bardney, Caistor, Coleby Grange, Folkingham, Hemswell, Ludford Magna, Melton Mowbray and North Luffenham. However, in a Cabinet reshuffle, Harold Watkinson took over from Duncan Sandys as Minister of Defence in 1959, and in April 1960 Watkinson cancelled *Blue Streak*, expressing more than a passing interest in the American Skybolt.

Vulcan B.1 XA903 carries a Blue Steel test round, painted red and white for photographic recording when released. Gordon Bartley BAS

134

With Blue Steel trials coming to fruition, Vulcan B.1 XA903 joined the two Valiants in Australia in the late 1950s, not only to participate in final clearance trials but to evaluate the Vulcan as a Blue Steel carrier. XH539 was meanwhile engaged in parallel trials at Boscombe Down, under the auspices of the A&AEE. The Victor had been cleared by Boscombe Down to carry the weapon and at least two B.2s, XH674 and XL161, were deployed on trials in the early 1960s. XL161 went to Avro's plant at Woodford in December 1961 to commence trials on the Victor's compatibility with Blue Steel, while XH674 flew out to Edinburgh Field. XL161 joined it a few months later, to make live drops on the Woomera range.

Blue Steel was a good stand-off weapon and it attained a 90 per cent accuracy level during its final trials at Woomera. It had a self-contained guidance system developed by Elliott Brothers at Newbury and could not be diverted or jammed by

Victor B.2 XH675 engaged in Blue Steel trials relative to the type. Gordon Bartley BAS

ECM. It was capable of flying at 110,000ft (33,530m), although the Stentor's main combustion chamber was prone to cut out, so the service ceiling was set at a maximum of 80,000ft (24,385m). When released by its parent aircraft, the weapon fell free for 300ft (91m) before the Stentor fired. The weapon's controls unlocked and it sped off to its pre-set altitude, on course to its target.

Vulcan B.2 and Victor B.2 aircraft began returning to their respective manufacturers for modifications that would enable Blue Steel to be carried. In 1962, No.617 Squadron at Scampton was the first Vulcan squadron to start sending its aircraft to Woodford. In the case of the Victor B.2, it was felt that the 17,250lb (7,825kg) thrust of the Conway RCo.11 would not be sufficient to get a Blue Steel-laden aircraft up to 60,000ft (18,290m), so the stand-off weapon conversion included the fitting of Conway RCo.17s, rated at 20,000lb (9,072kg) static thrust, which had initially been fight tested in B.2 XL159 in November/December 1961.

The modifications needed to make the Vulcan and Victor compatible with Blue

Taken by the 35mm bomb-bay camera, a Blue Steel round ignites its engine. Avro Heritage

Specification – Avro W-100 Blue Steel Mk.1

Powerplant: One Bristol Siddeley Stentor rocket motor producing 20,000lb (9,072kg) thrust, supplemented by a secondary chamber for initial light-up, producing 4,000lb (1,815kg) thrust.

Weight: 16,500 to 17,000lb (7,480 to 7,710kg).

Dimension: Span 13ft 0in (4m); foreplane span 6ft 6in (2m); length 35ft 0in (10.7m); maximum body diameter 4ft 2in (1.27m).

Performance: Maximum speed Mach 1.6.
Maximum range 100 miles (161km) at Mach 1.6
200 miles (322km) at Mach 0.85
Service ceiling 70,000ft to 80,000ft (21,335m to 24,385m)
Service low-level limit 1,000ft (305m)
Warhead yield approximately 1 megaton.

Avro Blue Steel Mk.2 project to Specification 1159 – same main body as Mk.1 but powerplant changed to four Bristol Siddeley ramjets superimposed in pairs at the wing-tips, plus twin solid-fuel booster rockets on the main body. A maximum speed of Mach 3 and a range of 700 to 800 miles (1,125 to 1,290km) at 70,000ft (21,335m) was projected.

Blue Steel Mk.2 was cancelled in December 1959, after nearly £850,000 had been spent on the project.

Blue Steel production at Avro, August 1959. Harry Holmes

Steel operations were quite extensive. On the Vulcan, the forward bomb-bay spar had a crank put in it, while the rear spar required a cut-out in order that the weapon could be installed. Bomb-bay doors were removed and a fairing tailored around the weapon when it was *in situ*. An additional fuel tank was installed in the bomb-bay, in the space above the Blue Steel's tapered front section. In this guise, the aircraft has sometimes been referred to as Vulcan B.2A.

Victor B.2 conversions were more extensive. Besides the engine change already mentioned, the bomb-bay doors were removed and fairings that fitted around the weapon, with a rubber sealing strip, were held in place by quick-release connectors. Once a Blue Steel round had been installed, special replacement bomb doors were put in place, which, once the weapon had been launched, closed so that the aerodynamics of the under-fuselage could be maintained. The additional bomb-bay fuel tank that was fitted in the Vulcan could not be incorporated in the Victor, therefore underwing tanks were installed. In fact, the Victor's wings became quite involved with the conversion. Fixed-droop leading edges were installed and the aircraft's *Window* (the foil anti-radar strips nowadays called chaff) capacity was increased by the addition of two container-fairings attached to the upper-surface wing surface, that protruded aft of the trailing edge. Colloquially referred to as 'Küchemann carrots', the fairings were the brainchild of the RAE's Dr Küchemann working with R.T. Whitcomb of the NACA Langley Laboratory. They served to delay shock waves on wings at high subsonic speed and low-altitude flying by holding back the separation of the boundary layer. Their use as *Window* dispensers was an added bonus to their aerodynamic properties so far as the Victor was concerned and they were introduced into the Victor B.2 production line. The converted aircraft were known as Victor B.2Rs, the 'R' denoting retrofit. Once again, the shape of the ram air inlet for cold air to the tail fin anti-icing pump, positioned at the base of the fin, was changed. This was the fourth time that the inlet's contours had been redesigned in the life of the Victor and the humped-back appearance on the B.2R certainly had no aesthetic merit, but no doubt it was necessary for the aircraft's new environment. At the extreme rear end, a new housing was designed to take the *Red Steer* tail warning system, with six aerials in small blisters around its circumference. The system had originated at the Telecommunications Research Establishment, in conjunction with E.K.Cole Ltd (EKCO) in the early 1950s, as the first post-war A.I. radar intended for single-seat fighters, being designated A.I.20, with the codename *Green Willow*. It was flown in the TRE-modified Canberra B.6 WH953 during 1954, but in the course of the programme the decision was made to fit the later A.I.23, developed by TRE and Ferranti, as the Lightning's interceptor radar and adapt the A.I.20 to a tail-warning radar for the V-bomber force, with Gerald Steer as the project scientist handling the programme at the TRE.

Vulcan B.2 XL321 of No.617 Squadron, the first unit cleared to operate Blue Steel. Derek N. James

No.44 Squadron B.2 XL445 carries an operational Blue Steel round. Gordon Bartley BAS

Victor B.2R XL233 with a production Blue Steel stand-off bomb installed. The limited ground clearance of the Victor, plus Blue Steel, is very apparent. Author's collection

On both types, dedicated Blue Steel control panels were positioned in the rear crew compartment, with the captain having the flight safety lock switches fitted in his operating area. Within the respective bomb-bays, a contoured box-structure carrier was held to the roof with strong connectors and the weapon itself was secured by crutches fixed at each corner of the carrier. All supplementary services for the weapon, such as the electric arming circuitry and temperature control systems, ran through the box structure, as did a pneumatic release unit on the carrier's underside that detached the round from the aircraft at the determined time. While the bomb-bay installations were tailored for the two different types, the fundamental operation was very similar.

In February 1963, No.617 Squadron, with its Vulcan B.2s, became fully operational with Blue Steel. Similarly equipped Nos 27 and 83 Squadrons made Scampton an all Blue Steel base, while Nos 100 and 139 Squadrons at Wittering were the only two Victor B.2 units carrying the weapon. As already said, Blue Steel was a good weapon, but getting it under its two different carrier aircraft were entirely different operations. The difference in ground clearance between the Vulcan and Victor presented problems at first, with two different loader designs being required. The Vulcan's loader was electrically operated, while the low-loader for the Victor operated hydraulically. Later, a common hydraulic loader was developed, which had an adaptor for the higher Vulcan.

For Abingdon's Air Show on 15 June 1968, No.83 Squadron's Vulcan B.2 XL386 from Scampton carried an inert Blue Steel round. George Pennick

A Scampton Wing Vulcan B.2 XL443, complete with inert Blue Steel round, was present at Alconbury on 4 July 1969. George Pennick

An anonymous B.2, plus Blue Steel, comes in to land at Woodford. Derek N. James

The Vulcan's weapons bay was a good 6ft (1.8m) above the ground, whereas the Victor, carrying Blue Steel, had a 14in (35.6cm) clearance between the weapon and terra ferma. All Blue Steel rounds had their lower fin adapted to fold through 90 degrees, but for the Victor the upper fin was removed for loading and replaced once the weapon had been installed in the bomb-bay.

Avro designed a training variant of Blue Steel, without warhead or rocket motor, for loading instruction. Several examples were built and employed at the Bomber Command Bombing School (BCBS) based at Lindholme, to acquaint ground crews of the weapon's characteristics, as well as aircrews, on the operational requirements of delivering the weapon to

Vulcan B.2 XH538 carries Skybolt rounds on the specially developed underwing hard points. Avro Heritage

a target. In the four-week course, pilots and Air Electronic Officers (AEOs) were detached to the BCBS for seven days, before moving to the OCU at Gaydon for a further three weeks, while navigators remained at Lindholme for the whole month. The crews were then reunited for an airborne conversion course carried out under the instructions of qualified Blue Steel operators. The Blue Steel Services Pack was installed in the front section of the bomb-bay and its operations were monitored by the AEO throughout its whole time from readiness to release, up to target impact.

Blue Steel remained operational right up to 1970, with No.617 Squadron being the last to relinquish the weapon. By this time, the Royal Navy had won the day, after many years of battling, and nuclear-powered submarines armed with Polaris missiles took over the thermonuclear deterrent role for the United Kingdom.

Skybolt

Blue Steel Mk.1 was not a cheap or easy system to develop and these factors effectively ensured that the Mk.2 variant never got beyond the mock-up stage. With sixty Thor intercontinental ballistic missiles (ICBMs) on 'permanent loan' from the United States, which had control of the warheads, and *Blue Streak* still under development (although on the verge of being cancelled), 1960 was the year when the Air Staff turned their attention to the Douglas Aircraft Co. of Santa Monica in California. The company had been contracted to design an air-launched ballistic missile (ALBM) with a nuclear warhead for the American Strategic Air Command (SAC), who wanted to have the weapon carried by the Convair B-58 Hustler and Boeing B-52. Later, the B-58 application was dropped and the B-52 became the sole intended delivery system for the missile.

Originally referred to as the WS-138A, the weapon was re-designated XGAM-87A during its experimental stage and GAM-87A when it acquired the name Skybolt. With a length of 38ft (11.6m), it was a two-stage, solid fuel missile with a maximum range of 1,150 miles (1,850km) and a design speed of Mach 5.0. The size of Skybolt was determined by the proposal to fit up to four on pylons under the SAC aircraft, each having its own designated target and the carrier aircraft releasing them 1,000 miles (1,610km) from the target areas.

During March 1960, Prime Minister Harold Macmillan had a meeting with President Dwight D. Eisenhower at the Camp David presidential retreat. One subject high on the agenda was the possibility of Britain purchasing a number of Skybolt missiles. A Memorandum of Agreement was drawn up to the effect that Skybolt would be supplied to the RAF after its introduction into SAC service, which was anticipated as being around the end of 1963. Furthermore, whereas the nuclear warheads for Thor were American, with their release for installation on the ICBM in time of war being subject to US approval, no objection was raised when Britain insisted on designing and manufacturing its own nuclear warhead for Skybolt. This agreement was the catalyst for the cancellation of *Blue Streak* and the future of the V-bomber force looked to be getting centred around Skybolt, as fifty-seven Blue Steel stand-off bombs could not last for ever.

In January 1961, Vulcan B.2 XH563 of No.83 Squadron at Scampton flew to the Douglas plant to undergo a programme of electrical compatibility tests with the company, after which it went to Wright-Patterson AFB in Ohio, where the Wright Air Development Division had an experimental facility. The development of Skybolt in America was split into four elements, with Douglas being the prime manufacturer. The two-stage power system became the responsibility of Aerojet-General, the Northrop electronic division Nortronics handled the astro-inertial

XH537 lifts off with a pair of matching Skybolt rounds. Derek N. James

Seen taxiing at Woodford, XH537 carries two different Skybolt aerodynamic shapes. Avro Heritage

and ballistics computers, while General Electric's contribution was the re-entry vehicle.

Following its success with Blue Steel, Avro was to manage Skybolt in the United Kingdom and become the associate contractor. Vulcan B.2s XH537, XH538 and XH563 were allocated to the Skybolt development programme, with Hawker Siddeley engineering the modifications required for them to carry the weapon. AEI received the contract to produce the interface equipment, including an analogue/digital converter, for the aircraft/missile combination. AWRE at Aldermaston were tasked with the design of a thermonuclear warhead to fit in the small Skybolt nose-cone which, with a new pre-launch computer designed to accept data from the Vulcan B.2's standard navigation and bombing systems, placed Skybolt on course for subsequent RAF service.

November 1961 saw XH537 make its maiden flight with a dummy Skybolt suspended from a pylon under each wing. The dummy missile under the starboard wing had a more streamlined nose-cone than the port side one for aerodynamic comparison trials and cameras were installed in blister housings under each wing-tip. The following month, on 9 December, XH538 carried out the first release of dummy missiles, over the West Freugh range in Scotland, from 45,000ft. Early in 1962, Wg Cdr Charles Ness led a team of 200 RAF personnel on detachment to Elgin AFB in Florida, where the American Skybolt trials teams had their headquarters. There they formed the

British Joint Trials Force, to evaluate the Vulcan/Skybolt marriage from an operational point of view.

However, despite Bomber Command's enthusiasm, the Skybolt development programme in Americas was not a 'happy ship'. The missile was carried on the B-52 on pylons positioned between the fuselage and inner pair of engines. The first live launch was made on 19 April 1962, but the second-stage booster failed to ignite and the round was lost. On 29 June, the second live launch was equally discouraging, as the first-stage motor would not ignite as programmed and the range safety officers had to destroy the missile. In the third firing, on 13 September, both stages of the propulsion system fired successfully, but the guidance system failed and, when the round veered off course, the safety officers were again in action. Two weeks later, on 25 September, the fourth launch started as scheduled, but again the second stage failed, this time after only 15 seconds of activity and the programmed range was not accomplished.

Undeterred, the Trials Force prepared for Vulcan live firings early in 1963; however, before this, politics had taken charge. Dwight D. Eisenhower had retired and John F. Kennedy was in the White House. He had appointed Robert McNamara as Secretary of Defense, who looked into the American defence programmes very thoroughly. These already consisted of Minuteman and Polaris nuclear missiles, which McNamara considered to be adequate. In his opinion, there was no requirement for a third missile and the test-firing failures of

Skybolt encouraged official thinking to question the continuation of the programme.

In Britain, these rumblings of discontent across the Atlantic prompted the government to decide how many Skybolts were needed and in July 1962 they placed an official order with the American government, which was accepted. From XM597, the sixty-first Vulcan on the production line, wings were strengthened and attachment points incorporated to accept a pylon-mounted Skybolt under each wing. The failures of test firings three and four in September were the last straw so far as McNamara was concerned. Skybolt had already cost over $500 million and this figure, together with a timescale slippage that was proportional to the cost, convinced him that, British order or no British order, things had to come to a halt.

On 8 November 1963, the British Ambassador in Washington was informed of McNamara's recommendation to cancel the Skybolt programme. The reaction in Britain was such that a meeting was set up at Nassau in the Bahamas between Prime Minister Macmillan and President Kennedy, in which the strength of British feeling came as a surprise to the US president. The agreement with President Eisenhower in 1960 had been coupled with the United Kingdom granting the US Navy's nuclear submarine fleet unrestricted facilities at Holy Loch in Scotland, of which President Kennedy appeared to be unaware; nor did he seem to know that the future strategy of the V-bomber force was tailored around Skybolt. To British eyes, the whole scenario gave the impression that the United States wanted to discourage Britain's independent nuclear capabilities.

In retrospect, it must be admitted that Britain placed too much reliance on past relationships with America and on the Skybolt programme, to the exclusion of any other alternative, particularly its own capabilities. President Kennedy insisted that the Skybolt cancellation was purely a question of economics so far as the United States was concerned. He underlined this by making a munificent offer to the Prime Minister. If Britain wanted Skybolt so badly, the United States would pay half of all future development costs, with Britain paying the balance. However, in a broadcast made before the Nassau meeting, President Kennedy had already justified the American cancellation on the grounds

XH537 carries cinecameras in housings under each wing-tip and ahead of the bomb-bay doors to record dummy Skybolt releases. Gordon Bartley BAS

progress at Nassau, on 19 December 1962 a B-52F took off from Elgin AFB with a live Skybolt round, released it at the designated launch point and it hit its target 1,000 miles down range in the south Atlantic, right on the button. Irony does not come much stronger than that!

The Vulcan featured exclusively in the Skybolt saga, for the simple reason that the Victor was too low on the ground to accept it. Handley Page made attempts to get three under a Victor, but there was insufficient ground clearance. The company proposed a two-under-each-wing installation, with the aircraft having a widened centre section containing four Conway Co22 engines, the bomb-bay filled with a large fuel tank, wing-tip tanks and a new taller twelve-wheeled undercarriage. The company sent Peter Wall, the Victor Project Engineer, to Douglas to become the company's representative during the Skybolt programme and H.P. himself, appearing on British television in 1960, underlined the Victor's ability to carry Skybolt without any modification to the wings or undercarriage. In terms of weight carrying, this was true, but it came to naught as the Victor and Skybolt were just aerodynamically incompatible.

that the weapon was not coming up to expectations. In this case, no matter how generous the American gesture was, the Prime Minister was not interested in even partially financing a product that was considered to be inferior by its country of origin. Furthermore, the trials programme, Vulcan conversions (including modifications to aircraft on the assembly line), the British Joint Trials Force at Elgin AFB, plus project work at De Havilland and Vickers-Armstrongs, had cost the British taxpayer £27 million, for which there was absolutely nothing to show.

The President tried to appease the Prime Minister by offering the North American AGM-28 Hound Dog strategic air-to-surface missile (ASM), but this was not much of an improvement over Blue Steel, so it was rejected and eventually the US President offered Polaris. This was a more viable proposition so far as the Premier was concerned, and also in the opinion of the Admiralty and British shipbuilding. The only dissenting voice came from the Air Staff, but the die was cast. As if to rub salt into the already smarting wound, while the four-day meeting was in

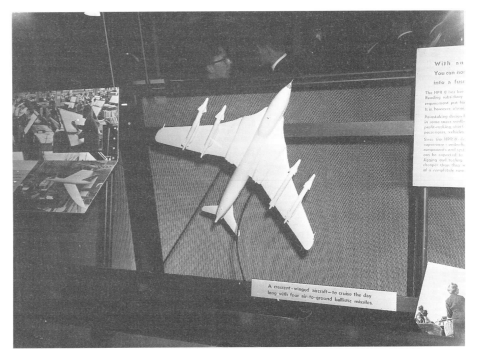

Considering the Victor's limited ground clearance, this model of a Victor with four Skybolts, at the 1960 SBAC Display, seems a bit optimistic, although a Victor modification with longer undercarriage legs and wings had been mooted. Author's collection

The British desire to operate Skybolt can be gathered by the fact that not only the Vulcan was envisaged as its carrier. Proposals had been lodged with the MoS by De Havilland for a Trident variant carrying four underwing Skybolts, and Vickers-Armstrongs had investigated a VC10, with a 4,000-mile range, carrying four of the missiles on underwing pylons. Avro themselves had also drawn up the Phase 6 Vulcan, with increased wing area and more powerful Olympus engines, carrying three Skybolts under each wing. Whether Prime Minister Macmillan was unwise to reject the President's offer is open to conjecture. The one certainty is that the RAF had lost its British nuclear deterrent role for ever.

Iron Bombs

The cancellation of Skybolt, added to the already acknowledged fact that high altitude over the target no longer gave immunity from interception, brought home the truth that Bomber Command would have to change its operational tactics. The only option open now was to go low down, even though all three V-bombers had been designed to operate in a high-altitude environment. Getting in under enemy radar required a maximum flying height of approximately 3,000ft (915m) to ensure being lost in the echoes from the ground, and low-level trials were carried out at Woomera with a Vulcan armed with a Blue Steel round. The weapon was released at low altitude, climbed to over 15,000ft (4,570m) to follow its set course, then dived at Mach 1.5+ to strike the target. Blue Steel was cleared for low level, with the stored altitude data amended for its new role.

The small number of Valiant B(K).1s not employed in the tanker role (principally aircraft of Nos 49, 148 and 207 Squadrons assigned to SACEUR) were the first designated for low-level operations in 1963. They could each carry up to twenty-one 1,000lb conventional bombs, set in three pre-loaded carriers each containing five bombs and two con-taining three each. There was also the ability to carry American-designed Mk.5 tactical nuclear weapons, which later were returned to the United States, which replaced them with Mk.28 bombs of 100-kt yield. The aircraft were repainted in the grey/green camouflage of the period, with Light Aircraft Grey on the lower fuselage and under-surfaces.

Bomber Command initiated Quick Reaction Alert (QRA). First set up at Marham, QRA consisted of a special tarmac Operational Readiness Platform (ORP) set at the side of the runway threshold. Four aircraft could park on this hardstanding, facing towards the runway at an angle of approximately 30 degrees to its centre line. The quartet comprised air-craft from each squadron, all maintained in an armed condition, with the crews in their flying suits at all times and living in caravans beside the ORP. On the sound of the alert, crews abandoned whatever they were doing, including eating, sleeping or ablutions, and officially 15 minutes had been set as the time required between

A typical V-bomber carrier for seven 1,000lb conventional bombs. *Aeroplane*

A Vulcan B.2 releases a stick of 1,000lb retarded bombs, fitted with umbrella-like retardation parachutes, to obviate low-level released bombs exploding while the aircraft was in the near vicinity. Author's collection

the first decibel of the alert and getting the undercarriage clear of the runway. Squadron pride decreed that this was too long and regular times of 6 to 8 minutes were recorded at nearly all QRA stations. The 1960 SBAC Display at Farnborough was opened by a demonstration of 'scrambling' the crews of four aircraft each day. The crews and aircraft (Valiant B(K).1s of No.148 Squadron operated on the Monday, Thursday and Sunday, Vulcan B.1s of No.617 Squadron took over on Tuesday and Saturday, while No.15 Squadron's Victor B.1s performed on the Wednesday and Friday) were set in motion by a starter's gun, fired from the SBAC President's enclosure. On the Monday, No.148 Squadron was airborne in 1min 56sec and by Sunday, they had reduced this to 1min 37sec. However, as recalled in Chapter 9, fatigue cracks in the wings brought an unexpectedly early termination to Valiant operations.

The dropping of conventional bombs from high altitude had featured heavily in both the Vulcan and Victor clearance trials, although the aircraft were initially designed for the *Blue Danube*- type nuclear bomb, with *Yellow Sun* Mk.1 becoming a part of the arsenal in the late 1950s, followed by *Yellow Sun* Mk.2 in the 1960s. There was also the *Red Beard* tactical nuclear weapon, produced in the Mk.1 15-kt and Mk.2 25-kt versions. A number of WE177 lay-down nuclear weapons were tested with Cottesmore-based Vulcan B.2s. The weapon had an overall length of 12ft (3.7m) and 1ft 4in (0.4m) diameter. Two variants, the 200-kt WE177A, weighing 600lb (272kg) and the 400-kt WE177B, weighing 950lb (430kg) were evaluated and delivery of the weapons commenced in the late summer of 1966.

One further post-Skybolt Avro project must be mentioned at this stage. This was a fighter-support variant of the Vulcan. It

entailed a B.2 carrying three piloted Folland Gnats, one under each wing suspended from the Skybolt hardpoints and one carried in a specially modified bomb-bay. Reports on the project have intimated that the Gnats would be released in enemy airspace, to provide fighter cover, or released to deliver nuclear weapons of their own. Whatever their intentions were, it was considered that they could either land in friendly territory or take on fuel from the Mother aircraft via a specially installed in-flight refuelling drogue. The whole scheme sounds to have the merits of an ashtray on a motorcycle and it quietly evaporated.

In March 1963, the decision to change to low-level operations affected Nos 44, 50 and 101 Squadrons, flying Vulcan B.1As from Waddington, as well as Nos 10 and 15 Squadrons at Cottesmore, plus Nos 55 and 57 Squadrons at Honington, all operating with Victor B.1As. The overall white

The scene at the 1960 SBAC Display, with the four Valiants being towed to their temporary ORP position.

The first of the quartet starting its takle-off run . . .

. . . and the last aircraft rolling as the number two rotates and number three reaches **V1**. Author's collection

Vulcan B.2s from No.101 Squadron in the foreground, with representatives of Nos 9, 44 and 50 Squadrons, on the ORP at Waddington. Author's collection

first time in its life, the Vulcan's tail profile changed shape, when a passive ECM antenna was fitted on the tip. Several Terrain-Following Radar systems were tried, to assist both types in contour-flying at low altitude, and a General Dynamics product was eventually chosen. A small thimble-like antenna was mounted on the nose tip of the Vulcan, while Victors had it positioned directly above the ram air intake that supplied pressure to the bellows of the artificial feel system. In order to preserve airframe fatigue life, two-thirds of training flights were executed at 1,000ft, with the balance being flown at 500ft. This preservation of airframe life particularly affected the Victor, which rode the turbulent air well but at the expense of wing flexing, while the Vulcan, built as a much more sturdy airframe, had no such problems.

No.617 Squadron was the last to operate Blue Steel, with the weapon's last flight being made on 21 December 1970. As the Vulcans and Victors ceased carrying the stand-off bomb, their bomb-bays were modified to take conventional ordnance. The Vulcan B.2 was cleared to carry twenty-one 1,000lb 'iron bombs', set in three carriers, with each holding seven bombs. Handley Page's Victor B.2 had a capacious bomb-bay, holding thirty-five 1,000lb conventional weapons in seven pre-loaded carriers, each containing five bombs, as its standard armament. However, the aircraft was capable of carrying up to forty-eight 1,000lb short-length bombs, three 10,000lb bombs, two 12,000lb bombs or one 22,000lb bomb. The last two were based on the World War II 'Tallboy' and 'Grand Slam' weapons, respectively.

When Avro proposed the Vulcan's Phase 6 wing to carry six Skybolts, they also submitted a variant with the same wing, giving the aircraft a thirty-eight conventional 1,000lb bomb load. Ten were to be carried within a shorter bomb-bay, while a large pod containing fourteen bombs was to be fitted flush under each wing, at approximately mid-span. With the cancellation of Skybolt, both applications of the Phase 6 wing project disappeared.

colour scheme gave way to camouflage and numerous training sorties were flown over the next two months. Sidescan radar and rolling-view maps were installed, as well as an improved ECM suite conducive with the aircraft's new environment. For the

CHAPTER TWELVE

Tanking and Surveying

The sudden loss of the Valiant tankers, in January 1965, kick-started the Air Staff into putting impetus behind provisional plans already in hand. Three years earlier, in 1962, they had been considering the use of Victor B.1s after Bomber Command had its full complement of B.2s. They appreciated that in-flight refuelling requirements were growing and the existing Valiant tanker fleet may not be enough to meet forthcoming demands.

Victor B(K).1A

To ease the situation and by working in non-stop shifts, Handley Page had six Victor B.1As converted to carry two underwing flight-refuelling pods and delivered to No.55 Squadron at Marham by May 1965. Before going to Marham, the first of the six, XH620, went to the A&AEE at Boscombe Down to have the system cleared for service. With just the underwing Mk.20 pods, the six two-pointer tankers retained their bomber role and as such, were designated Victor

B(K).1As. Later, further B(K).1As, fitted with Mk.7 HDUs in the bomb-bay, as well as the underwing pods, to become three-pointer tankers, were delivered to the RAF. The original six two-pointers were re-designated Victor B.1A(K.2P), which was supposed to simplify nomenclature, but in my opinion, merely confused it! No.55 Squadron's two-pointer Victors arrived in time to supply in-flight refuelling to No.74 Squadron's Lightning F.3s on deployment to Akrotiri in August, which was only three months after the Marham unit started tanker operations. Having previously been flying Victor B.1s, they found the tanker's handling to be very similar and had little difficulty in converting to the demands of making over 3,000 re-fuelling link-ups during the two years that they operated the aircraft.

Victor K.1 Prototype

The second production Victor B.1, XA918, having been a Controller (Air) aircraft since 23 June 1956, was selected

for conversion to the full tanker role. The aircraft still had the overall white colour scheme applied on the assembly line in March 1956 and retained the four Sapphire ASSa.7 engines. As the Flight Refuelling Ltd FR.Mk.7 hose and drogue unit installed in the rear of the bomb-bay protruded slightly below the fuselage line, it was enclosed in a neat housing. A 13ft 6in (4.1m) FR.Mk.20B hose and drogue pod, which had first been flight-tested as the FR.Mk.20 in a ventral position on Canberra B.2 WK143, was to be fitted under each wing as an interchangeable unit with the underwing duel tanks, using the same strong points. However, such an installation was seen to give rise to a potential hazard, as the drogues would be close to the tail assembly when trailed. Therefore, the pods, which each weighed over 2,000lb, were moved further outboard, although in this position they were liable to damage unless the pilot took great care when landing in a crosswind. But compromises had to be made and future operations would not prove the pod's positioning to be too unduly troublesome. The underwing pod's outer location gave the added bonus of the external fuel tanks being retained, but not on B.1s, as the Sapphire's 11,050lb (5,012kg) thrust was just not enough to handle the increased weight – although B.1 XA930 is reported to have been used for trials with the tanks *in situ*, but the length of take-off run has not been recorded!

XA918, by this conversion, had become the prototype fully appointed Victor tanker and, as such, was designated the K.1, making its maiden flight in the new configuration on 8 July 1964. Trials were conducted in conjunction with FRL and the A&AEE starting in August, using FRL's Valiant WZ376 at the usual pace for getting equipment cleared for service, when the service Valiant's fatigue problem was encountered. The programme suddenly took on great urgency and the tempo of work at Radlett increased dramatically.

An anonymous Victor B.1A(K.2P) with a pair of Lightnings, hooked up at Le Bourget on 7 June 1969. George Pennick

Victor B.1A(K.2P) XH588 carries No.55 Squadron's crest on its fin. Author's collection

B(K).1A XH650 lands at Wethersfield on 28 October 1968. George Pennick

Victor K.1A XH649 of No.57 Squadron at Marham. Jeff Ball

147

Seen at the Cottesmore Battle of Britain display on 18 September 1965, XH620 was the first Victor converted to B.1A(K.2P) standard. Geoffrey Hunter

Victor B.B.1A(K.2P) XH648 of No.57 Squadron makes its final flight into Duxford on 2 June 1976. Archer/Fenn

The prototype K.1, with everything trailing, shows the nose intake problem had not been solved at this time. Handley Page Association

Victor K.1

Ten Victor B.1s were returned to Radlett for conversion to K.1 three-pointer tanker standard, starting with XA937, which had arrived on 30 April 1964. It made its first flight after conversion on 2 November 1965, with two additional fuel tanks fitted in the bomb-bay, ahead of the Mk.7 HDU. Sealed bomb doors enclosed these, but their rear portion was modified to open for maintenance and servicing of the HDU. When required for transferring fuel, the HDU housing was lowered below the fuselage underside, allowing the hose to trail for the receiving aircraft and three pairs of lights were installed at the rear of the housing for night operations. Initially having a fully extended length of 93ft (28.3m), the hose was shortened to 80ft (24.4m) following A&AEE trials in which the receivers had great difficulty mating with a violently oscillating drogue.

No.57 Squadron moved from Honington to Marham with their Victor B.1s on 1 December 1965, and on 14 February 1966 the unit took delivery of its first Victor K.1. Also at Marham, on 1 March 1965, the Valiant B(PR)K.1- and B(K).1-operating No.214 Squadron was disbanded. Just over a year later, on 1 July 1966, it was re-formed as a Victor tanker squadron, receiving its first K.1 on the same day. Thus Marham became an all-Victor tanker station and remained that way for over ten years. A Tanker Training Flight (TTF) was formed at the base, in which three of the original six B.1/B.1A(K.2P) aircraft operated until May 1970, when

Victor K.1 XH592, as a Tanker Training Flight aircraft, with TTF on its fin, when attending a Coltishall air show on 14 September 1968. George Pennick

the Flight was expanded and changed its name to No.232 OCU, the title of the original Gaydon-based conversion unit that had disbanded there in June 1965.

Victor K.1A

Starting in September 1964, XH650 was the first of fourteen Victor B.1As that were gradually released by their squadrons and returned to Radlett for conversion to three-pointer tanker standard, designated Victor K.1A. No.55 Squadron was the first unit to receive the new variant, commencing in February 1967, where they replaced the original B.1A(K.2P) two-point tankers and the squadron operated with them until August 1976.

XA926, the tenth production B.1, attended an Abingdon display on 15 June 1968, as a K.1 belonging to No.57 Squadron. George Pennick

Victor K.2

The Armstrong Siddeley Sapphire ASSa.7 engines were always going to impede the Victor, so far as realizing its true potential as a tanker was concerned, but the Conway-powered Mk.2 was a different story. No.100 Squadron was disbanded on 30 September 1968, with its fellow Wittering Wing unit, No.139 Squadron, following suit on 31 December of the same year. Therefore, within the space of three months, twenty-one Victor Mk.2s were placed in storage and inspection showed that fatigue cracks in the lower boom forgings had been induced by the years of low-level operations.

Handley Page drew up a design recommendation and schedule for converting the aircraft into tankers, but the Ministry of Defence played the political card. The company had a severe financial problem, mainly due to going over budget in the development of their H.P.137 Jetstream, which had destroyed the MoD's faith in their future. Consequently, the B.2-to-tanker contract was placed with the Hawker Siddeley Group, who undertook the conversions in the Avro works at Woodford, where the original race to get the Avro 698 into the air before the Handley Page H.P.80, had taken place in 1952. The last twenty-five Victor B.2s in Contract No.6/ACFT/15566/CB6(a) had already been cancelled, and the break-even figure for the Jetstream had gone up from 400 to 1,000 units; Handley Page's very existence had depended on the tanker conversion contract. Therefore, on 8 August 1969 the company went into

Victor-to-Victor viewpoint, as an unknown K.1 is approached with the signal lights on the HDU housing showing well. Author's collection

the approach of aircraft requiring refuelling, and the cockpit's fuel control panel was redesigned. When the K.2 conversion was completed, each aircraft was anticipated to have fourteen years of fatigue-free life ahead.

The seventy-fourth Victor to be built, XL231, came off the Radlett assembly line on 31 January 1962 and was converted to B.2R standard in 1963. On 1 March 1972 it made its maiden flight from Woodford, as the prototype Victor K.2, and went to Boscombe Down for refuelling pod trials with dayglo orange paintwork on the outer wings to guide recipients to the pods. Two years later, on 7 May 1974, the first fully-equipped Victor K.2 had its first flight and the following day joined No.232 OCU at Marham. No.543 Squadron at Wyton, flying Victor B.2(SR)s, was disbanded on 24 May 1974 and its aircraft allocated to the K.2 conversion programme, which was scheduled as twenty-eight airframes. However, the Treasury decreed that this would take the programme over budget, so the total was set at twenty-four aircraft, which was considered sufficient to equip two squadrons, this number of units being deemed enough for RAF requirements. Nos 55 and 57 Squadrons at Marham had been flying Victor K.1s and K.1As for over seven years, so the replacement of these aircraft with K.2s commenced in July 1975, the two squadrons collectively being designated the Marham Wing. No.214 Squadron at the same base also gave up its K.1s and K.1As when it was disbanded on 28 January 1977.

The Wing carried out a heavy work schedule, year after year, refuelling RAF air defence Lightnings and Phantoms, as well as Strike Command Buccaneers and

voluntary liquidation and, although assistance was offered from the United States provided that the tanker conversion work could be regained, the MoD would not relent. On 2 March 1970, the main workforce at Radlett was laid off, leaving just a small group to handle support for Victors already in service.

In the spring of 1970, the former Wittering Wing B.2s stored at Radlett were relocated to Woodford, starting with XH671 on 9 April, together with the Ministry's trials B.1, XA922, which had gone the day before. The conversion contract stipulated that there was to be no built-in capability for reversion to the bomber role. Therefore, all weapon-carrying ability was removed, together with the ECM equipment, except for the *Blue Sage* passive warning receiver, which was retained in the tail-cone. The chaff-dispensing mechanisms were taken out, although the 'Küchemann carrots' were retained for their aerodynamic properties. The underwing fuel tanks remained, but as fixed items and not capable of being jettisoned as on the B.2. Handley Page's conversion proposals had included the fitting of an additional 350-gallon (1,590-litre) fuel tank on each wing-tip, with the dual purpose of bob weights, but Hawker

Siddeley preferred to reduce the wingspan by 3ft (0.91m), in order to bring the centre of pressure further inboard.

Considerable work was done on the wing structure, not only to repair the cracks sustained in the low-level bomber operations but also to strengthen areas found to be prone to fatigue. Skin gauge was increased and riveting employed in place of spot welding in the reworked wing structural areas. A new rear-view periscope with a swivelling eyepiece was installed, for rear crewmembers to monitor

XH672, a No.55 Squadron Victor K.2, shares a Mildenhall pan with a KC-135 and C-141. Author's collection

150

Conversion to K.2 standard in full swing at Woodford, with Nimrod production under the same roof.

Gordon Bartley BAE Systems

Jaguars. Bomber Command Vulcans took part in refuelling link-ups on many of their exercise sorties, while Victor-to-Victor tanker top-ups in day or night operations became a regular routine.

The potential hazards of in-flight refuelling were demonstrated by an event on 24 March 1975. No.57 Squadron Victor K.2 XH618, piloted by Flt Lt Keith Handscomb, had a rendezvous point over the North Sea, about 100 miles north-east of Newcastle-upon-Tyne. The recipients were Honington-based Buccaneer S.2s and at the appointed time two of them duly appeared. The first aircraft made contact with the port-side drogue and in two minutes withdrew, having been replenished.

For the pilot of the second Honington aircraft, it was his first participation in an in-flight refuelling, and in order to initi-

ate him in the procedure, he was instructed to make two 'dry' contacts, without receiving any fuel. He made his first contact successfully and withdrew after a minute, to allow the Victor to execute a 180-degree turn. Following the tanker round, the Buccaneer's pilot approached for his second dry contact but, on appreciating that his speed was too fast, he drew back just as he was level with the drogue, which, on striking his probe, caused the hose to snake round and the drogue to hit the Victor. The drogue ricocheted off the tanker's fuselage, striking the Buccaneer's canopy and causing the hose to wrap itself around the fuselage. The pilot made a quick nose-down manouevre, but his starboard wing hit the Victor's port elevator, causing Flt Lt Handscomb to lose control; this placed too great a load on the tail and it broke

off. The captain ordered the crew to bale out, but just as he made his ejection, the Victor exploded. Handscomb was found in a dinghy by the German freighter *Hoheburg* and recovered from his injuries to fly again. The rest of the tanker's crew perished, while the Buccaneer survived to make landfall.

In the early spring of 1982, the proficiency of the Marham Wing was put under the spotlight in the biggest possible way, when Argentine forces invaded the Falkland group of islands in the south Atlantic and the RAF went to war once more.

Again, when British forces became an element in the Gulf War in 1990–91, No.55 Squadron supplied eight Victor K.2s, later increased to ten, to provide in-flight refuelling for the Jaguar, Tornado GR.1s and F.3s engaged, plus all Canadian,

K.2 XH672 of No.55 Squadron stands by to receive two Buccaneers and a Tornado, on its underwing hoses only. *Gordon Bartley BAE Systems*

French and US aircraft that were compatible with the probe/drogue system. Taking over from the VC10s of No.101 Squadron, which had been operating in the Gulf area since October 1990, No.55 Squadron's detachment landed at Muharraq, Bahrain, on 14 December of the same year.

Until 18 March 1991, when eight aircraft recovered to Marham, adorned with the inevitable nose-art of wartime operations, the squadron's K.2s had completed 417 sorties in 1,150 flying hours. Of this total, 299 sorties in 870 hours had been in support of combat operations during the forty-two days of actual warfare. Although operating under extreme pressure, the squadron met every scheduled in-flight refuelling rendezvous, in the established *Olive Trail* route on the Iraq border and had 100 per cent serviceability, thanks to some excellent engineering support. Considering all ten aircraft had been built

Victor Tankers
The conversion of Victor bomber aircraft into in-flight refuelling tankers involved a total of fifty-five airframes.

Victor K.1
Eleven aircraft obtained by conversion of existing B.1s by Handley Page.

XA918	XA926	XA927	XA928	XA930	XA932	XA936
XA937	XA938	XA939	XA941			

Victor B(K).1A/B.1A(K.2P)
Six aircraft obtained by conversion of existing B.1As by Handley Page.

XH615	XH620	XH646	XH647	XH648	XH667

Victor K.1A
Fourteen aircraft obtained by conversion of existing B.1As by Handley Page.

XH587	XH588	XH589	XH590	XH591	XH614	XH616
XH618	XH619	XH621	XH645	XH649	XH650	XH651

Victor K.2
Twenty-four aircraft obtained by conversion of existing B.2s by Hawker Siddeley.

XH669	XH671	XH672	XH673	XH675	XL158	XL160
XL161	XL162	XL163	XL164	XL188	XL189	XL190
XL191	XL192	XL231	XL232	XL233	XL511	XL512
XL513	XM715	XM717				

Conversion to K.2 standard of Vulcans XM561, XM571 and XJ825 under way at Woodford.

Gordon Bartley BAE Systems

between 1960 and 1962, with the newest K.2 converted aircraft first flying as such in July 1977, this was a great achievement for an aircraft in the twilight of its years.

Deployments to the Middle East continued until 8 September 1993, and on 15 October of that year, No.55 Squadron was disbanded at Marham, still with seven airworthy Victor K.2s on their inventory. This finally closed the book on thirty-eight years of V-bomber service in the RAF.

Vulcan K.2

The war in the south Atlantic had thrown into relief the urgent need for more in-flight refuelling capacity than the Marham Wing could provide. The RAF had four-teen Vickers-Armstrongs VC10 C.Mk.1s in service with Transport Command. Ten more ex-British Airways VC10s, including the larger Super variant, were held at Abingdon awaiting conversion to military service. On 5 July 1983, the first of six ex-British Airways Lockheed L1011 TriStars, ZD948, entered service as a passenger transport, pending a future conversion by Marshall of Cambridge to an air-to-air refuelling capability.

It would take well over a year before the first of either of these conversions would come to fruition and what was wanted was more tanker availability, as of yesterday! The Vulcan B.2 was a logical candidate and six aircraft were selected for a rapid conversion to a dual bomber/tanker role, for which the designation B(K).2 was allocated, later to be amended to K.2. Following on from the Valiant and Victor

Vulcan K.2 XH560 on trials with K.2 XL445 receiving. Author's collection

tankers, the bomb-bay was the obvious place to install the Mk.17 HDU, but when the slide rules were brought out, it became apparent that such a location would place the receiving aircraft in too close a proximity to the tanker. The delta con-figuration placed the wing trailing edge much further aft than was the case with any other type. Further calculations showed that the ECM bay was large enough to take the top portion of the HDU and the lower half could be faired in. This also had the added attraction of leaving room for an additional fuel tank in the bomb-bay, without jeopardizing too much of the aircraft's bomb-carrying capacity. Optimistically and rashly, the MoD was informed that Woodford could do a conversion in three weeks.

An HDU was delivered to Woodford on 9 May 1982 and two FRL engineers

arrived the next day, to separate the top half of the Unit from its bottom, coincid-ing with the MoD giving the go-ahead to the project. XH561, the fifteenth Vulcan B.2 to be built, arrived at Woodford on 11 May and shifts of workers were organized so that there was no let-up on the work in hand. The top of the Mk.17 HDU was fitted in the space left by the removal of the ECM suite, so that the lower half could be mated to it *in situ*, and a rather ungainly, but effective, square-sectioned cover was placed over the protruding Unit, complete with a group of three lights on either side for guidance to the receiver's probe.

The conversion of XH561 was com-pleted in exactly six weeks, on 18 June, but no one at the MoD seems to have minded the time slippage. It received an interim CA release five days later, on 23 June, and was ferried back to No.50 Squadron on the same day. The type was considered to be a very good tanker, with the only reservations being that it was only a single-pointer and there were so few of them. Their operational life was also short-lived, because the HDUs installed in such meritoriously quick time at Woodford were only available because they were being held pending the com-pletion of VC10 conversions at Filton. As the Vickers-Armstrongs airframes became ready for their HDUs to be installed, a Vulcan K.2 was withdrawn from service and surrendered its flight-refuelling capabilities. On 31 March 1984, No.50 Squadron was disbanded and the twenty-seven years of Vulcan opera-tions, started with No.230 OCU in May

A fine shot of K.2 XH560 with its single HDU deployed. Avro Heritage

1956, was officially closed, with the demise of the HDU-less K.2 airframes varying.

Reconnaissance

Right from the beginning, Specifications B.35/46 and B.9/48 stipulated that the three aircraft selected for production would be developed with dual roles, principally as bombers, but with a strategic reconnaissance capacity. Vickers-Armstrongs were the only company to apply this on the original assembly line, and the seventh production Valiant, WP205, was the first B(PR).1, which No.543 Squadron started operating in June 1955. The Vulcan and Victor both differed from the Valiant approach in so far as neither was produced as new-build reconnaissance aircraft, but attained the capability by conversion of existing airframes. Although both of their respective prototypes had undertaken photographic reconnaissance trials (four Victor B.1s actually went to work alongside No.543 Squadron's Valiant B(PR).1s in 1958, as the Victor Radar Reconnaissance Flight, which was so under-utilized that it just disappeared as a unit), the introduction of the Victor to the operational role was hastened by the Valiant's premature withdrawl from service. Rather ironically, the Canberra, which was the RAF's first turbojet-powered reconnaissance aircraft, the PR.3 commencing service with No.540 Squadron at Benson in December 1952, has seen off all three of the four-engined types and today is still serving at Marham in the PR.9 variant.

Victor B(SR).2/SR.2

During 1959, the Controller (Air) B.1, XA920, was fitted with a photographic reconnaissance conversion pack and undertook trials at Radlett and Boscombe Down for a time. Prior to this, the RRE at Malvern had been investigating high-resolution radars for reconnaissance navigation and bombing, with the sideways-looking mode being dictated by aerial technology at that time. This was due to resolution being a function of aerial length, so that the longer the aerial, the better the definition. (When Avro designed their Type 730 for the original strategic reconnaissance role, they provided for a 50ft (15.25m) aerial in the lower fuselage.) The RRE produced a 15ft (4.6m) Q-Band aerial, with a beam width of 0.1 degrees, for airborne installation and the project, designated the codename *Red Neck*, was intended for operational application on the Victor B.2. The Q-Brand aerial was test-flown by the RRE as a ventral installation on a Valetta C.2, that was delivered to Defford on 3 May 1951.

The *Red Neck* system called for a reconnaissance installation carried in pods under both wings. One pod contained a Q-Band transmitter with a 15ft (4.6m) aerial, while the other pod carried an X-Band (9G.Hz) transmitter with a 30ft (9m) aerial. Although this work by the RRE was directed at the reconnaissance application, parallel interest was shown in the possibility of the Q-Band high-resolution system being adapted for V-bombers, in a high-altitude NBS role. However, the NBS Mk.1 system incorporating the H_2S Mk.9 radar was considered satisfactory by the Air Staff, although when the TSR.2 was on the drawing boards at Weybridge and Preston, a Q-Band aerial was designed to be installed in a lower-fuselage pallet, developed by Mullard Equipment Laboratories.

The Red Neck **aerodynamic test pod is under the port wing of an unknown B.2.** Handley Page Association

**XA918 carrying two
Red Neck pods,
when evaluating
the system.** Handley
Page Association

Victor SR.2 XL193, on a rain-soaked Farnborough tarmac, in 1966. Author's collection

An aerodynamic test pod was installed on a pylon under the port wing of an unidentified B.2 and full trials of the sideways-looking *Red Neck* system were conducted with XA918, before it had the extended outer wing chord and fixed wing nose flaps. The units were carried in pods, attached to the underwing strong points normally used to carry the external fuel tanks. *Red Neck* performed well and was reliable enough for consideration to be

given to operating it with No.543 Squadron at Wyton, but eventually the idea was discarded. With the development of the Synthetic Aperture Radar small aerial heads by the Malvern Airborne Radar Group in the early 1970s, which had trials in Canberra WT327, the use of very long aerial arrays was discontinued.

The long-range photographic reconnaissance role for the Victor had trials in B.2 XL165, which became the prototype

for the Victor B(SR).2, a designation which in time has given way to Victor SR.2. Due to the gap left by the Valiant, its trials were hastened and the aircraft flew to the A&AEE for assessment of its operational capabilities, following which it was allocated to No.543 Squadron in February 1966, by which time four more SR.2s were with the squadron at Wyton. A total of eight aircraft went to Radlett for conversion to the PR role between May 1964 and April 1965.

The photo-reconnaissance fit in the SR.2 consisted of a camera crate containing F49 and F96 cameras for daytime, while F89 cameras were employed for nocturnal operations. Four F49s were usually installed, with up to eight F96s included in the crate, which was situated centrally in the bomb-bay. Unlike the PR Valiants, which had glazed panels incorporated in the bomb doors, the Victor SR.2 opened its bomb doors in the usual fashion and the air deflector grille actuated by the door-opening sequence for weapon dropping was still deployed.

Forward of the camera crate in the bomb-bay, the space could be fitted with either two additional fuel tanks, two photo-flash canisters or a combination of one of each, and in this configuration in

XL165, the prototype SR.2, at Upper Heyford on 14 June 1969. George Pennick

No.543 Squadron sent SR.2 XM718 to the 1969 Air Fête at Mildenhall. George Pennick

three aircraft went to Woodford for conversion to Victor K.2 standard. Three more, XH674, XL165 and XL193, remained at Wyton to form the Victor Flight. This was a unit dedicated to monitoring French nuclear testing in the Pacific, which operated until May 1975, when nuclear testing was discontinued. XH674 joined the Marham Wing until being struck off charge on 22 July 1976, while the remaining two went from the Victor Flight to St Athan, to be struck off charge at the end of 1975.

Vulcan B.2(MRR)/SR.2

With the impending closure of No.543 Squadron and the urgent need for some of its Victor SR.2s to be converted to fill the tanker shortfall, a decision was made to convert a small number of Vulcan B.2s into the long-distance strategic reconnaissance role, to replace the Victors temporarily. Five ex-*Blue Steel* aircraft, plus four that had previously been converted for conventional 'iron bomb' operations, were selected and No.27 Squadron was re-formed at Scampton on 1 November 1973

the early 1970s Victor SR.2s were of great assistance to the Royal Navy in plotting the positions of large numbers of Soviet Navy vessels. However, when the economics of flying Victor photo-reconnaissance missions was compared with the Canberra PR.9, it was found that the English Electric aircraft was a more

viable proposition and the nine Victor SR.2s began concentrating on radar reconnaissance operations.

On 24 May 1974, No.543 Squadron at Wyton was disbanded. Two aircraft, XL230 and XM716, had crashed in the nine years that the squadron had been operating the SR.2, and on disbanding

A No.27 Squadron Vulcan B.2(MRR) makes itself known to a Soviet helicopter carrier with Kamov Ka-25 'Hormones' aboard. Author's collection

---

Photographic and Radar Reconnaissance

Victor B(SR).2/SR.2
Eight aircraft obtained by conversion of existing B.2s by Handley Page:
XH672   XH674   XL161   XL165   XL193   XL230   XM715   XM716

Vulcan SR.2/B.2(MRR)
Five aircraft obtained by conversion of existing *Blue Steel* B.2s by Hawker Siddeley:
XH534   XH537   XH558   XH560   XH563

Four aircraft obtained by conversion of existing 'iron bomb' B.2s by Hawker Siddeley:
XJ780   XJ782   XJ823   XJ825

---

to operate them. The squadron had been a Vulcan B.2 unit for eleven years before being disbanded at Scampton on 29 March 1972, so knew its way around the delta.

Once more, some confusion arose concerning the designation of the converted aircraft. First referred to as the Vulcan SR.2, their principal application for maritime radar reconnaissance was recognized by the official designation Vulcan B.2 (MRR), which does not exactly trip off the tongue too well. For the new role, the aircraft were fitted with Loran C navigation equipment and the General Dynamics terrain-following radar was removed, thereby getting rid of the thimble-shaped aerial on the tip of the nose (strangely, this aerial housing was not removed from the Victor when it was adapted for the role). Some of the B.2(MRR)s had upper-air sampling pods fitted on small pylons, attached to the underwing hardpoints originally built in for Skybolt, the main body of these pods having been manufactured by the conversion of former Hawker Hunter external fuel tanks. A small 'localizer' sensor, with the appearance of a vacuum flask, was carried further inboard, under the port wing.

The reconnaissance Vulcans remained at Scampton, with No.27 Squadron, for nine years, until the unit was disbanded on 31 March 1982, this being the seventh time in its sixty-seven-year history – I cannot help thinking that a phoenix might be a more appropriate motif to have in its squadron badge, rather than the elephant, which it has as a reminder of its interwar Indian 'colonial policing' duties.

After the squadron's disbanding, its aircraft were distributed to various locations. XJ823 and XJ825 remained at Scampton, while XH563 became Instructional Airframe 8744M, together with XJ782 (8766M). XH558 and XH560 went to Waddington, with XH560 later being converted to K.2 standard. XH534 was sent to St Athan, where it was sold for scrap, as was XJ780, while XH537 became another Instructional Airframe, 8749M, at Abingdon. Today their maritime reconnaissance role is in the safe hands of the 'Mighty Hunter', the Nimrod.

CHAPTER THIRTEEN

War Games and War

Joint USAF Exercises

From the first time that the United States invited Bomber Command to take part in the SAC Bombing Competition, at Pinecastle AFB, Florida, in October 1957, regular inter-Service competitions and exercises have been held. The 1957 event involved a single Valiant from each of Nos 138 and 214 Squadrons, plus three Vulcan B.1s from No.230 OCU's inventory. It was considered necessary for V-bomber crews to gain experience from the different operational techniques of the USAF and it has been placed on record that, although the Bomber Command quartet did not exactly shine, nevertheless a lot was learned from the venture – one thing being that the RAF should not underestimate the professionalism of SAC as a force. It was also good to learn that the Valiant and Vulcan, which had only been in service for a short time compared to the Boeing B-47s that they were competing against, were operationally as good as the American aircraft, while being superior in terms of weapon load and altitude performance. But the RAF V-bomber crews had quite a lot to

learn and it is to their credit that they did just that.

In 1958, the SAC competition was held at March AFB in California, where Bomber Command acquitted itself much better. The regularity of the contests, plus the desire to gain experience of long-distance navigation sorties over featureless terrain, led to the establishment of a training base at Goose Bay, in Labrador, which had been a busy ferry station during World War II, handling a large percentage of transatlantic Allied air traffic. V-bomber detachments operated out of an expanded Goose Bay and the experience of having to rely on pinpoint navigation over thousands of miles of virtually uninhabited, frozen wastelands of the North American continent was invaluable. Flying at the speed and altitude of a V-bomber over the United Kingdom, with its great number of landmarks, could almost be accomplished with an AA map book and was no great test to an experienced navigator.

The December 1971 competition was attended by Nos 27 and 101 Squadrons, with Vulcan B.2s XM600, XM602, XM650 and XM654. Also present was Vulcan B.2

XL392, which was flown into McCoy AFB in Florida by Air Vice Marshal B.P.T. Horsley, Air Officer Commanding No.1 Bomber Group, carrying the inscription, written on the nose-wheel door, 'Flown by HRH Prince Charles on 27 July 1971'. Whether SAC were suitably impressed has not been recorded.

Exercise *Skyshield*

By October 1961, a joint early-warning system had been established by Canada and the United States, to shield the North American eastern coastline. It involved an automated and integrated system of communications for the continent's SAM missile batteries, working with the fighter defence squadrons of the Royal Canadian Air Force (RCAF) and the USAF, in what was designated the North American Air Defense Command (NAADC). For the first full-scale test of the system, Exercise *Skyshield* was set up and RAF Bomber Command was invited to participate. The exercise was as near as the Command was going to get at that time, in terms of true operational conditions, without actually going to war and it would provide good testing experience for them as well as for the NAADC.

Nos 27 and 83 Squadrons, both based at Scampton, were each ordered to supply four Vulcan B.2s, which would be the first time that the variant had been used for such an exercise and the first time that the USAF was able properly to assess the 'aluminum cloud', as the Vulcan was euphemistically called in the USA. No.27 Squadron deployed to Kindley AFB, on the island of Bermuda, to attack from the south, while No.83 Squadron had to stay nearer to home and fly their sorties against the northern areas from Lossiemouth.

Exercise *Skyshield* started on 14 October and No.27 Squadron attacked from the south, using their jamming ECM to good effect, but Convair F-102A Delta Daggers intercepted three of their aircraft near the

The No.230 OCU Vulcan B.1s at Pinecastle AFB in October 1957. *Aeroplane*

B.2 meets B-52 . . .

. . . and KC-135s.
Harry Holmes and
author's collection

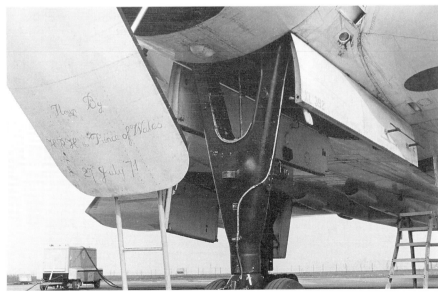

Vulcan B.2 XL392 with its inscription. Dave Thomas

Vulcan B.2 of No.44 Squadron, with the Eagle Squadron's F-15s. Author's collection

A smoky B.2 at Abbotsford in 1972. Author's collection

coast. The fourth, however, changed course to the north and flew across the American mainland before eventually landing at Plattsburgh AFB, in New York State, not far from the Canadian border. Against the northern defences, B-47s flew low-level attacks to neutralize the ground radar units, with B-52s, combined with B-57s, attacking from 35,000 to 40,000ft. With their greater operational altitude, No.83 Squadron's Vulcan B.2s attacked from 56,000ft and, after attacking the lower formations, the intercepting fighter units did not have enough fuel to climb to the Vulcan's altitude. Consequently, the squadron had no interceptions and flew serenely on their allotted course, to land at Stephenville in Newfoundland.

The consensus of opinion by the United States on *Skyshield* was that the NAADC was reasonably effective, but at a disadvantage against a high-altitude attacking force. The F-101C Voodoo's service ceiling was 52,000ft (15,850m) and the Delta Dagger could make 57,000ft (17,370m), but both had a very limited endurance once they had attained these altitudes, while Bomber Command's Vulcan B.2 still had nearly 10,000ft (3,050m) in reserve. From the RAF's point of view, it was an interesting exercise and the Vulcan's high-altitude ability gave it a measure of defence over a wide range, but, of course, this was not total immunity, as Gary Powers had discovered the previous year – although it has to be pointed out that he was deep inside Soviet air space, without any ECM, before he received the undivided attention of an SA-2 missile.

The Malayan Emergency

The deep consternation felt by many countries regarding the emergence of Mao Tse-tung as Chairman of the Chinese Communist Party was enough for Australia, Britain, France, New Zealand, Pakistan, the Philippine Republic, Thailand and the United States to draw up the South East Asia Collective Defence Treaty. Signed in Manila on 19 February 1955, it agreed that the signatories would 'separately and jointly, by means of continuous and effective help and mutual aid, to maintain and develop the individual and collective capacity to resist armed attack and to prevent any counter-subversive activities directed against members' territorial integrity and political stability'.

Communist influence in the 'rubber state' of Malaya was led by Chin Peng, who had been awarded the Order of the British Empire for services against the Japanese occupying forces during World War II. Now his ambition was to evict all 'Imperialist' influences and when three rubber planters were murdered by Communist terrorists on 16 June 1948, a National State of Emergency was declared, with the aim of overthrowing the Malayan Races Liberation Army. The Emergency was to last twelve years and RAF Canberras were heavily involved, operating alongside the air forces of Australia and New Zealand.

During the conflict, the airfield at Butterworth, in northern Malaya, was expanded and in 1960, although the Emergency was no longer in force, the first of an annual detachment of Victor B.1As flew into Butterworth. These were No.10 Squadron aircraft and during their stay, they spent hours unloading the contents of their bomb-bays on the China Rock and Song Song ranges. While being useful exercises, the Victor deployments at Butterworth had the dual purpose of being a visible reminder to the surrounding states of the potential capabilities of the RAF, should anyone step out of line.

Trouble with Indonesia

Britain and Malaya signed a defence agreement on 16 September 1957 and when in December 1962 an armed rebellion broke out in the Sultanate of Brunei, swift action by both countries was called for, in order to contain the uprising. The unrest had its foundations in the ambitions of President Sukarno of Indonesia to form an Indonesian 'super-state' by annexing the whole of Borneo. Canberra B.2s of Nos 45 and 81 Squadrons took care of the immediate unrest, but by 1964 there had occurred a dangerous escalation of the conflict. Increased numbers of Indonesian rebel troops were crossing the North Borneo borders, despite the formation of the State of Malaysia in September 1963 by uniting the provinces of Malaya, Sabah, Sarawak and Singapore. A condition of the treaty forming the State had been that Britain gained permission to maintain forces and bases within Malaysia, in order to preserve peace within the area.

The increase in Indonesian guerrilla activities was supported by Indonesian Air Force (IAF) B-25 Mitchell flights over the peninsula, as well as Soviet-built Tu-16 Badgers, which the IAF had recently obtained and which regularly flew close to Singapore. Once again, Canberras were heavily engaged in attacks on rebel forces. A three-monthly rotation of Canberra detachments to Tengah, on the island of Singapore, was initiated, to counter any large-scale assaults on the Malaysian state. The British government viewed the situation as volatile enough to order eight Victor B.1As to join the Far East Air Force (FEAF) in December 1963. These were drawn from Nos 10 and 15 Squadrons at Cottesmore, which each supplied four aircraft.

These were rotated with Nos 55 and 57 Squadrons from Honington the following year, and during one of these deployments a B.1A pilot earned the Air Force Cross (AFC). On 24 November, Flt Lt Terry Filing flew XH614 out from Tengah, to encounter an engine phenomenon peculiar to tropical conditions and the Armstrong Siddeley Sapphire, called 'centre-line closure'. During the climb out of Singapore, the aircraft encountered thick rain cloud at 14,000ft and he was still flying in it when, at 23,000ft, the crew heard a loud bang. No.1 engine quickly lost power, an orange glow was reflected from the cloud and the established fire drill was set in motion, which included shutting down No.2 engine. The reflected glow disappeared, but as the aircraft descended, a second bang was heard and No.3 engine's instruments showed that this too had failed, although at no time was there any fire warning indication.

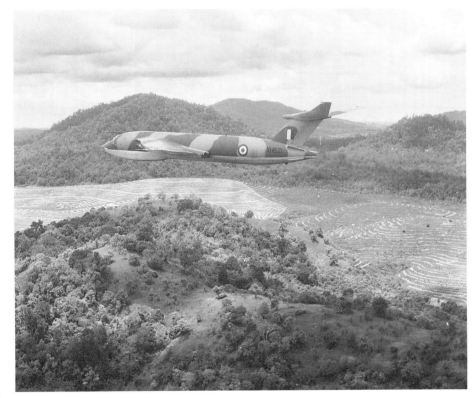

Victor B.1A XH621 of No.57 Squadron when it was a bomber unit, over a typical Malaysian landscape.
Author's collection

With only one Sapphire in action, all electrics and fuel switching were aligned to it and a course to Tengah was set, during which it was decided to try to relight the No.2 engine that had been shut down during the fire drill and which everyone hoped was still in working condition. If not, the unpalatable question of abandoning the aircraft had to be faced. XH614 broke cloud at 12,000ft and, after three abortive attempts, No.2 Sapphire burst back into life, enabling Flt Lt Filing to touch down at Tengah, coming to rest just off the end of the runway.

Examination showed that Nos 1 and 3 engines had shattered, severing the fire warning systems circuitry in the process. Because the compressor blades expand when on full power, enough clearance exists between the compressor casing and the blades to allow for this. When XH614 entered the rain cloud, being of different metals the casing cooled quicker than the blades, so that their tips came in contact with the contracting casing and disintegrated. An economical solution was found, by coating the inside of the casing with an abrasive ceramic, which helped more or less to reduce the rate of heat loss equally between the blades and casing. If, however, the blades did come into contact with the casing, the tips would be ground down, instead of the whole blade shattering. As a result of this 'exceptional feat of leadership, airmanship and courage', Flt Lt Terry Filing was awarded the AFC.

IAF activity increased during 1964 and seaborne raids were made by Indonesian troops against the Malaysian mainland. Troops were dropped by IAF Hercules on the Malaysian state of Johor and the situation became dangerous enough for Canberras to be deployed from Germany. Some of the Akrotiri Strike Wing's Canberras were also despatched, together with four Vulcan B.2s of No.12 Squadron, which were held at Gan, the most southern of the Maldives, in the Indian Ocean. With each B.2 carrying a full load of 1,000lb 'iron' bombs, they, together with the Victors at Tengah, constituted a genuine threat to Indonesia's ambitions, so that within a month tension in the area had been relieved enough for the Vulcans to leave Gan and start returning to Coningsby, just in time for No.12 Squadron's move to Cottesmore on 17 November.

The Far East Air Force

The Cottesmore Wing of Nos 9, 12 and 35 Squadrons was handed the responsibility of reinforcing the FEAF should any further emergencies arise, and in April 1965 No.35 Squadron took part in Exercise *Spherical*. This was an operational exercise, during which the squadron was called into action without any prior warning, by a request from the FEAF received on 26 April at 14.00hr, for im-

mediate reinforcements. By 00.15hr on 27 April, the squadron's Commanding Officer, Wg Cdr David Craig, was lifting his Vulcan B.2 off Cottesmore's operational runway and within less than 36 hours, eight of his squadron's B.2s, including XM597, XM598, XM599, XM600 and XM604, were basking in the heat on Gan's dispersals, before going on to Butterworth, with four aircraft diverting to Tengah.

Fourteen-week long detachments were made to the Far East under the *Matterhorn Rotation* programme, which gave assurance to Commonwealth countries within that vast area; India, in particular, appreciated these actions, as China had made its first nuclear test on 16 October 1964.

Exercises to test Australian defences were flown at altitudes well above 60,000ft (18,300m), where the Vulcan B.2's speed was just keeping ahead of the stall. Neither the RAAF's CA-27 Sabre Mk.32, with its service ceiling of 55,000ft (16,760m), nor Mirage IIIO, capable of reaching 59,000ft (18,000m), could make any interceptions.

In 1970, No.44 Squadron at Waddington took over the FEAF reinforcement rotation and flew its Vulcan B.2s to Tengah for Exercise *Bersatu Padu*. At

Tengah, new facilities had been constructed, to cater for the increased amount of V-bomber activities in the area that were proving their global capabilities under the codenames of *Sunflower* and *Moonflower*, denoting whether the particular exercise was a daylight or night operation. How the presence of V-bombers in the area affected various decisions made by those who wanted changes to the status quo may never be known, but during their times of deployment, not a single Vulcan or Victor dropped any ordnance in anger. Canberra crews most likely thought 'No, we are doing it all!'

Beating SAC in the USA

The November 1974 SAC Bombing Competition displayed the great strides that Bomber Command crews had made since their first attendance at Pinecastle seventeen years earlier. Based at Barksdale AFB, outside Bossier City in Louisiana, four Vulcan B.2s were ranged against representatives of nearly every B-52 and F-111 base in the whole of the USAF's Strategic and Tactical Air Commands. It was to be the biggest strategic bombing

On their way to Giant Voice, **four Vulcan B.2s overfly an assortment of HC-130P, KC-135 and EC-121 at Barksdale AFB.** Author's collection

war game yet held, entitled *Giant Voice*. The fifty-one aircraft taking part each flew four missions, mostly at night. High- and low-altitude bombing sorties, scored by radar trackers and a bomb release 'bleeper' in the bomb-aimer's button, were followed by an inertial or celestial navigation exercise, with low-level navigation flights made across Louisiana, together with the neighbouring states of Mississippi and Arkansas.

In one of these sorties, a Vulcan crew from No.230 OCU, commanded by Flt Lt Peter Perry, suffered the embarrassment of a large part of its navigational system malfunctioning just prior to take-off. This did nothing to impede their mission, however, as they promptly opted to continue, using maps and pencils, for an old-fashioned manually navigated sortie that proved to be more accurate than that flown by any other participant. For their efforts, the RAF contingent took the Mathis Trophy, awarded for the best results by one crew in bombing and navigation, plus the Navigation Trophy for the best individual crew performance. Air Vice Marshal David Evans, No.1 Group's AOC, voiced his jubilation by declaring that 'we did what everybody said couldn't be done – beat Strategic Air Command in the USA. I don't believe in good luck ... you can only *make* good luck for yourself.' From the USAF point of view, they found it hard to come to terms with a bombed-up Vulcan leaping off the tarmac halfway along the runway and climbing at an alarming angle towards the heavens, while the B-52 ate up every inch of runway before it got airborne, only to dip again before really getting going.

Exercise *Red Flag*

Three years later, in 1977, Bomber Command Vulcan B.2 crews were invited to join Exercise *Red Flag* in Nevada. Based at Nellis AFB, outside Las Vegas, this was an exercise initiated in the USAF to maintain combat capabilities in the aftermath of the Vietnam War. It ranged over a vast area, with targets as large as industrial sites protected by missile defences or as small as individual vehicles. Combat-experienced fighter pilots flying Northrop F-5s, which had become the standard simulated-Soviet fighter, were the defending force. Each crew undertook five missions, ranging from 'as high as' 300ft to below

Vulcan B.2s, including a No.35 Squadron aircraft, when attending Red Flag **at Nellis AFB in 1977.** Author's collection

200ft over featureless desert and mountain ranges. The Vulcan crew's high standard of professionalism, in which they flew many sorties without a single interception, impressed even the most hardened USAF crews.

One lesson that came out of *Red Flag* was the fact that a Vulcan turning away from an interceptor presented a large planform, which, painted in the existing Light Aircraft Grey, was an easily seen target. Consequently, for the low-altitude role that they were now assuming, B.2s were

painted in a 'wrap-round' camouflage pattern, extending over the whole underside of the aircraft, and national roundels on the wing's lower surfaces were removed.

Operation *Black Buck* – the Preparations

In 1967, the Royal Navy's nuclear-powered submarines, armed with Polaris ICBMs, had wrested the strategic nuclear deterrent role from Bomber Command, which had brought about a change in Vulcan B.2 operations, for which it no longer used in-flight refuelling.

It is doubtful if that was of any interest to the President of Argentina when, on 2 April 1982, he ordered his forces to invade South Georgia and the Falkland Islands, in the south Atlantic. The immediate response from the British government was to organize a Task Force, under the code-name *Corporate*, in which the Royal Navy would convey ground troops, together with RAF personnel and aircraft, to attempt a recapture of the British territory. The only airfield in the area, at Port Stanley, was an obvious target and an ambitious operation was initiated, whereby the airfield would be attacked by Vulcan B.2s carrying conventional 'iron bombs', supported by Victor K.2 tankers. Just how ambitious these operational plans were has to be viewed against the background of there being only three Vulcan squadrons in existence and these were scheduled to be disbanded in two months' time, with the subsequent disposal of their aircraft. Furthermore, such an operation would virtually denude the RAF in Europe of its air-to-air refuelling capability, for it

was 8,000 miles from Waddington to Port Stanley – and the same distance back!

Given the codename Operation *Black Buck*, the attack would require at least ten bombers to be available and the first task was to find ten Vulcan B.2s capable of undertaking such a mission. Although some of the Vulcans in the three squadrons still retained their refuelling probes, together with the internal plumbing, fifteen years of inactivity had given rise to the deterioration of nearly all valves and seals, to such an extent that they were useless. There was the added complication that quite a few Vulcan probes had already been removed, to be donated to Hercules and Nimrods, prior to the retirement of Roy Chadwick's delta, so the net to obtain replacement parts had to be spread as far as the other side of the Atlantic. One further obstacle was the fact that Vulcan-experienced personnel, ground crew as well as aircrew, who had already been posted in view of the forthcoming retirement of the type, had to be recalled to Waddington.

Eventually, enough parts and personnel were obtained to restore ten aircraft to active in-flight refuelling standard and of these, five B.2s – XM597, XM607 and

XM612 from No.44 Squadron, XM598 from No.50 Squadron, plus XL391 from No.101 Squadron – were chosen for restoring to conventional bombing standard, because they were the only aircraft that had retained the full Skybolt attachments, together with the associated services. These would be necessary for the carrying of external stores required for the mission. The Vulcan B.2's full capacity of twenty-one 1,000lb high-explosive bombs would be carried and the attack would be made at night, using the aircraft's H_2S blind-bombing equipment.

In the Atlantic Ocean, 1,000 miles south-west of the African state of Liberia, stands the small Ascension Island, governed by the British dependency of St Helena. The several military installations on the island, including a satellite and missile tracking station, are American owned, with Britain retaining rights of use of the Wideawake airfield, with its single 10,000ft runway. There is no taxiway or holding loop, but a large concrete parking apron at the western end of the runway, sufficient for the average of fifty-five aircraft movements per month that the airfield enjoys. This unimposing tract of 60 square miles of solidified volcanic rock, by

The Black Buck **dark grey underside is shown to advantage in this shot.** Author's collection

its geographical position, was to become the staging 'halfway house' for the aerial element of *Corporate* and at the height of the operations the airfield would be almost overwhelmed, with some 800 aircraft movements being recorded in a single day.

At Waddington, preparing the five selected B.2s plus their crews was an all-encompassing activity, not the least element being the reintroduction of in-flight refuelling. This entailed a very concentrated training programme, which revealed that the aircraft's probe was very susceptible to leakage and fuel spillage. This presented the captain and co-pilot with a torrent of AVTUR over the windscreen, completely obscuring their forward vision. Despite much experimenting, no really satisfactory cure was found, although the fitting of two rows of small vortex generator-like flat plates, diverging from the nose to either side of the windscreen, directing the stream of fuel away from the canopy, was found to be the best compromise, to which Flight Refuelling Ltd had considerable input.

Because the Argentine forces were known to have installed ground-to-air radar on the Falklands and the *Fuerza Aérea Argentina* operated at least one Boeing 707 in an airborne early warning (AEW) capacity, Waddington's engineering facilities were faced with the task of installing a suitable ECM capability on each Vulcan. The only compatible system readily available was the Westinghouse AN/ALQ-101, E-10 pod, carried by No.208 Squadron's Buccaneer S.2s at Honington and to carry this, pylons were fabricated out of surplus mild steel girders, in store at Waddington. A pylon was installed under the starboard wing of four of the aircraft, attached at the built-in Skybolt pick-up points, with the necessary electrics routed through the coolant pipes required for the missile and wired into a control panel at the Air Electronics Officer's desk. The ability to install these pylons was one of the determining factors when selection of the individual Vulcans was made, because late production aircraft, such as XM645 which had originally been short-listed, were built after Skybolt's cancellation and consequently did not have the missile's hardpoints or internal ducting. The pylons could also be used for carrying Sparrow, Martel and Shrike missiles for defensive purposes.

A Delco inertial navigation system for each aircraft had to be extracted from

former British Airways Super VC10 aircraft that were in open storage at Abingdon, awaiting conversion into tankers, and a number were purchased from British Airways, as the Victor tankers required to be similarly equipped. One of the final processes for the Vulcan B.2s' conversion was the re-spraying of their undersides with a coat of a darker grey than standard, removing the underwing roundels, and the relative squadron insignia carried on fins was also overpainted.

While all the Vulcan preparations were being implemented at Waddington, Marham was equally active. Although they were not actually carrying out any bombing, their involvement was more intense than Waddington's and, furthermore, they had more operational Victors than there were Vulcans in existence. No.232 OCU had already assigned an air-to-air refuelling instructor (AARI) to each Vulcan crew for daylight training link-ups over the Jurby range on the Isle of Man and night contacts over the Scottish western isles. Although there had been a shortage of Vulcans able to be made ready for the *Black Buck* missions, the fact that it took a good dozen tankers to sustain one bomber, not only to reach Ascension Island but to attack Port Stanley, put a great strain on Marham's resources. Nos 55 and 57 Squadrons, together with No.232 OCU, had only about twenty operable Victor K.2s between them, assuming that they were all serviceable at the same time, while there was also not exactly a glut of fully trained crews.

Six Victor K.2s deployed to Wideawake on 18 April and some idea of the amount of flying involved in operating from the staging airfield can be gathered from their first mission. Before the Task Force could make a successful landing on the Falkland Islands, the disposition of Argentina's naval elements had to be ascertained. On 31 March, a few days before the south Atlantic crisis arose, No.27 Squadron had disbanded at Scampton, retiring their last Vulcan B.2(MRR). This reduced the RAF's maritime radar reconnaissance capabilities, for Nos 120 and 201 Squadrons were still working up with their Nimrod MR.2s and they had yet to get in-flight refuelling experience. Consequently, by 20 April, Victor K.2 XL192 had been hastily adapted for an MRR mission and it left Wideawake to reconnoitre the area around the South Georgia

islands. Four K.2 tankers followed and, having refuelled XL192 on its outward leg, they returned to Wideawake. About an hour and a half was spent in a search pattern around the area, before a course was set for returning to Ascension. On the inward leg, another four tankers were required to replenish the reconnaissance Victor and after 14hr 45min flying time, covering over 6,500 miles, XL192 landed, with evidence of the absence of any significant Argentine naval activity in the south Atlantic area. The required ratio of support for XL192 was eight to one, the reason being that over the great distances involved, the refuelling tankers themselves required refuelling. This ratio would be greatly increased for *Black Buck* missions. To put XL192's achievement into the realities of Service life, within two years the aircraft was reduced to the role of base fire training on Marham's fire dump.

Operation *Black Buck* – The Missions

Black Buck was initiated as a single mission, involving one attacking aircraft, mounted with the intention of damaging the single runway at Port Stanley to such an extent that its use was denied to the *Fuerza Aérea Argentina*, for their Mirage IIIEA, Pucara and Skyhawk aircraft that formed its airborne defences, together with the transports used to sustain the ground forces. Should the mission be unsuccessful, contingency plans were made for a second strike at a later date.

The reasons for the attack being made by a 'singleton' were two-fold. The target was too small for any formation attack and, furthermore, there just were not enough Victor tankers to support more than one aircraft over such a far-ranging sortie. On 29 April 1982, Vulcan B.2 XM598, together with XM607, left Waddington for the Ascension Island, followed later by a reserve aircraft, XM597, which returned to base when it was established that the two were trouble-free and on course. During the 4,100 mile flight, Victor K.2s replenished each Vulcan twice and the tankers themselves required numerous fuel transfers to complete the flight. This deployment gave some indication of the amount that a *Black Buck* aircraft would require for the flight from Wideawake to Port Stanley and back.

XM598 of No.44 Squadron, the Black Buck 1 **primary aircraft that had to abort because of an unsealing DV window, seen displayed at the RAF Museum at Cosford in 1985.** Author's collection

XM598 and XM607 arrived at Wideawake nine hours after take-off from Waddington, and throughout 30 April, a veritable armada of Victor K.2s arrived from Marham, in time to be prepared for *Black Buck 1*, scheduled for the following day. Briefing was held in the evening of 30 April and just before 23.59hr, the two Vulcan B.2s took off, preceded by four Victor K.2s, one of which was a reserve, at one-minute intervals. The primary Vulcan was XM598, but shortly after take-off, the direct vision window was found to be incapable of sealing after closure, so the aircraft aborted its intended mission and XM607 took its place. Five minutes after the two Vulcans, a further seven Victor tankers took off, again one being a reserve.

The timetable called for the primary Vulcan to be refuelled six times on the outward journey to Port Stanley, but several factors conspired to make XM607 require one more than had been scheduled, as its fuel consumption was heavier than had been calculated. The heavily-laden Victor tankers, with 54.9 tons (55,780kg) of transferable fuel contributing to their all-up weight of 106.25 tons (107,950kg), were unable to attain the 33,000ft (10,060m) cruising altitude of *Black Buck 1*, and fuel transfers made around 28,000ft (8,535m) meant that extra fuel was being burnt by the Vulcan flying at the Victor's height and on every

climb back to its own optimum altitude.

Bad weather was encountered on the outward leg, which, while not affecting XM607, had repercussions in the Victor fleet. Nine tankers were involved in getting the twenty-one bombs onto Port Stanley's airfield, the two reserves having returned to Ascension. Tanker had to refuel tanker on five occasions and one Victor, XH669 piloted by Flt Lt Steve Biglands, had been selected as the key tanker, which would go nearly all the way, topping up the Vulcan before it descended to 300ft in order to get below the Argentine radar for the attack. However, when XH669 rendezvoused with its tanker, XL189, above the turbulence of a raging thunderstorm, its probe broke before the fuel transfer had been completed and the aircraft had to return to Wideawake, as, without a probe, it was unable to be replenished. Sqn Ldr Bob Tuxford, flying XL189, assumed the role of key tanker and took on fuel from XH669 before it withdrew. This fuel, however, was not enough for the Vulcan to have a full transfer prior to the strike and Flt Lt Martin Withers, together with his co-pilot Flg Off Peter Taylor, were rather surprised during the final transfer to receive the light signal from the Victor's HDU housing, indicating that the transfer was complete, when they knew that they had not been fully replenished. The tanker

pulled away and as there was complete radio silence before the raid, XM607 kept on course in the firm belief that Wideawake would not let them down.

XM607 began its descent to 250ft for the run-in under the radar screen at 400mph, before zooming up to 10,000ft for a straight bomb run. The target made a perfect display on the H_2S screen and when the Argentine radar was picked up, the E-10 pod was triggered and the illumination closed. At 04.45 local time, the bomb run was made at a diagonal to the single runway and all twenty-one bombs were released in one stick, some having 30min or 60min delay fuses, while the majority were fused for impact detonation. On completion of the strike, the codeword *Superfuse* was relayed back to Wideawake and a reserve tanker was immediately scrambled to meet up with XL189, as it was known that Sqn Ldr Tuxford did not have sufficient fuel to make base. The two met up some 500 miles south of Ascension for a satisfactory transfer and both made recoveries at Wideawake.

Meanwhile, Flt Lt Withers in XM607 had to improvise on the initial plan because of his fuel state. The briefing called for the aircraft to withdraw from Port Stanley at 300ft, but the pilot decided to climb to 8,000ft, which was a more economical cruising altitude than low level. The time for the arranged rendezvous with a Victor tanker passed and the thought of 'flying on vapour' did not have much appeal to the crew. However, a Nimrod MR.2, with its sophisticated radar reconnaissance suite, had been scrambled from Wideawake and it vectored XM607, with about one hour's flying time sloshing about in its tanks, onto one of a pair of tankers. The fuel transfer was plagued with leakage and visibility in the Vulcan was so bad that the AARI, Flt Lt Richard Russell, who had accompanied the crew for the mission, had to direct the operation while peering through a small area of clarity at the bottom of the windscreen.

With the transfer safely completed, XM607's crew made Wideawake for a successful touchdown, secure in the knowledge that they had taken part in the longest RAF bombing mission ever flown, and photographs showed that their first bomb had landed on the runway, with subsequent craters running into the airfield's buildings, which were destroyed, together with one of the hangars.

Many lessons were learned with *Black Buck 1* and it was decided that the assault on Port Stanley's airfield would not be confined to the one raid. When *Black Buck 2* was planned for 3 May, changes were made in the pattern of Victor support. Again Vulcan B.2 XM607 was used, but with Sqn Ldr R. Reeve and Flt Lt D. Dibbens as pilots. They took off with a small group of Victors and a larger tanker formation left Wideawake later, to fly at a higher speed than on *Black Buck 1*, thereby catching up with XM607 well down the course. The plan worked perfectly, with the key tanker replenished enough to fill XM607 to the brim, in readiness for its descent and a run in to the target at 16,000ft. The runway was not hit on this raid but considerable damage was inflicted on parked aircraft and buildings associated with the airfield.

Confidence in the RAF's ability to attack the Port Stanley facility had grown and *Black Buck 3* was scheduled for 16 May, again using XM607, with XM612 as reserve, this having replaced XM598, which had returned to Waddington. However, weather conditions between Ascension and the Falkland Islands were bad enough to force a cancellation of the mission. There was a limit to how many Victor tankers were available, for weather conditions affected fuel consumption to a point where it required too many refuellings of both bomber and tankers to make an attack a viable proposition.

Strategy changed for the next Vulcan mission to the south Atlantic. Argentine forces on the Falklands were using a Westinghouse AN/TPS-43 surveillance radar to direct air strikes against the Task Force, together with Fledermans and Skyguard gun-laying control radars. The destruction of these radars became a matter of some urgency and a *Black Buck* mission was viewed as the best way of achieving this. Buccaneers were equipped with the Martel AS.37 ASM anti-radar missile, but it was impossible to get that aircraft down to the Falklands. Therefore, the Waddington engineers had been tasked with adapting their Vulcan pylon, the design of which had been refined by No.32 Maintenance Unit at St Athan since it had first been fabricated, to carry the Martel ASM.

While modifying the pylon itself was no great undertaking, wiring up the system required a lot of burning of the midnight oil. The adaptation was implemented on XM597 and it made the first flight of a Martel-armed Vulcan, on 4 May, with a round fitted on the port wing pylon, the starboard pylon carrying an E-10 pod. The following day a live firing was carried out over the Aberporth range, but, although this trial was successful, doubts were expressed as to how the weapon would stand up to a long, high-altitude flight over the south Atlantic.

The US Secretary of State, Alexander Haig, had expressed an 'even-handed' approach to the Falklands conflict, for valuable commercial trading was involved with both the combatants. Nevertheless, he considered that the offer of the AGM-45A Shrike to the RAF for anti-radar missions was in line with this approach. The Shrike was an ASM, developed by Sperry Rand together with Texas Instruments, to target in particular the radars associated with anti-aircraft guns and missile systems. More work by the Waddington engineering team enabled a Shrike to be fitted on the Vulcan pylon, but ever ambitious, within ten days they had adapted the pylons to take a two-missile launcher, and on 26 May XM596 flew from Waddington to Wideawake, equipped with a twin-missile installation under each wing. The next day, XM597 made the same journey, but with empty pylons, a consignment of Shrikes having been transported to Ascension for them to be installed on site.

The first anti-radar mission, *Black Buck 4*, officially designated a 'defence suppression mission', was flown on the night of 28 May, by XM597, but five hours out from Ascension, the HDU failed in the key Victor and everyone had to return to base. Carrying a quartet of Shrike missiles and no bomb load meant that the Vulcan's bomb-bay could accommodate two auxiliary tanks, which increased the internal fuel capacity by just over 7 tons, this in turn reducing the in-flight refuelling requirements to four transfers on the outward leg and just one on the return.

Two nights later, on 30 May, *Black Buck 5*, again with XM597, captained this time by Sqn Ldr Neil McDougall, with Fg Off Chris Lackman as co-pilot, hoped to carry on where *Black Buck 4* had unavoidably left off. On reaching the Falklands, radio silence was broken in order to get a simultaneous Harrier strike laid on and during the time spent in the target area, which was nearly one hour, some Shrikes were fired, damaging the TPS-43 antenna, but the Vulcan's fuel situation required it to set course for Widwawake, with a refuel en route.

Black Buck 6, flown on 2 June, was a repeat mission, although weather condi-

The Black Buck 6 **XM597 that was forced to land at Rio de Janeiro with a broken probe.** Author's collection tions precluded the Harrier strike. Argentine radars were switched off once XM597 was in the vicinity, with a game of 'cat-and-mouse' being played over the next 45 minutes, where radars were switched on briefly and XM597's AEOs tried to lock on. Fuel state again decreed that a return to Ascension should be started and a Nimrod vectored the Vulcan onto the Victor tanker, which had drifted off course. This link-up started diplomatic activities that continued for some time.

On making contact with the Victor's drogue, the tip of XM597's probe broke off, dousing the windscreen with fuel, which was of less consequence than the fact that the aircraft's fuel state was none too healthy. It had been an understanding on all *Black Buck* missions that, in an emergency, Brazil would permit a landing at Rio de Janeiro international airport, but the gauges on XM597 indicated that there was a strong possibility that it might not be able to make such a journey. Flying at an optimum altitude of 40,000ft to conserve what fuel they had, the crew fired off the remaining Shrike missiles and gathered into a flight bag everything that they felt could jeopardize diplomatic arrangements, ready to be jettisoned once they had reached a lower altitude. However, one Shrike was reluctant to abandon the aircraft and the crew knew that this could be a problem, but it was beyond their control. A *Mayday* transmission was relayed to the tower at Rio, when the aircraft was less than 200 miles out and a straight-in landing was made with insufficient fuel remaining to allow anything else.

During the week's stay in Brazil, the hung-up Shrike was removed from the pylon to be impounded, but the crew were well treated by all the Brazilian officials. Contact between Britain and Brazil established that XM597 could be refuelled to full capacity, for a return to Ascension, where a new probe was fitted, enabling the aircraft to return to Waddington.

The last *Black Buck* sortie involved a return to the bombing of Port Stanley's airfield, but with the runway specifically omitted from the target list, as the progress of the land fighting indicated that it could soon be in use by the RAF. *Black Buck 7* was flown on 11 June by XM607, with the variation from the two previous bombing missions being an engine flame-out that required three attempts at relighting. A

V-bomber Participation in Operation _Corporate_

Vulcan B.2
Three aircraft from No.44 Squadron confirmed as converted for *Black Buck* operations:
XM598   XM607   XM612

Two aircraft from No.101 Squadron confirmed as converted for *Black Buck* operations:
XL391 (not used operationally)   XM597

Victor K.2
Thirteen aircraft from No.55 Squadron confirmed as supporting *Black Buck* operations:
XH671   XH675   XL161   XL162   XL164   XL188   XL190
XL191   XL232   XL233   XL511   XM715   XM717

Ten aircraft from No.57 Squadron confirmed as supporting *Black Buck* operations:
XH669   XH672   XH673   XL158   XL160
XL163   XL189   XL192   XL231   XL512

---

full load of 1,000lb high-explosive and anti-personnel bombs was dropped, as briefed, without hitting the runway. Four days later, on 15 June 1982, Argentine forces on the Falkland Islands surrendered and within a week the Vulcans returned to Waddington. Some anti-radar training flights were carried out, in the light of the enforced and unrehearsed operations in the Falklands, but the days of the Vulcan as a bomber were numbered, despite the reprieve gained by the south Atlantic conflict, so that on 21 December, No.44 Squadron was disbanded.

During Operation *Corporate*, Victor K.2 XL190 suffered the indignity of the nosewheel failing to lock down on landing at Wideawake. A satisfactory touch-down was made and the damage incurred was repaired, although, by necessity, the standard of workmanship was not up to the home-base standard made possible by a full engineering facility. The repairs enabled XL190 to return to Marham but, before departing Wideawake, a shark's mouth nose-art was applied over the patch-up. On the port side of the under-nose radar housing, the names of all involved were added, under the respective headings, 'Them that broke it', 'Them that lifted it' and 'Them that mended it'.

It has always been a moot point as to whether Operation *Black Buck* was a cost-effective contribution to the Falklands conflict, but maybe that is not the way to consider the operations. What is undeniable is the fact that they were prime examples of logistics matching any operation during World War II and an excellent testimony to the design teams at Chadderton and Radlett.

Operations *Granby* and *Desert Storm*

By the time that Iraq had declared its aspirations towards Kuwait, much of the RAF's tanker operations were being served by a No.101 Squadron's VC10 K.2 and K.3s, plus No.216 Squadron with their TriStar KC.1s. No.57 Squadron had disbanded at Marham on 30 June 1986, four years after the south Atlantic conflict, leaving just No.55 Squadron to soldier on with its Victor K.2s. It had inherited twelve K.2s when its fellow Marham squadron disbanded, plus a couple from No.232 OCU when that had disbanded.

The needs of Operation *Granby*, so far as No.55 Squadron was concerned, started in August 1990, when the squadron was engaged in providing support to Jaguar GR.1s being flown at the Reconnaissance Air Meeting in Texas. A signal was sent, recalling all Victor K.2s to the UK, which meant that 48 hours later the squadron was refuelling Jaguars, plus Tornado GR.1s and F.3s, en route to the Gulf, where they deployed to Dhahran, Muharraq and Tabuk, in the build-up preparations for Operation *Desert Storm*, the air offensive against Iraqi forces in Kuwait.

On 14 December, a detachment from No.55 Squadron took over from the elements of No.101 Squadron at Al-Muharraq, in Al-Bahrayn. One K.2 arrived for the take-over, and the next day a further three aircraft arrived from Marham. Their brief was to provide in-flight refuelling for Jaguar and Tornado F.3 operations only, while VC10s would supply Tornado GR.1s. Operations began on this basis on 16 December, but the impracticalities of such an arrangement soon manifested themselves, with Strike Command aircraft hunting around for a Victor while VC10s were available in the vicinity. The original brief was kicked into touch and No.55 Squadron supplied probe/drogue-compatible aircraft from Canada, France, the USAF and US Navy, as well as the RAF.

Two weeks of such operations made the four K.2 crews involved proficient enough to return to Marham, allowing another four crews to be rotated to the area, so that by 12 January 1991 the first crews delivered an additional four Victor K.2 tankers. Four days later, a pair of No.55 Squadron tankers supported the first Operation *Desert Storm* Tornado GR.1 strike into Iraq, the target being Tallil airbase, in the south-east of the country. A designated route for the tankers to refuel strike aircraft, referred to as the *Olive Trail*, ran along the southern Iraqi border and in the early stages of *Desert Storm*, the K.2s carried a full 55 tons fuel load, but this placed a heavy fatigue strain on the airframes and, with experience, fuel loads were adjusted to meet specific requirements, thereby lessening the fatigue factor.

An additional K.2 flew in from Marham on 19 January, as the fourteen refuelling sorties being flown each day were placing a strain on both aircraft and aircrews. Thankfully, from this point of view, the Gulf War ended after forty-two days, when the Allied Commander, Gen Norman Schwarzkopf, called a halt to proceedings after the Iraqi invading forces had been forced back across the Kuwait border. Whether this was the right decision at the time is one of those talking points that will most likely never be agreed upon. It has been placed on record that all the participating tanker aircraft

Victor K.2 XM715 Teasin Tina, **which shows proof of thirty-five fuel transfers during the Gulf War, is now a resident of the British Aviation Heritage Collection at Bruntingthorpe.** Dave Jackson

---

Gulf War Victors

Ten aircraft from No.55 Squadron confirmed as supporting *Granby* and *Desert Storm* operations:
XH671 *Sweet Sue*, originally *Slinky Sue* XH672 *Maid Marion* XL161 XL162 XL164 *Saucy Sal* XL188 XL190 XL231 *Lusty Lindy* XM715 *Teasing Tina* XM717 *Lucky Lou*

---

established a reputation for reliability that enabled *Desert Storm* to be waged so successfully.

No.55 Squadron alone, with by far the oldest aircraft in the campaign, flew 299 sorties, which averaged out at thirty-three missions per crew. There was not a single case of the squadron missing its scheduled rendezvous, which echoes well the high standard of maintenance and engineering that was applied to the aircraft.

By 18 March 1991, No.55 Squadron and its Victor K.2s were back at Marham, for both to enjoy a more leisurely path to retirement. The squadron was disbanded at Marham on 15 October 1993 and the last Victor flight was made six weeks later, on 30 November, when K.2 XH672 *Maid Marion* from the Gulf War landed at Shawbury in Shropshire, prior to being dismantled for transportation by road to the RAF Museum at Cosford.

CHAPTER FOURTEEN

Testing Times

By the very nature of their design, the Valiant and Victor were not easily adapted for trials or flying test-bed roles, their principal disadvantage being their limited ground clearance. In this respect, the Valiant was better than the Victor and it did serve as a flight-test vehicle for one engine, as well as being a trials aircraft for the RRE at Pershore. No doubt it would have had a longer life in these spheres, had not the wing fatigue problem signalled its death knell.

The Vulcan, on the other hand, because of the large delta's inherent requirement to have legs that can reach the ground through its generated cushion of compressed air when landing, had ground clearance in abundance and several aircraft had active lives as engine flying test-beds, principally at the Patchway side of Bristol's Filton airfield.

None of the V-bombers had the inbuilt adaptability of the Meteor or Canberra that allowed them to be aerodynamically mutilated in the name of science or research. They were much more complex aeroplanes than either of the twin-engined types and considering that the Meteor was a 1940 design, that is not too surprising. Also, the Gloster and English Electric designers, George Carter and 'Teddy' Petter, were both denounced as being too orthodox in the approach to their respective designs, but it was this very factor that made the two aircraft so readily able to be used in the trials and test-bed spheres. The Vulcan and Victor were both very complex aeroplanes, designed for the task of delivering nuclear weapons at high speed, from high altitudes. Even the Valiant, built to a less demanding specification and therefore slightly less sophisticated, lacked the ability to be too drastically modified as an aerodynamic shape.

Valiant

Pegasus

The first pre-production Type 674 Valiant B.1, WP199, had its maiden flight on 21 December 1953 and from that date was instrumental in proving the type as an operational tool for Bomber Command, at the numerous development establishments that existed to 'iron the bugs' out of a new design before it reached the squadrons.

By 1962 the aeroplane had served its purpose in this respect and Bristol Siddeley required a flying test-bed for their latest variant of the Pegasus vectored-thrust engine. This was Dr Stanley (later Sir Stanley) Hooker's masterpiece that he and his young team working for Bristol Aero Engines at Patchway had developed from Frenchman Michel Wibault's original *Gyroptere* concept based on the Bristol Orion, with rotating jet outlet nozzles. At Patchway, Hooker's team collaborated with Ralph Hooper, the project designer responsible to Hawker's Chief Designer Sir Sydney Camm and

John Fozard, the company's Senior Project Designer, to produce the P.1127. This went into limited production as the Kestrel precursor of the Harrier, powered by the Pegasus and a vectored-thrust turbofan variant, the Pegasus 104, developing 21,500lb (9,525kg) static thrust, was the subject of WP199's flight test programme.

A dummy Harrier centre fuselage was installed beneath the Valiant's fuselage, with separate fuel tanks for the Pegasus in the bomb-bay above it and, after considerable ground running at Patchway, the combination first became airborne on 24 March 1963. The successful flight test programme was continued into 1964 when, during that year, the cracked wing-spar troubles became apparent. This put a stop to plans already in hand, to use the aircraft for testing later Pegasus variants, and WP199 was struck off charge.

Rear Crew Ejection Seats

The one bone of contention, common to aircrews of all three types, was the absence of ejector seats for all except the two

The first rear crew dummy ejection from the Valiant at Chalgrove in 1960. Martin-Baker

Front and rear views of Martin-Baker's test rig for V-bomber rear crew ejection. Martin-Baker

pilots. Martin-Baker had recognized this anomaly very early on, after the original emergency evacuation proposal in Specifications B.35/46 and B.9/48 had been discarded. Specification B.35/46 stipulated that 'the complete pressure cabin must be jettisonable. Such a cabin must be provided with parachutes to reduce the falling speed to a value at which the occupants will be unhurt when hitting the ground while strapped in their seats. If such a jettisonable cabin cannot be provided, the seats must be jettisonable.'

All three designing companies found that such a facility just could not be provided, with Vickers-Armstrongs going further when, at an Advisory Design Conference, GRE went on record as saying that the installation of ejector seats for all Type 660 crew members would be detrimental to the design and structure of the cabin canopy. Therefore, Specification B.9/48 was phrased as 'a completely jettisonable cabin is desired. If this is not practicable, arrangements

should be made for good emergency escape means for the crew.' This was about as ambiguous as one could get and was the subject of debate for nearly as long as there were V-bombers.

As the answer, so far as Weybridge, Chadderton and Radlett were concerned, was to supply an entrance doorway through which the three rear-facing crew members could clamber if they were lucky, Martin-Baker, ever open for a challenge, set about designing an ejector seat system for them. Whether the company was so occupied with contracted design work or the system took so long to perfect, is open to interpretation, but the fact is that it was 1960 before any meaningful tests were made. Martin-Baker obtained the services of an early pre-production Valiant and the Bomber Command Development Unit provided a crew for the tests. A rearwards-facing Mk.3 ejector seat, specially modified for the trials, was installed in the position of the central of the three crew members at the rear desk, with a curved

sheet of metal around it as a screen. An aperture had been cut through the aircraft's skin, above the seat.

A programme of three dummy ejections was carried out at Chalgrove during May-June 1960, one being made during take-off, before the Valiant's nose-wheels had cleared the runway, followed by two at a height of 200ft, with the aircraft flying at indicated speeds of 295mph and 353mph. To round off the series of tests, a live ejection was made on 1 July by W.T.H. 'Doddy' Hay, from the Valiant, which was based at Finningley. The ejection was made at a height of 1,000ft and speed of 295mph, observed by several RAF officers from the Ministry of Aviation and Bomber Command headquarters. It was completely successful and Hay landed in the middle of Chalgrove airfield after a perfectly controlled parachute descent. As far as is known, this was the first rearward-facing live ejection in the world, which fully proved the feasibility of such means of emergency exit. 'Doddy' Hay commented afterwards on the unusual sight of the Valiant's huge fin passing beneath him as he continued on his trajectory upwards, before the drogue-chute gun was fired.

The Martin-Baker V-bomber system was based on the Vulcan, but obviously could be adapted for any of them. A sequence was set in motion when the pilot or co-pilot operated the canopy jettison. This tilted the rear crew table and opened a hatch above the central crewman's position. The centre seat tilted forward and ejected, after which the port side seat slid to the vacated central position, tilted forward prior to ejection, with the starboard seat making a similar operation, for the ejection of all three rearward-facing operators to be completed in 2.68sec. A total of twenty test firings on a specially built rig were carried out with dummies, their trajectories being calculated as proving that the firings would carry each seat, plus occupant, 5.5ft above a Vulcan's fin and 6.5 ft above the empennage of a Victor.

However, nothing came from all these efforts, the prime objections being the costs involved in incorporating the system into the production lines, together with the inevitable delay in the build-up of V-bomber squadrons that would occur. As examples of all three types were already in service, a retrospective modification programme was an even more horrendous prospect, which nobody had the courage to suggest.

RRE Trials

The Aircraft Department of the Radar Research Establishment (later the Royal Radar Establishment) had no primary requirement for large V-bomber aircraft, except for final proving trials of systems in which the Establishment had development interests. It had a basic fleet of some two dozen Canberras, which increased or decreased according to the electronics being developed at the time, and was sufficient to meet the majority of their requirements.

However, in 1954, the second pre-production Type 674 Valiant B.1, WP200, was allocated to the RRE, for the final approval trials of the NBS Mk.1 system and it stayed with the Establishment for some years. Pending the transfer in 1957, from Defford to Pershore, with its reinforced and extended runway, an RRE

The demise of WP200 at Pershore, after its aborted take-off accident. William H Sleigh

detachment based with No.232 OCU at Gaydon got the programme. Once the Establishment had moved to Pershore, WP200 was employed on NBS development until 14 March 1961, when the pilot aborted a take-off while the aircraft was in manual (instead of powered) control selection. In the overshoot area between runway 21's threshold and the airfield's security fencing, an unfilled cable trench ripped off the aircraft's nose-wheel, which induced major structural damage that was compounded as the aircraft went through the 6ft high wire fencing, which acted as an 'arrester net'. With its back broken aft of the pressure cabin, the aircraft was deemed to be damaged beyond economical repair and was struck off charge.

The following year, WP200 was replaced at Pershore by Type 706 Valiant B.1s WZ370 to complete the trials programme and WZ375, as a back-up aircraft, which was retained at the end of the NBS programme, for a further RRE project. The Establishment had been engaged on the development of continuous wave (CW) airborne interception (AI) radars for some considerable time, the trials originally being conducted in the modified wing-tip tanks of Canberra B.6 WH953. Valiant WZ375 was nominated as a back-up for this programme, which

Vulcan

Conway

Rolls-Royce developed their first bypass turbojet, the Conway, in the early 1950s, although the bypass principle was not as efficiently employed as in modern engines. This family of powerplants started with the civil market in mind, but in 1955 Rolls-Royce commenced preparing variants with much higher thrusts than the 13,000lb (5,896kg) outputs of the RCo.5 type tested in 1954, for military aircraft application. Avro Ashton Mk.2 WB491 had a ventral pod engineered by D. Napier and Son at Luton, to accommodate the first Conway series 500 engine, the 505, which was later replaced by a 508, producing 17,500lb (7,938kg) static thrust which, although basically being a military engine, was produced for BOAC's 707-420 aircraft. Another Ashton, the Mk.3 WE670, which had been flight-testing various Avon engines for some time, had a military Conway RCo.11, developing 17,250lb (7,825kg) thrust, installed in the pod, to commence flight-testing on 12 February 1958 of the engine that would power the Victor B.2.

Prior to this, in 1957, the first Avro 698 prototype, VX770, which had flown with a quartet of 6,500lb (2,948kg) thrust Avon RA.3s and 8,000lb (3,629kg) thrust Sapphire ASSa.7s, was fitted with four Conway RCo.7s, each giving 15,000lb (6,804kg) static thrust. This was in reality a 'stepping-stone' engine in the development of the RCo.11, and during twelve months of testing was flown by VX770, including appearances at the 1957 and 1958 SBAC Displays, before it broke up, on 14 September 1958, at the Air Display at Syerston, as recounted in Chapter 6.

No further RCo.7 test-flying was carried out and Vulcan B.1 XA902, which first went to No.230 OCU on 10 May 1957, was passed over to Hucknall later in the year, to undertake Conway RCo.11 testing. Four examples were installed for a 1,000hr endurance programme that commenced in the latter part of 1958, running into 1959.

Spey

Originally designed in the late 1950s as a civil engine, designated the RB.168, the Spey two-shaft turbofan was first run in the test house in December 1960.

The RRE mock-up and finished conversion on Valiant B.1 WZ375's port external wing tank, for the MRCA radar nose profile tests. Author's collection

was being conducted for eventual service in the Panavia Multi Role Combat Aircraft (MRCA), which eventually evolved as the Tornado.

To this end, the engineering department at Pershore designed a modification to WZ375's port underwing fuel tank, where the forward section had an extended structure profiled as the MRCA nose. A wooden mock-up was first constructed, after which the Valiant had a purpose-built new section, complete with the AI, installed on the front of the tank. These trials too had to be abandoned,

because of the Valiant's withdrawal from service and actual flight-testing of the AI system was transferred to Canberra B.6 WH953.

Super Sprite

The fitting of two de Havilland Super Sprites on the second prototype Type 667 Valiant WB215 is covered in Chapter 9 and was a trial installation geared to rocket-assisted take-offs for the Valiant, rather than a trials programme for the development of the rocket motor itself.

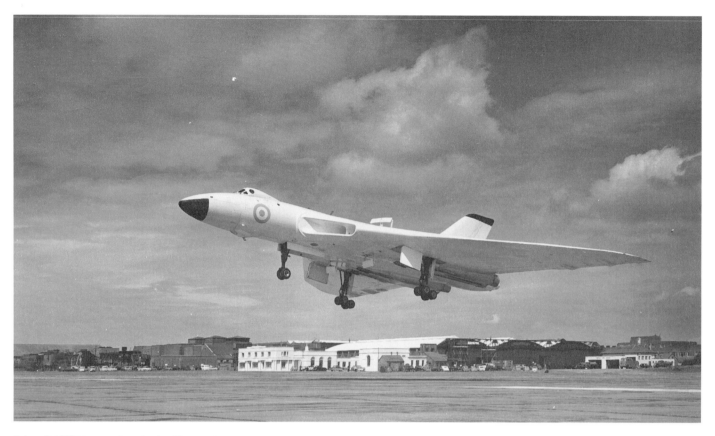

Vulcan B.2 XH557 comes in to land at Filton, under the power of four Olympus 300 series engines. Author's collection

A military variant, the 101 series, was scheduled to be the powerplant for the Buccaneer S.2 and, in 1961, Vulcan XA902 joined the Spey testing programme. It went into Hucknall's engineering facility for the two inboard Conway RCo.11s to be replaced by RB.168 1A Speys, each developing 11,200lb (5,080kg) static thrust. The new combination had its maiden flight on 12 October 1961, with Rolls-Royce CTP Jim Heyworth at the controls. Spey testing was continued with XA902 until 1963, when the aircraft was scrapped at Hucknall.

Olympus

There is no doubt that the Olympus was one of the most important turbojet engines produced by the British aero-engine industry. I remember Bill Gunston telling me, when he was Technical Editor of *Flight*, how he was down at Patchway watching an early engine in the test house and it was the first time that he had observed the needle on the thrust recording gauge moving up the scale at the same speed as the operator's hand on the power controls, with no time lag whatsoever.

The second generation Olympus Mks 201/202 engines were first flight-tested in XA891, the third production Vulcan B.1, although they were a very tight fit within the standard engine bays. Producing 16,000lb (7,258kg) thrust at a compression ratio of 10:1, they started their flight trials in Spring 1958, operating from both Patchway and Woodford, plus appearing at that year's SBAC Display at Farnborough. However, the aircraft crashed at Walkington, outside Hull, on 24 July 1959, when it suffered a total electrical failure shortly after taking off from Woodford. The B.1 had emergency batteries, which should have supplied 12 minutes of operation, but as this quite often did not happen, 'Jummy' Harrison played safe by retaining control while the rest of the crew made emergency exits, before he ejected.

When the Olympus 201 entered RAF service in the Vulcan B.2, the engine was sometimes found to be prone to surging, which resulted in flame-outs when double engine handling was being employed at medium to high altitudes. This occasionally presented a pilot with the loss of two engines on the same side. On 1 October 1960, the fourteenth production B.2, XH560, returned to Woodford after having suffered several double-engine surges. Flight-testing, to determine the cause and find a cure, commenced in February 1961 and it was not until 1962 that XH560 rejoined No.230 OCU at Waddington. A cure had been implemented by reducing the length of the low-pressure (LP) turbine stators by 2 per cent and revising the fuel system schedule.

In January 1959, first bench running of the Olympus 301 was conducted at Patchway and a potential output of 20,000lb (9,070kg) thrust was apparent. Calculations indicated that the fitting of this engine in the Vulcan B.2 would require a larger air intake than was standard on the current aircraft and XH557 was allocated for trials of the Olympus 301 itself, as well as a revised air intake. The aircraft was delivered on 16 September 1960, arriving over the Filton airfield that was shared by the Patchway-based engine company with Bristol Aircraft, who were

Four marks of Olympus engines are airborne in this picture. XH557 has 301s on the port side (with their larger jet-pipe nozzles) and 201s on the starboard, while XA894 has four 101s in their proper places, plus a 22R in the ventral nacelle.
Rolls-Royce Heritage

sited on the opposite side of the runway. With Flt Lt Wareham at the controls, the aircraft made its approach late in the afternoon, with rain and low cloud combining to give very poor visibility. Touch-down was made more than halfway down the runway and the braking parachute had been streamed, but it would not deploy. The pilot was instantly aware that there was a distinct shortage of tarmac ahead of him, so he opened the throttles wide and hauled on the controls, in order to go round again.

XH557 was running light and lifted off Filton's runway without much effort, but the dragging braking parachute, plus the blast from 64,000lb (29,030kg) of Olympus 201 thrust, removed a lamp standard, steel fencing and four petrol pumps in a garage that was directly in line with the runway, on the opposite side of the busy A38 trunk road bordering the airfield. The windscreens of two cars, unfortunate enough to be travelling along the A38 at the time, were also shattered. The garage was appropriately named the 'Runway Garage', and coincidentally the driver of one of the two cars with broken windscreens had already suffered a similar experience a couple of years before at the hands of a Meteor, outside Gloster Aircraft's Moreton Valence airfield. XH557's crew were unsure of the damage,

if any, they may have sustained when hitting the lamp standard, so made a diversion to St Mawgan in Cornwall, which was enjoying better weather. A Boeing 707 was in the vicinity of St Mawgan when the Vulcan arrived and its crew were requested to have a good look at XH557's underside. As they gave a clean report, the Vulcan landed at the Cornish base and was thoroughly inspected before returning to Filton on 4 October, with the undercarriage locked down.

Considerable structural modifications had to be made to the aircraft before it could accept the larger Olympus 301, and it was 19 May 1961 before it flew again, for assessment by an Avro test flight team, with the new engines in the outboard positions only, before later being fitted with four. High-altitude relights were achieved up to 56,000ft (17,070m) and prolonged cruising at this altitude was made to study the behaviour of the oil system, but, ironically, while these trials were in progress low-level operations were introduced by the RAF and a new flight-test programme had to be initiated, in order to test the engines in the new environment. Flying at speeds up to 500mph at 500ft (805km/h at 152m), revealed resonant vibration on the zero stage blades, and for a time Vulcan B.2s

powered by Olympus 301 engines were restricted to a maximum speed of 295mph (475km/h) below 10,000ft (3,000m), until the phenomenon was cured by resetting the angle of the blades. Early in 1964, XH557 was returned to Woodford, where it was converted back to operational B.2 standard, to join the Cottesmore Wing on 12 December.

The twenty-second Vulcan B.2 off the Woodford assembly line, XJ784, was converted to accept a quartet of Olympus 301s, and in April 1962 it went to Boscombe Down for assessment. The Establishment fitted vortex generators to the inboard wall of the port air intake, in an attempt to improve the handling of the inboard engine, but the resultant small improvement was not sufficient for the installation to become mandatory.

When OR339 was first raised, in September 1957, a number of projects were submitted to the MoS, from which the proposals by English Electric and Vickers-Armstrongs were similar enough to warrant collaboration by the two companies, which crystallized as the British Aircraft Corporation (BAC). Their combined designs emerged as the TSR.2 and the first choice of engines was the Rolls-Royce Medway, which was in an embryonic stage of development at Derby. Politics enforced Bristol Aero Engine to merge with Coventry-based Armstrong Siddeley Motors, to form Bristol Siddeley Engines Ltd in April 1959, in order to gain the contract for the TSR.2 power-plants and a reheat variant of a developed Olympus 301, the Mk.320, was designated the Olympus 22R. The bench running programme involved six engines and the English Electric Lightning was suggested as the test-bed for a 400hr flight trial.

The Lightning was discarded in favour of a Vulcan B.1 and XA894, the sixth production aircraft, was delivered to Patchway on 19 July 1960. A ventral nacelle was designed to carry the test engine and the intake, profiled for subsonic engine testing only, was bifurcated for an undisturbed airflow to pass either side of the nose-wheel leg. Engine number 2205 was installed in the nacelle, for ground running to start early in January 1962, and Patchway was contracted to complete this part of the programme by the last day of the month, which was achieved by running the engine until 02.00hr on 1 February, but as this portion of the flight clearance test had begun on 31 January, the contract terms were considered to have been met.

XA894 made its first flight with the Olympus 22R on 23 February 1962, with Canberra B.2 WK141 as chase aircraft, and the Vulcan flew a demonstration routine at the 1962 SBAC Display, after which the full three-ring reheat system was first employed on 12 November during the test-bed's forty-eighth flight. 'Bee' Beamont flew the aircraft on 20 November as part of the run-up to the TSR.2 and he told me that he had Bristol Siddeley's CTP Tom Frost with him for the flight. He added, 'I found it easy and likeable for such a big aircraft. I didn't like its restricted view from the cockpit though – but then I was biased!'

One week later, XA894 was on the detuner for a ground run, to include a full power check. Maximum reheat was being applied by approximately 15.00hr, when there was a loud rumble, plus a burst of orange flame above and below the aircraft, which induced the four test observers in the cabin to make a hasty evacuation, accomplished just before burning fuel poured around the hardstanding, setting alight the obligatory fire engine parked nearby. The whole parking bay, with XA894, the fire engine and numerous support trailers, burned out of control for the rest of the afternoon, showering burning magnesium alloy like a fireworks display. When the fire had burned itself out, it was found that the LP turbine disc had been ejected from the engine, travelling through the two bomb-bay fuel tanks, before hitting the ground. It ricocheted up to remove over 10ft of the port wing leading edge, then travelled like a Barnes Wallis bouncing bomb across the airfield in the direction of a prototype Bristol 188 parked nearly half a mile away, but its impetus ran out shortly before reaching the 188. Examination of the remains of XA894 showed that the LP disc's ejection caused all the turbine blades to shower around in a great arc, rupturing every fuel tank in the aircraft.

Following the loss of XA894, Vulcan B.1 XA899 was selected as a replacement, but the time required to convert it to the required configuration, coupled with the cost involved, inspired a re-think by the MoS and Bristol Siddeley. The National Gas Turbine Establishment at Pyestock had upgraded its facilities and further development of the TSR.2's powerplant was transferred to them.

XA894, the sixth production Vulcan B.1, as the test-bed for the TSR.2's Olympus 22R. Author's collection

The first meeting of the Supersonic Transport Advisory Committee was held in London on 5 November 1956, with Sir Morien Morgan, who had led the Advanced Bomber Project Group that evaluated the B.35/46 submissions back in 1947, as chairman. Over the next five years, various projects materialized, and the Bristol Aircraft Type 198 was so similar to a Super Caravelle proposal made by Sud Aviation of France that a combination of the two countries' projects was ratified as one design by the signing of a contract on 29 November 1962, from which came Concorde – with an 'e' to pacify Gallic nationalism.

Both countries had selected the Olympus for their original designs and Concorde's engines would be designed by Bristol Siddeley, with the French engine company SNECMA handling the reheat system. The engine was at first a civil variant of the Olympus 22R, designated the Olympus 591, but a subsequent redesign of the airframe in 1963 necessitated a different engine design, which emerged as the

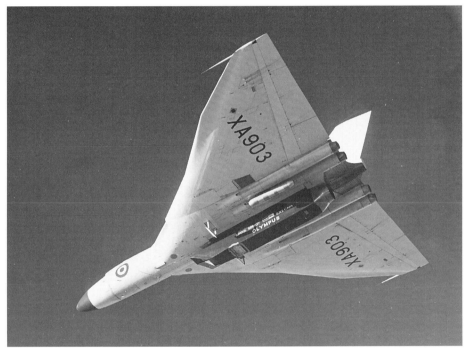

Vulcan B.1 XA903 had its standard visual bomb-aimer's blister and tail-cone removed for early Olympus 593 trials. Author's collection

Olympus 593D in 1964, which by September was producing 28,100lb (12,746kg) thrust on the test bench.

Vulcan B.1 XA903, which had been a primary *Blue Steel* trials aircraft with both the A&AEE and RAE Farnborough, was allocated as the Olympus 593 flying test-bed. It arrived at Patchway on 3 January 1964 for a thirty-month conversion to fulfil its new role, the major constituent of which was a large ventral nacelle, profiled as half a Concorde engine installation, containing one engine. Above the nacelle, the bomb-bay carried water and fuel tanks, together with instrumentation and avionics associated with the test programme, which commenced on 9 September 1966 with XA903's first flight

carrying the Concorde installation. With Tom Frost as captain and Harry Pollitt as co-pilot, the aircraft's intake ramp suffered an involuntary opening at 27,000ft (8,230m), setting up heavy oscillations owing to air spillage from the Olympus intake, which continued until the airspeed had been reduced to less than 235mph (378km/h). The ramp would not close and a landing had to be made at Filton, with a risk of foreign-object damage to the engine, which fortunately did not occur.

The ventral nacelle's geometry allowed various standards of engines to be installed and the only real problem occurred during Flight No.167, made on 6 February 1970. A hydraulic pipe fractured when the aircraft was flying over Filton, which pro-

duced a complete loss of fluid and pressure. The Vulcan B.1's undercarriage and Maxaret braking system were hydraulically operated, so the loss of anti-skid braking decreed a landing on a longer runway than was available at Filton.

The aircraft was initially diverted to Boscombe Down, but it was after 16.00hr on a Friday and the airfield was closed! A second diversion to Fairford proved more satisfactory and the undercarriage was lowered in free fall, but the nose-wheel would not lock down. Nevertheless, a landing had to be made and when the aircraft's forward speed was lessened, with the main wheels on the runway, the aerodynamic loads on the nose leg were reduced enough for the unit to lock. The braking parachute did not deploy, resulting in a small fire breaking out in the port brakes, but this was soon extinguished. A subsequent inspection, made once everything had been shut down, revealed that a large portion of the aircraft's underside had been stained bright red by the escaping hydraulic fluid.

By early March 1971, a water-spray grid, containing over 100 nozzles, had been fitted ahead of the test-engine's nacelle, for de-icing trials. Water was to be sprayed into the intake at various concentrations, with the de-icing system operating. The first flight with this unit was made on 12 March, but not as an engine test flight. The spray grid, plus its supporting structure, was positioned around the ventral crew access hatch and the main object of the flight was to make a dummy drop in order to test the ability of the crew to escape, should an emergency arise. A similar programme of dummy dropping had taken place early in the programme, when the Olympus test installation was first flown in 1966 and now, as then, no adverse effects were encountered.

The green light was given for the de-icing trials, which occupied three months. A series of television cameras installed around the intake monitored the operation of the whole system and the results were so successful that, when it went into service, Concorde was granted a Special Category icing clearance, based entirely on the results of the trials with XA903.

An Olympus 593-602, which was to be the original production engine, was ready to be installed in the middle of 1971, when the programme had to be closed, due to the aircraft being required for a new series of engine trials which, being for mil-

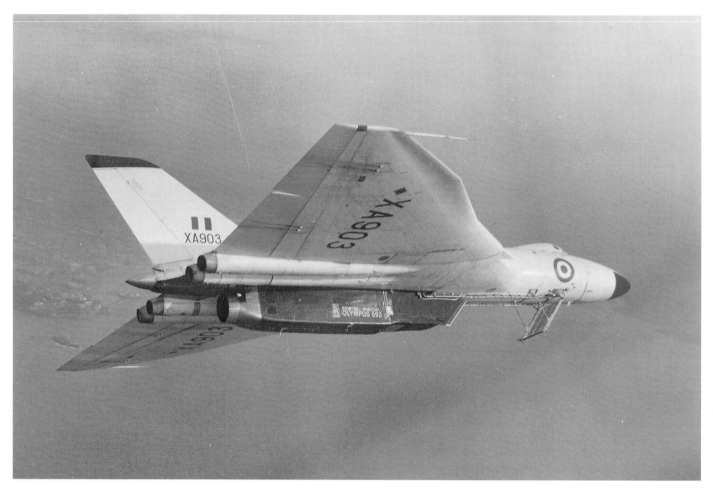

XA903 rigged up with a water spray for Olympus 593 de-icing trials, with its tail-cone restored. Author's collection

itary application, took precedence. The 219th and last Concorde engine test flight took place on 21 July 1971, when again there was trouble with the braking parachute, which would not deploy or be jettisoned. Several circuits of Filton were made with the trailing parachute gradually being torn to shreds, before it eventually fell away. On landing this time, there was no fire in the brakes, as occurred in the Fairford landing, and having ended its Olympus associations, XA903 went in August to Marshall of Cambridge.

RB.199

The deployment to Marshall of XA903 was for the required conversion to fulfil the role of the flying test-bed for the Turbo-Union RB.199-34A engine. Aeritalia co-operated with the Cambridge company in designing a near-representation of the left half of an MRCA centre body, as a ventral pod for the Vulcan.

On 30 September 1969, an international consortium was formed to produce an engine, that had been originated by Bristol Siddeley's Patchway design team as the M45G turbofan, fitted with reheat. Bristol Siddeley had become a part of Rolls-Royce in 1966 and as the RB.199, the engine was developed into the RB.199-34A, the powerplant for the MRCA design that had been spawned by BAC Warton. The consortium Panavia was formed on 26 March 1969, with BAC, MBB of Germany and Aeritalia of Italy, to produce the MRCA, which was named Tornado. The RB.199 engine was also to be manufactured by a consortium, named Turbo-Union Ltd, the members being Rolls-Royce and Germany's MTU, each holding 40 per cent, together with Fiat's aero division, Aeritalia, having 20 per cent.

XA903 left Marshall in February 1972, flying cross-country to Patchway to receive a flight-cleared RB.199 in the

ventral pod, which had a functioning variable intake, a dummy reverser and provision for a cannon. The engine's installation was completed and ground tested for a maiden flight to be made on 19 April 1973. Harry Pollitt was now CTP for Rolls-Royce at Patchway and he captained the first flight, which was an aerodynamic test flight only, with the RB.199 not being run. Similar flights were made until 26 July, when the test engine was first run and its behaviour was examined up to 50,000ft, where Mach 0.92 was achieved. Reheat trials were started in April 1974 and, while there were several failures of test engines during the five years that the programme was active, the RB.199 was found to be a smooth-running engine, with very good fuel consumption.

Various RB.199 variants were installed in XA903's ventral nacelle, with the first production-standard -34 engine being tested during 1976. During the same year, a 27mm Mauser Mk.27 cannon was installed in the housing incorporated in the nacelle for a series of A&AEE-sponsored trials. Butt-firing was carried out before live firings were made over the Irish Sea, to test for any gun-gas ingestion in the engine (possibly the problems incurred with the Hunter twenty years earlier were in mind, but the cannon firing produced no adverse effects).

In its production form, the RB.199-34R delivered 8,000lb (3,630kg) static thrust dry and 15,000lb (6,800kg) with full after-burner. By the middle of 1977, to say that XA903 was getting 'long in the tooth' is rather an understatement, as it had been flying since May 1957 and was the last Vulcan B.1 still airworthy. Spares were becoming a distinct problem and gate guardians were scoured for some parts, especially electrical fittings. The aircraft's wiring system had degraded to such a dangerous extent that it had to be completely renewed, after which an RB.199-34R Mk.101 was test-flown before being introduced into the first production batch of Tornado GR.1s. This was the last engine to be tested and Turbo-Union test-bed activity ceased on 18 August 1978, after a total of 203 flying hours accrued in 125 sorties. The aircraft left Patchway for RAE Farnborough on 22 February 1979, as the final flight by a Vulcan B.1. It was consigned to Farnborough's fire dump as a fire and crash rescue airframe, before being finally scrapped in 1980.

BS.100

In the latter half of 1961, Hawker Aircraft started design work on a supersonic Vertical/Standing Take-Off and Landing (V/STOL) strike fighter, designated the P.1154. An advanced version of the Pegasus vectored-thrust engine, the BS.100, was envisaged by Bristol Siddeley as being the powerplant for the aircraft. The principal change needed to develop the Pegasus into the BS.100 was the provision of the forward cold nozzles having a form of plenum-chamber burning. In order to provide flight-testing of the new engine, XA896, the eighth production Vulcan B.1, was flown to Rolls-Royce's test facility at Hucknall, on 24 June 1964.

The engineering required to design and manufacture a ventral pod to take a BS.100, was well in hand when, in February 1965, the Hawker P.1154 was cancelled. As the aircraft and the engine were integral elements, the engine was also killed off, after the combined projects had incurred an expenditure of £21 million.

After a total of 2,125.25hr flying, with No.230 OCU as well as Nos 44 and 83 Squadrons, XA896 was struck off charge in 1966. The nose and crew compartment were removed for instructional purposes and the rest of the aircraft was scrapped.

Victor

The Victor was never utilized as a test vehicle for anything other than to further its own potential. The *Red Neck* sideways-looking radar trials with XA918 were associated with its own conversion to the strategic reconnaissance role, in which it was designated the SR.2, but *Red Neck* never became a part of the aircraft's operational equipment.

Likewise, the testing of the de Havilland Spectre 4 rocket motor, as a means of RATOG for the Victor. A paired installation on B.1 XA930 was tried, with a Spectre 4 fitted under the wing centre section on each side. Only one take-off was flown, but the impending installing of the more powerful Conway engines, plus the Air Staff decision that the majority of V-bomber operations would be made from UK bases (a decision that proved not to be the case as time went on), negated any further thoughts of RATOG.

CHAPTER FIFTEEN

Debrief

Human nature being what it is, there is so very often a natural desire for one thing to be better than another, or at least, comparisons made when they are not really necessary. In aviation, this has been a maxim almost throughout its history. The Camel or the Pup, Wellington or Whitley, Spitfire or Hurricane, Lancaster or Halifax, have been subjects for debate and argument among many an aeronautical gathering.

So it is inevitable that the question is raised, 'Which was the best V-bomber?' Just as inevitable is the answer, 'It depends on what you mean by best'. While the Valiant was built as an 'interim' bomber to provide the British nuclear deterrent capability that the Lincoln could not give until the Vulcan came into service, the Vulcan had a rival in the shape of the Victor and everyone expected the two to be evaluated against each other, in order to provide a winner. The fact that both were ordered for service is a pointer to the Air Staff themselves not being wholly convinced that one was superior to the other.

Without hypothesizing too much, it has to be said that in not ordering the Valiant Mk.2 into production – a contract for seventeen was issued in April 1952, but subsequently cancelled – the Air Staff lost a purpose-designed low-level bomber that proved in testing to be better than either the Vulcan or Victor, in the environment in which they were eventually forced to operate. If only the word 'Pathfinder' had not been attached to the aircraft, for this was an archaic role which, I consider, clouded official thinking and had no place in the post-war Bomber Command. Had it been classified as a 'Bomber', I am sure it would have gone into production as the Valiant B.2 and operated in the low-level role, with its stablemate, the B.1, as a high-altitude bomber, plus tanker, with either the Vulcan *or* the Victor, and my money would have been on the Vulcan.

When the Handley Page design team got down to tackling Specification

B.35/46, it ensured that their bomber would not be second best, in terms of weapon carrying capacity, as the Halifax had been to Avro's Lancaster, in World War II. With an RAF-set limit of thirty-five 1,000lb bombs, the Victor could accommodate, by far, the superior bomb load. While the principal requirement was to carry the *Blue Danube* nuclear weapon, it was not at the expense of conventional bombs. The Victor's large bomb-bay is attributed to the design's crescent wing configuration of the highly-swept centre section, which enabled the three-web main spar box to be forward of the commencement of the weapon carrying area, whereas the Vulcan was limited to having the bomb-bay between the two wing spars. The Valiant too was not restricted in this way, as the wing root attachment beams ran above the bomb-bay roof, forming part of its actual structure. The Vulcan and Victor had very similar performance figures at high altitude, with the Victor being marginally better above 60,000ft (18,290m), and their *Blue Steel* capabilities were on a par with each other. However, when Skybolt came into the

picture, with future RAF plans built around it, the Victor, by virtue of its low ground clearance, was a non-starter.

The need to replace the Valiant tanker fleet put the Victor back in the frame and it was an excellent three-point tanker for many years. The eleventh-hour Vulcan conversion to a tanker role too proved it to be capable of undertaking the job, but it had the limitation of being only a one pointer. There is no doubt that had the Valiant survived, it would also have been capable of adaptation to three-pointer standard.

There was absolutely nothing wrong with the Valiant as a design to meet its specification. The Vulcan required a new wing and the Victor required lengthening before they were operationally acceptable. The Valiant went into production as it came off the drawing board. Its nemesis carried the cryptic designation DTD683. Rolls-Royce had a very extensive metallurgical research facility within its research laboratories at Derby and the roots of DTD683 go back to the early days of World War II. The laboratory formulated a very strong aluminium alloy for use

Victor SR.2 XM715 of No.100 Squadron. *Aeroplane*

Vulcan B.2 XL317 of No.617 Squadron disturbs the peace of the Lincolnshire village below. Dave Thomas

in forgings, which was quite light in weight but had a tensile strength of 32 tons per square inch, compared with only 10 tons per square inch for similar aluminium alloys being used in aircraft construction. It was registered as Alloy R.R.77 and was adopted by the Ministry of Aircraft Production (MAP) as DTD683, which proved to be an excellent material within the operational performances of aircraft *circa* 1945/46.

Post-World War II, the MAP's title was changed to Ministry of Supply and this government department was enamoured of the alloy's properties. To be fair to the MoS, they had no reason to think otherwise. Consequently, DTD683 was advocated for many late 1940s designs, with Vickers-Armstrongs, together with Handley Page, opting for the material for their respective bomber's load-bearing strong components, such as centre-section main spars, engine attachment brackets, undercarriage structure items and fuselage interface attachments. W.E.W. Petter had

selected DTD683 for his Canberra and at one time the aircraft came close to being killed off, due to structural failures that caused a number of fatal accidents.

Checks on several of the wrecks revealed that unpredictable fatigue characteristics had been initiated by stress corrosion. The cause was found to be the very high sensitivity of the alloy to such things as the chatter of the cutting tool during machining operations, insufficient radius at corners and wrong heat treatment temperatures, none of them being attributable to the aircraft's manufacturer. Extensive changes were made in processing techniques, which changed DTD683 and it became DTD5024, 5044 or 5114, according to the application.

The Victor B.1s too showed signs of the stress levels encountered by the Valiant, but in its case the B.2 was in production, to supersede the earlier variant, and the properties of the alloy were being understood. The Vulcan's delta configuration meant that it was a simpler design, but

with greater structural strength than either of its two contemporaries. This in turn gave it the ability to have, in its B.2 form, greater power reserves without losing manoeuvrability, together with a better flexibility than the Victor B.2.

There never has been a thriving export market for the large, technically sophisticated bomber, apart, I suppose, from the old Soviet Union, which was entirely politically motivated. Therefore, it is a little surprising to realize that, in 1960, when South Africa was looking for a light bomber for its Air Force, to use in a retaliation capacity in case it was attacked, it considered the Canberra, Buccaneer, Mirage IVA, Vulcan B.1 and Victor B.2. The Canberra was considered too old, the Buccaneer too new and the Mirage IVA too expensive. On what grounds the Vulcan and Victor were rejected is unknown, although one would think that, when the requirement was for a *light* bomber, the grounds were common sense. They finally ordered sixteen new-build

Valiant B(K).1 XD823 on manufacturer's air test before joining a squadron. Derek N. James

Buccaneers and had nine refurbished Canberras as 'stop gaps'.

So, which *was* the best of the trio? Without denigrating the Avro or Handley Page aircraft in any way, I consider that Weybridge gave the RAF the more superior aeroplane, which, bearing in mind the speed at which it was conceived and produced, was a truly remarkable achievement. Every delivery date, from the first prototype to the last production aircraft, was met or bettered. By designing an 'unfunny' bomber, with the requirements of a flight-refuelling tanker and photographic reconnaissance aircraft built in from the start, GRE's team produced an 'interim' aeroplane that pioneered a number of techniques for the British aircraft industry. In many terms of construction and avionics, it paved the way for its two successors, while the RAF had a first-class bomber, on which it could cut its

teeth in preparation for any threat to Britain or NATO in the new era of nuclear warfare. Its operational performance, which was never too far short of either the Vulcan or the Victor, was obtained with less than 50 per cent of the power available to either of them. In my mind, there is no doubt, DTD683 not withstanding, that the subsequent installation of more powerful engines, in line with the Vulcan and Victor, would have enabled the Valiant to have fulfilled its roles as well as, or better than, its contemporaries. Also, ready and able, was the Mk.2!

An aeronautical engineer once said to me 'To mass produce good aeroplanes, you need plenty of manpower, floorspace and money.' I think he was right and, with this in mind, the British aircraft industry did extremely well in the early 1950s. It was only five years since the end of a six-year conflict with Germany and Japan. The three commodities mentioned were far from being in abundance and the industry's designers were delving into areas for which they had virtually no previous experience to fall back on. Plus, they had to run the obstacle course of official procrastination and political ineptitude. The V-bombers were a credit to everyone, from the designers with their slide rules, to the shop floor with their 'windies', to the RAF that operated them. I doubt that we shall ever see such commitment by the industry, or the Service, again.

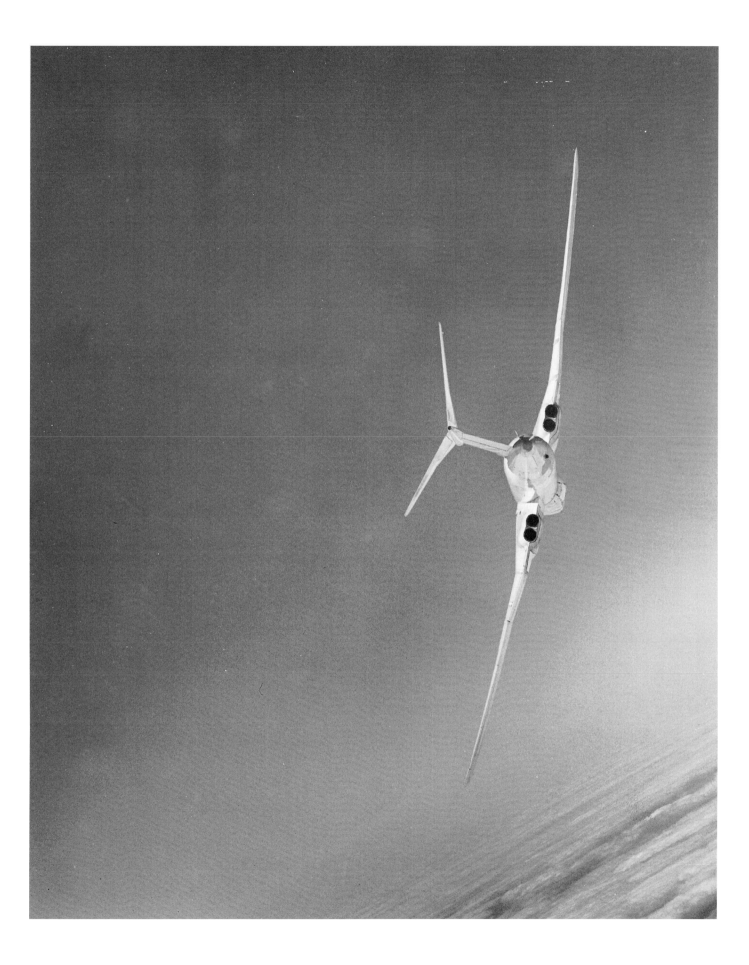

V-Bomber Production and Serial Blocks

Valiant
Type 660 prototype
WB210 (1 aircraft)
Type 667
WB215 (1 aircraft)

Contract No.6/ACFT/6313/CB6(c)
Type 674 Valiant B.1
WP199 to WP203 (5 aircraft)
Type 706 Valiant B.1
WP204, WP206 to WP216, WP218, WP220, WP222
(15 aircraft)
Type 710 Valiant B(PR).1
WP203, WP217, WP219, WP221, WP223
(5 aircraft)

Contract No.6/ACFT/7375/CB6(c)
Type 706 Valiant B.1
WZ361 to WZ375, WZ377 (16 aircraft)
Type 710 Valiant B(PR).1
WZ376, WZ378, WZ379, WZ381, WZ383, WZ384
(6 aircraft)
Type 733 Valiant B(PR)K.1
WZ380, WZ382 (2 aircraft)

Contract No.6/ACFT/7376/CB6(c)
Type 733 Valiant B(PR)K.1
WZ389 to WZ399 (11 aircraft)
Type 758 Valiant B(K).1
WZ400 to WZ405 (6 aircraft)

Contract No.6/ACFT/9446/CB6(c)
Type 758 Valiant B(K).1
XD812 to XD830, XD857 to XD875 (38 aircraft)
Intended Type 758 Valiant B(K).1
XD867 to XD893, XE294 to XE299 (24 aircraft)
cancelled.

Type 673 Valiant Mk.2 prototype
WJ954 (1 aircraft)

Total Valiant production, including 3 prototypes, 107.

Vulcan
Type 698 prototypes
Contract No.6/ACFT/1942/CB6(a)
VX770, VX771 (2 aircraft)

Vulcan B.1 and B.1A
Contract No.6/ACFT/8442/CB6(a)
XA889 to XA913 (25 aircraft)

Contract No.6/ACFT/11301/CB6(a)
XH475 to XH483, XH497 to XH506, XH532 (20 aircraft)

Vulcan B.2
Contract No.6/ACFT/11301/CB6(a)
XH533 to XH539, XH554 to XH563 (17 aircraft)

Contract No.6/ACFT/11830/CB6(a)
XJ780 to XJ784, XJ823 to XJ825 (8 aircraft)
Contract No.6/ACFT/13145/CB6(a)
XL317 to XL321, XL359 to XL361, XL384 to XL392,
XL425 to XL427, XL443 to XL446 (24 aircraft)

Contract No.KD/B/01/CB6(a)
XM569 to XM576, XM594, XM595, XM596*, XM597 to
XM612, XM645 to XM657 (40 aircraft)

Total Vulcan production, including 2 prototypes, 136.

*XM596 was the serial number allocated to the sixti-
eth production Vulcan, but it was never applied, as

the airframe was used as a fatigue test specimen. It
completed 41,100 simulated flights between May 1964
and September 1970, following which it was
employed on various test programmes until being
scrapped in late 1973.

Victor
Type HP80 prototypes
Contract No.6/ACFT/1875/CB6(a)
WB771, WB772 (2 aircraft)

Victor B.1 and B.1A
Contract No.6/ACFT/8441/CB6(a)
XA917 to XA941 (25 aircraft)

Contract No.6/ACFT/11303/CB6(a)
XH587 to XH594, XH613 to XH621, XH645 to XH651,
XH667 (25 aircraft)

Victor B.2
Contract No.6/ACFT/11303/CB6(a) – extension of B.1
and B.1A contract
XH668 to XH675 (8 aircraft)

Contract No.6/ACFT/12399/CB6(a)
XL158 to XL165, XL188 to XL193, XL230 to XL233,
XL511 to XL513 (21 aircraft)

Contract No.6/ACFT/15566/CB6
XM714 top XM718 (5 aircraft)
Intended Victor B.2
XM719 to XM721, XM745 to XM756, XM785 to
XM794 (25 aircraft) cancelled

Total Victor production, including 2 prototypes, 86.

V-Bomber Squadrons

VALIANT

No.232 Operational Conversion Unit

Formed at Gaydon in June 1955 to train Valiant air-crews and, initially, ground crews. The first course became the nucleus of No.138 Squadron, which transferred from Gaydon to Wittering, to become the RAF's first V-bomber squadron on 6 July 1955.

No.7 Squadron

The squadron had flown Stirlings and Lancasters throughout World War II and was equipped with Lincoln B.2s when disbanded at Upwood on 1 January 1956. Re-formed on 1 November of the same year, at Honington, it received its first Valiant B(PR).1 the same day, to be followed in 1957 by B.1s, B(K).1s and finally, in August 1961, after moving to Wittering, B(PR)K.1s. The squadron was disbanded as a V-bomber unit at Wittering on 30 September 1962 and eight years later went to St Mawgan to fly Canberra TT.18s.

No.18 Squadron

Having been disbanded five times since its formation at Northolt in 1915, the squadron was re-formed on 17 December 1958 at Finningley, from 'C' Flight of No.199 Squadron. It operated Valiant B.1s in a joint ECM role with Canberra B.2s, until being disbanded on 31 March 1963 and a year later, on 27 January 1964, it became a helicopter unit at Odiham.

No.49 Squadron

With a World War II record of flying Hampdens, Manchesters and Lancasters, the squadron was disbanded at Upwood on 1 August 1955 while operating with Lincoln B.2s. It was re-formed at Wittering on 1 May 1956, with Valiant B.1s, and supplied aircraft to the Operation *Grapple* programme, where it made the first British atomic and hydrogen bomb drops. The squadron became an element of SACEUR until the Valiant fatigue troubles arose, and was disbanded at Marham on 1 May 1965 when its Valiants had been withdrawn from service.

No.90 Squadron

Noted for being the first RAF unit to operate with the Fortress Mk.1, in May 1941, the squadron was re-formed at Honington on 1 January 1957 to fly Valiant B(K).1s, to which were added B(PR).1s and B(PR)K.1s, before it was disbanded on 1 March 1965.

No.138 Squadron

Formed from the first Valiant OCU course at Gaydon before transferring to Wittering, the squadron flew all four Valiant variants between February 1955 and April 1962. It was detached to Malta for bombing sorties during Operation *Musketeer* and was principally a tanker squadron when disbanded on 1 April 1962.

No.148 Squadron

Serving in the Middle East throughout World War II and returning to the UK to operate with Lincoln B.2s until disbanding at Upwood in July 1955, the squadron was re-formed at Marham on 1 July 1956, to operate with all four versions of the Valiant. It was back in the Middle East for Operation *Musketeer* and later was delegated to the low-level role with NATO, during which its aircraft suffered the wing fatigue problem,

Vulcan B.2 XL321 of No.230 OCU Scampton. Dave Thomas

forcing the unit to surrender its Valiants before disbanding on 1 May 1965.

No.199 Squadron

Based at Hemswell, the squadron received a few Valiant B.1s in May 1957, to operate alongside Lincoln B.2s and Canberra B.2s in an ECM role. It was detached to Honington on 1 October 1957, leaving the Lincolns at Hemswell as No.1321 Flight and on 17 December 1958 the Flight was renumbered as No.18 Squadron, at Finningley.

No.207 Squadron

With a pedigree going back to 1 November 1916, the squadron changed its Canberra B.2s for Valiant B(PR).1s at Marham in June 1956 and flew with B(K).1s, together with B.1s, in the low-level role with SACEUR for five years, commencing in 1960. It was disbanded on 1 May 1965 following the Valiant's withdrawal from service and four years later, in February 1969, it became a Communications Squadron, in which role it operated until being disbanded for the last time on 30 June 1984.

No.214 Squadron

Re-formed at Marham on 21 January 1956 as a Valiant unit, the squadron was just in time to participate in Operation *Musketeer*. All four Valiant variants served with the unit and in the spring of 1958, it became the RAF's first tanker squadron, with B(K).1s. The squadron served in this capacity until 1 March 1965, when it was disbanded.

No.543 Squadron

The second squadron to be formed from No.232 OCU, it was the first to operate with Valiant B(PR).1s. The squadron moved from Gaydon to Wyton on 18 November 1955 and replaced its B(PR).1s with B(PR)K.1s, but only operated with them until December 1964, when the Valiants were withdrawn from service.

VULCAN

No.230 Operational Conversion Unit

Being established at Waddington in August 1956, as the Vulcan OCU, the Unit's Vulcan B.1s first arrived in January 1957, to be joined by B.1As and, in June 1960, by Vulcan B.2s. The OCU became an all-B.2 Unit in 1965 and remained that way until 1980, when it was disbanded.

No.9 Squadron

The squadron's lineage goes back to 8 December 1914 and a vast miscellany of different types had been

on its inventory before it was re-formed at Coningsby on 1 March 1962, having been disbanded the previous year. Receiving its first Vulcan B.2s in April 1962, the unit moved to Cottesmore on 10 November 1964 and, five years later, on 26 February 1969, to Akrotiri as part of the Near East Bomber Wing. The squadron returned to the UK, to become an element of the Waddington Wing, on 15 January 1975, remaining as such until being disbanded as a Vulcan operator on 1 May 1982 and re-formed to receive its first Tornado GR.1 the following month.

No.12 Squadron

Another former Canberra squadron, it was re-formed at Coningsby on 1 July 1962 to become a part of the Coningsby Wing of three squadrons operating with Vulcan B.2s. It moved with its sister squadrons to Cottesmore, on 17 November 1964, to become the Cottesmore Wing, before disbanding on 31 December 1967. Two years later, the squadron again re-formed, this time as a Buccaneer S.2B unit.

No.27 Squadron

World War II saw the squadron operating in the Far East for the whole of its duration. Post-war, it disbanded and re-formed twice, before coming together at Scampton on 1 April 1961 to become the second Vulcan B.2 unit and an element of the Scampton Wing. It operated in this role until 29 March 1972, when it was disbanded and lay dormant as a squadron number until reforming, still at Scampton, on 1 November 1973. Vulcan B.2(MRR) aircraft were allotted to the squadron and it became engaged in maritime reconnaissance for the next nine years, before being disbanded, once again, on 31 March 1982. You cannot keep a good squadron down and a year later it was resurrected as a Tornado GR.1 operator at Marham.

No.35 Squadron

Having been the Boeing B-29 Washington Conversion Unit in the early 1950s, the squadron was disbanded and re-formed at Coningsby on 1 December 1962 as one of the three Vulcan B.2 units comprising the Coningsby Wing. Seven years later, on 1 January 1969, the squadron moved to Akrotiri, to join the Near East Bomber Wing, where it remained until 16 January 1975. On that date, the squadron returned to the UK, to be stationed at Scampton, until disbanding on 1 March 1982.

No.44 Squadron

Named the 'Rhodesia' squadron, the unit's re-forming at Waddington on 10 August 1960 was made with the nucleus of No.83 Squadron's Vulcan B.1s and it retained them for seven years, during which time the

majority were upgraded to B.1A standard. In September 1966, Vulcan B.2s started to arrive and by September 1967 the squadron was an all-B.2 unit, remaining that way until disbanding at Waddington on 21 December 1982.

No.50 Squadron

Reforming at Waddington on 3 May 1937, the squadron served as a piston-engined unit without a break, until becoming a Canberra B.2 operator in August 1952. Disbanded in October 1959, the squadron was reformed at Waddington on 1 August 1961, taking ex-No.617 Squadron Vulcan B.1s and B.1As, until its B.2s arrived in January 1966. Being a part of the Waddington Wing, the squadron also received a few Vulcan B.2(K) aircraft in June 1982, which it retained alongside the Vulcans until the unit was disbanded on 31 March 1984.

No.83 Squadron

The squadron had the distinction of being the first Vulcan B.1 unit when it re-formed at Waddington on 21 May 1957 and its first aircraft was delivered on 11 July. It was reduced to a cadre on 10 August 1960, only to be re-established as a squadron one month later and receive its first Vulcan B.2 in December. In 1963, the squadron became the second operational Blue Steel unit, which was finally disbanded on 31 August 1969.

No.101 Squadron

Having been the first RAF Canberra B.2 squadron, the unit was disbanded at Binbrook in February 1957 and re-formed at Finningley on 15 October of the same year, as the second Vulcan B.1 squadron. It moved to Waddington on 26 June 1961, by which time Vulcan B.1As were on the inventory and in December 1967 the first of the B.2s arrived, for the squadron to become one of the three Waddington Wing units. The status quo lasted until 4 August 1982, when the squadron was disbanded. Two years later, it was re-formed at Brize Norton, with VC10 K.1 and K.2 tankers.

No.617 Squadron

One of the very few RAF squadrons formed for a specific mission, its 'Dam Buster' origin is carried forward in the squadron crest. Disbanded as a Canberra B.6 unit in December 1955, the squadron was reformed at Scampton, the site of its birth, on 1 May 1958. First equipped with Vulcan B.1s, B.1As started arriving at the end of 1960 and the following year, in September 1961, the first of the squadron's Vulcan B.2s was delivered. The squadron became the first to be declared operational with Blue Steel and on the stand-off bomb's withdrawal from service, aircraft were converted to the conventional bombing role. Its Vulcan days ended on 31 December 1981 and a year later the squadron was re-formed at Marham, to operate the Tornado GR.1.

VICTOR

No.232 Operational Conversion Unit

On 28 November 1957, the Gaydon-based OCU received its first Victor B.1 and for the next seven years Victor crew training was conducted in parallel with Valiant training. When the Valiants were withdrawn from service, the OCU operated exclusively with Victors and moved to Cottesmore in September 1961. The OCU disbanded following the last Victor squadron's formation, but it rose again in February 1970, when Marham's Tanker Training Flight was renamed and the unit continued in this capacity until the demise of the Victor K.2.

No.10 Squadron

Re-formed at Cottesmore on 15 April 1958, the squadron was the first to take delivery of the Victor B.1, and operated with the type for six years before being disbanded on 1 March 1964. Two years later, the squadron was re-formed at Brize Norton on 1 July 1966, to become a transporting unit, flying the VC10 C.1.

No.15 Squadron

Five months after No.10 Squadron, this squadron too re-formed at Cottesmore and became the second RAF unit to be equipped with the Victor B.1. Its operational history followed its fellow Cottesmore squadron very closely, and on 1 October 1964 it was disbanded after also flying B.1s for six years. Its re-formation in October 1970 differed from No.10 squadron, as it became a Buccaneer-operator at Honington.

No.55 Squadron

Staying dormant as a squadron number since 1 December 1946, No.55 Squadron re-formed at Honington on 1 September 1960, to fly the Victor B.1, which was superseded by the B.1A. A move to Marham on 24 May 1965 heralded a change of role, when Victor B(K).1As were followed in February 1967 by Victor K.1s and K.1As, for the squadron to become a tanker unit, together with No.57 Squadron. In July 1975, Victor K.2s started replacing the earlier variants and the squadron operated with them in the south Atlantic, as well as the Gulf, before disbanding as the RAF's last Victor squadron, on 15 October 1993.

No.57 Squadron

Another Honington re-formed squadron, on 1 January 1959 the first Victor B.1s were delivered and B.1As followed. It operated with No.55 Squadron in 1963, during the troubles with Indonesia, before, on 1 December 1965, moving to Marham, where it rejoined No.55 Squadron once again, but this time as a tanker unit. Victor K.1s arrived in February 1966 and ten years later, in June 1976, K.2s became the squadron in-flight refuelling supplier. On 30 June 1986, the unit passed its aircraft over to its Marham partner and was disbanded.

No.100 Squadron

After operating with several different Canberra variants for five years, the squadron was disbanded in September 1959 and re-formed at Wittering on 1 May 1962 to become the second Victor B.2 squadron, with clearance to operate Blue Steel being given in January 1964. It was disbanded on 30 September 1968, reverting to a Canberra squadron in February 1972 and today is the only RAF squadron still operating the type.

No.139 Squadron

On 1 February 1962, the squadron was re-formed at Wittering, to become the first Victor B.2 operator and the following year these were replaced by Blue Steel compatible B.2Rs, which the unit retained until it disbanded on 31 December 1968.

No.214 Squadron

When the Valiant was withdrawn, the squadron disbanded as a tanker unit at Marham on 1 March 1965. Sixteen months later, on 1 July 1966, it was re-formed, still at Marham, to resume the tanker role with Victor K.1s. The squadron continued in this employment for over ten years, before disbanding for the last time on 28 January 1977.

No.543 Squadron

Another former Valiant tanker unit, the squadron differed from the majority of similarly placed units by not disbanding when the Valiants left, as the first Victor B.2(SR) was delivered in May 1965 and for nine years it flew this version of the Victor, until being disbanded on 24 May 1974.

V-Bomber Conservation

The following aircraft have been confirmed at the time of writing as existing in the form described.

SERIAL   PRESENT LOCATION

Valiant B.1

XD875   British Aviation Heritage Collection, Bruntingthorpe, Leicestershire *(front fuselage only)*

Valiant B(K).1

XD816   Brooklands Museum, Weybridge, Surrey *(front fuselage only)*

XD818   Royal Air Force Museum, Hendon, Greater London

XD826   The Cockpit Collection, Rayleigh, Essex *(front fuselage only)*

XD857   On private loan to RAF Manston History Museum *(sectioned flight deck only)*

Vulcan B.1

XA893   Royal Air Force Museum, Cosford, Shropshire

XA903   Paul Hartley Wellesbourne Wartime Museum, Wellesbourne Mountford, Warwickshire *(front fuselage only)*

Vulcan B.2

XH558   British Aviation Heritage Collection, Bruntingthorpe, Leicestershire

XH560   The Cockpit Collection, Rayleigh, Essex *(front fuselage only)*

XJ823   Solway Aviation Museum, Carlisle Airport, Cheshire

XJ824   Imperial War Museum, Duxford, Cambridgeshire

XL318   Royal Air Force Museum, Hendon, Greater London

XL319   North East Aircraft Museum, Sunderland, Tyne & Wear

XL360   Midland Air Museum, Baginton, Coventry, West Midlands

XL361   Last heard of at Happy Valley, Goose Bay, Canada

XL391   Squires Gate, Blackpool Airport, Lancashire *(front fuselage only)*

XL426   Vulcan Restoration Trust, Southend Airport, Essex

XM569   Jet Age Museum, Staverton, Gloucestershire *(front fuselage only)*

XM573   Offutt Air Force Base, Nebraska, USA

XM575   East Midlands Aero Park, East Midlands Airport, Castle Donington, Derbyshire

XM594   Newark Air Museum, Winthorpe Show Ground, Newark

XM597   Museum of Flight, East Fortune Airfield, Scotland

XM598   Royal Air Force Museum, Cosford, Shropshire

XM602   Avro Heritage Society, Woodford Airfield, Lancashire *(front fuselage only)*

XM603   Avro Heritage Society, Woodford Airfield, Lancashire

XM605   Castle Air Force Base, California, USA

XM606   Barksdale Air Force Base, Louisiana, USA

XM607   Waddington Airfield, Lincolnshire

XM612   City of Norwich Museum, Horsham St Faith, Norwich, Norfolk

XM652   Sue and Roy Jerman, Welshpool, Powys *(front fuselage only)*

XM655   Wellesbourne Mountford Airfield, nr Stratford, Warwickshire

Vulcan B.2(MRR)

XH537   British Aviation Heritage Collection, Bruntingthorpe, Leicestershire *(front fuselage only)*

XH563   Donald Milne, Banchory, Scotland *(front fuselage only)*

Victor B.1

XA917   Private collector, Cupar, Fife, Scotland *(front fuselage only)*

Victor B.1A

XH592   Phoenix Aviation, Bruntingthorpe, Leicestershire *(front fuselage only)*

Victor B.1A(K.2P)

XH648   Imperial War Museum, Duxford, Cambridgeshire

Victor B.2

XH670   The Cockpit Collection, Rayleigh, Essex *(front fuselage only)*

Victor K.2

XH669   The Cockpit Collection, Rayleigh, Essex *(front fuselage only)*

XH672   *(Maid Marion)*, Royal Air Force Museum, Cosford, Shropshire

XH673   Marham Airfield, Swaffham, Norfolk

XL160   Blyth Valley Aviation Collection, Norwich, Norfolk *(front fuselage only)*

XL164   Peter Vallence Collection, Charlwood, Surrey *(front fuselage only)*

XL188   Last heard of at Kinloss dump

XL190   Last heard of at North Coates, Lincolnshire

XL231   Yorkshire Air Museum, Elvington, East Yorkshire

XM715   British Aviation Heritage Collection, Bruntingthorpe, Leicestershire

XM717   *(Lucky Lou)*, Royal Air Force Museum, Hendon, Greater London *(front fuselage only)*

Index